Facilitating Change through Intergroup Dialogue

In order both to prepare for an increasingly diverse society and to help students navigate diverse learning environments, many institutions of higher education have developed programs that support student learning and competencies around inter- and intra-group relations. *Facilitating Change through Intergroup Dialogue: Social Justice Advocacy in Practice* traces the impact of Intergroup Dialogue (IGD) courses on peer-facilitators who delivered Skidmore College's IGD curricula over a five-year period. Through a series of in-depth qualitative interviews and auto-ethnographies, this book explores how former IGD facilitators are applying what they learned to their personal and professional lives three to five years post-college. By exploring facilitators' application of IGD skills, understanding of social justice, and the challenges inherent in this work, *Facilitating Change through Intergroup Dialogue* offers concrete strategies for supporting undergraduate students in their enduring efforts towards justice.

Kristie A. Ford is Professor of Sociology and Director of the Intergroup Relations Program at Skidmore College, USA.

Facilitating Change through Intergroup Dialogue
Social Justice Advocacy in Practice

Edited by Kristie A. Ford

NEW YORK AND LONDON

First published 2018
by Routledge
711 Third Avenue, New York, NY 10017

and by Routledge
2 Park Square, Milton Park, Abingdon, Oxon, OX14 4RN

Routledge is an imprint of the Taylor & Francis Group, an informa business

© 2018 Taylor & Francis

The right of Kristie A. Ford to be identified as the author of the editorial material, and of the authors for their individual chapters, has been asserted in accordance with sections 77 and 78 of the Copyright, Designs and Patents Act 1988.

All rights reserved. No part of this book may be reprinted or reproduced or utilised in any form or by any electronic, mechanical, or other means, now known or hereafter invented, including photocopying and recording, or in any information storage or retrieval system, without permission in writing from the publishers.

Trademark notice: Product or corporate names may be trademarks or registered trademarks, and are used only for identification and explanation without intent to infringe.

Library of Congress Cataloging-in-Publication Data

A catalog record for this book has been requested

ISBN: 978-1-138-23643-1 (hbk)
ISBN: 978-1-138-23644-8 (pbk)
ISBN: 978-1-315-30223-2 (ebk)

Typeset in Goudy
by diacriTech, Chennai

To those who came before me, paving the road for a more just world.
To intergroup dialogue (IGD) facilitators who have taught me so much about how to work towards social change within themselves and others.
And, to my daughter, Kayla, who continually inspires me to do better.

Contents

List of Figures and Tables	*ix*
Foreword	*xi*
Acknowledgments	*xiii*
List of Abbreviations	*xv*

PART I
Contextualizing Intergroup Dialogue (IGD) Facilitation   1

1 **Introduction: The Power of Dialogue**   3
KRISTIE A. FORD

2 **Skidmore College as a National Leader: Institutional Context
and Methods of Inquiry**   16
KRISTIE A. FORD

PART II
IGD Facilitator Reflections   27

II A. Individual Narratives of Change

Preface to the Auto-Ethnographies   29
KRISTIE A. FORD

3 **On Becoming a Social Justice Advocate**   36
VICTORIA K. MALANEY

4 **Social Justice in Action and Inaction**   46
SARAH FAUDE

viii *Contents*

5 Leaning the True Meaning of Advocacy   54
TESHIKA R. HATCH

6 Interrogating Privilege   65
LUNA MALACHOWSKI BAJAK

7 Toward a New Operational Paradigm for Social Justice   73
STEPHEN A. BISSONNETTE

II B. Synthesizing Change Patterns: Across the Interview Data

8 Communicating Differently Post-College: An Analysis
of IGD Skills and Outcomes   85
HEATHER J. LIPKIN AND KRISTIE A. FORD

9 Working Towards Social Justice Advocacy   102
KRISTIE A. FORD AND HEATHER J. LIPKIN

10 A White Male's Post-College Reflections on Race,
Resistance, and Social Change   123
KRISTIE A. FORD

PART III
Beyond IGD Facilitation   131

11 "I Wouldn't Be the Person I Am Without IGR":
Implications and Conclusions   133
KRISTIE A. FORD AND HEATHER J. LIPKIN

12 The Dialogue Continues: The Future of IGR   142
STEPHEN A. BISSONNETTE AND VICTORIA K. MALANEY

Contributors   151

Index   153

Figures and Tables

Figure 1.1	Critical-Dialogic Theoretical Model of Intergroup Dialogue	7
Table 2.1	Participant Demographics	21
Table 3.1	Summary of Auto-Ethnography Themes	30
Table 8.1	Summary of Results	86
Table 9.1	Summary of Results	103

Foreword
Mark A. Chesler

Kristie Ford's new book challenges us to think anew about how to deal with the splintering of our national culture.

Current public discourse in the United States is marked by an increasing awareness of major inequities in access to critical social opportunities and resources. These inequities occur along the vectors of socioeconomic class, race/ethnicity, sexual orientation, and religion, among others. As awareness grows, so do feelings of disaffection with historic and current inequality and injustice. Challenges to the prevailing social order, on behalf of marginalized and oppressed groups, and feelings of threat and potential dispossession from members of privileged groups, dominate our national conversations. Too often, these "conversations" involve little listening and less hearing, and more talk than action.

We see these challenges and responses, and the great difficulty in dealing with them, in our city streets and rural communities, our national congress and state legislatures, and our nation's public schools and colleges/universities. Potential collaborations and effective problem-solving efforts founder on the rocks of inadequate means of cross-group conversation. Without knowing and practicing ways of talking honestly and meaningfully with one another, without even understanding fully the impacts of inequality and injustice on all our lives, we are left without a sturdy ship in these stormy seas.

Into this breach step Dr. Ford and her collaborators—and this book. She and her team describe and explore the practice of intergroup dialogue as a way of increasing people's awareness of social identity, difference, and inequality, and consequently their ability to engage in effective communication and action for change across social groupings. Dialogue, as a form of social engagement, and as an alternative to harassment, aggression, and warfare, has been with us since the development of human consciousness. Intergroup dialogue, as a form of academic enlightenment and social justice education, is a much more recent phenomenon.

A number of public agencies, communities and community groups, and many colleges and universities have developed forms of intergroup dialogue. In this volume, Dr. Ford tells the story of one such program on the campus of Skidmore College, a small liberal arts college in upstate New York. Formed eight years ago,

xii *Foreword*

Dr. Ford and the Skidmore program have achieved a position of national leadership for their curricular efforts, evaluative and research studies, and practical pedagogical advances in this realm. The work reported in this volume concentrates on one form of intergroup dialogues (IGD) – those involving matters of race – but a focus on race that consistently explores the intersectionalities of race with other forms of social division.

Dr. Ford and Skidmore are not alone in this effort. Similar programs were initiated at the University of Michigan 25 years ago and have been adopted and adapted at many colleges and universities. Some such efforts have been accompanied by evaluations and by thoughtful research on IGD and student learning outcomes. This book adds to the growing literature in this area and it additionally represents a marked expansion and advance in our practice of and knowledge about IGD in higher education.

Facilitating Change through Intergroup Dialogue is uniquely marked by four outstanding features. First, we see here theoretical clarity about the nature of social justice education and the grounding of the Skidmore program in the literature on IGD. This should be immediately helpful to others interested in creating and sustaining such programs in their own and different educational settings. Second, rigorous qualitative research portrays the longitudinal impacts of IGDs on a group of student facilitators some years after they completed their studies. These students were involved in the democratic process of leading their peers through the processes of self- and other-discovery. We learn important things about how these young people grew through the dialogic process. In particular, the book highlights how they continued to link their social justice learning to their careers, despite their struggles with resistance and feelings of being overwhelmed by the demands of social justice advocacy. Third, traditional research reporting is enhanced by a series of rich personal autobiographies and portraits (case studies) of five students' voyages of discovery of their own social identities, skills, and commitments to social justice advocacy. Kristie Ford models the best of dialogic practice in this research: she is a collaborator who writes with her (former) students as colleagues, much as she teaches with them as co-practitioner and co-learner/educator. And fourth, the volume provides fulsome descriptions of the successes and challenges that produced life-changing orientations in this group of students.

Dr. Ford's work, its findings and implications, will be immediately recognizable to those currently practicing or conducting research with IGDs. It also provides guidance to anyone in the public sphere wishing to increase the possibilities of effective civic conversations across social groupings and through the practice of social justice. This is an excellent and thought-provoking story.

Acknowledgments

I am eternally grateful to the countless people who helped bring *Facilitating Change through Intergroup Dialogue: Social Justice Advocacy in Practice* to fruition. In particular, I would like to acknowledge the following individuals:

The founders of the Program on Intergroup Relations (IGR) at the University of Michigan – Mark Chesler, Patricia Gurin, Ratnesh Nadga, David Schoem, Todd Sevig, Luis Sfeir-Younis, and Ximena Zúñiga – your vision and expertise continue to inspire me.

Mark Chesler, who initially introduced me to IGR when I entered the Sociology graduate program at the University of Michigan in 2001. I am forever grateful for your support and encouragement, as it furthered my social justice values and ultimately shaped my career trajectory to this point.

Kelly Maxwell, for providing me with the initial encouragement and inspiration needed to launch this book project.

Charles Behling and Monita Thompson, for so skillfully facilitating Skidmore College's IGR faculty/staff workshops throughout the years; watching you in action continues to shape my work in and outside the classroom.

Past and present IGR instructors at Skidmore College – Lei Bryant, Rochelle Calhoun, Mary Campo, Silvena Chan, Michael Ennis-McMillan, Sarah Goodwin, Rubén Graciani, Lisa Grady-Willis, Susan Layden, Peter McCarthy, Leya Moore, Jennifer Mueller, Joshua Nelson, Viviana Rangil, Nate Richardson, Jamin Totino, Brian Woods, and Adrienne Zuerner. This is an extremely labor-intensive endeavor; your passion and energy for social justice work, active engagement in the intergroup dialogue process, and insightful critiques have made our program stronger.

The 28 facilitators who generously opened up their hearts and lives to me – providing the rich data from which this book is based.

The ongoing collaborations with many current and former undergraduate students at Skidmore College – Eric Beriguete, Kali Block-Steele, Heather Lipkin, Victoria Malaney, Joseph Miranda, Eric Moretti, Josephine Orlandella, Elizabeth Pattison, Ashley Polanco, Jasmin Suarez, Kavey Vidal, Kali Villarosa, DyAnna Washington, and Mollie Weisenfeld. I greatly appreciate your thoughtfulness and attention to detail when assisting with transcription, coding, data analysis, and (in some cases) co-authorship.

xiv *Acknowledgments*

Linda Santagato, IGR's administrative professional, for managing our day-to-day programmatic operations. This would not be possible without your organizational support, wisdom, and get-it-done attitude.

The Dean of Faculty's Office at Skidmore College for funding our IGR program.

The entire University of Michigan and Skidmore College IGR family for embracing me and helping me to learn with and from you over the years. IGR not only allowed me to find a home in academia, but it has also given me a clear sense of purpose.

Catherine Bernard and the Taylor & Francis Editorial Board for believing in this project and guiding this process so diligently and professionally.

Finally, I would like to thank the publishers who granted permission for us to reprint or adapt the following journal articles:

Ford, K. A. (2012). Shifting white ideological scripts: The educational benefits of inter- and intraracial curricular dialogues on the experiences of white college students. *Journal of Diversity in Higher Education, 5*(3), 138–158.

- Adapted with permission from APA.

Ford, K. A., & Malaney, V. K. (2012). I now harbor more pride in my race: The educational benefits of inter- and intraracial dialogues on the experiences of students of color and multiracial students. *Equity & Excellence in Education, 45*(1), 14–35.

- Reprinted by permission of Taylor & Francis, Ltd, http://www.tandfonline.com.
- Reprinted by permission of the University of Massachusetts Amherst, College of Education, www.umass.edu/education.

Ford, K. A., & Orlandella, J. (2015). The "Not So Final Remark": The journey to becoming white allies. *Sociology of Race and Ethnicity, 1*(2), 287–301.

- Adapted with permission from ASA.

Sorensen, N., Nagda, B. A., Gurin, P., & Maxwell, K. E. (2009). Taking a "hands on" approach to diversity in higher education: A critical-dialogic model for effective intergroup interaction. *Analyses of Social Issues and Public Policy, 9*(1), 3–35.

- Figure 1.1: Reprinted with permission from John Wiley & Sons.

Thank you!

Abbreviations

IGD	Intergroup Dialogue
IGR	Intergroup Relations
HWI	Historically White Institution
LGBTQA	Lesbian, Gay, Bisexual, Transgendered, Queer/Questioning, and Allies
MRID	Multiracial Identity Dialogue
POC/WHITE	People of Color/White People Dialogue
UM	University of Michigan
WRID	White Racial Identity Dialogue

Part I

Contextualizing Intergroup Dialogue (IGD) Facilitation

1 Introduction
The Power of Dialogue

Kristie A. Ford

> The work is the work ... I am also human, and I am also doing the work internally too ... I can't turn away from it ... it's there ... Social injustice keeps me motivated every day. (Jennifer)

Since Michael Brown, an unarmed Black teenager, was fatally shot by a White police officer in Ferguson, Missouri, in 2014, activism on U.S. college campuses has refocused public attention on racial inequities. Students continue to unite to raise awareness about racialized police brutality and shootings through Black Lives Matter rallies and Die-Ins (Natarajan, 2014). On an institutional level, students of color have also worked to highlight racial microaggressions, or the subtle daily comments or actions that communicate hostility towards people of color (Hunter, 2013, p. 62; Ross, 2015; Sue, Capodilupo, Torino, Bucceri, Holder, Nadal, & Esquilin, 2007), through campaigns like "I, Too, Am Harvard" (http://itooamharvard.tumblr.com/) and, more recently, #thisis2016 (Woo & Al-Hlou, 2016).

In 2015, support for student demands to improve the racial climate at the University of Missouri sparked similar protests across the country (Libresco, 2015). Since then, other grassroots movements have also emerged, including Black college athletes refusing to stand for the national anthem, controversy surrounding racialized mascots or buildings named after problematic historical figures, and free speech versus hate speech conversations in the wake of the 2016 Clinton-Trump presidential election (Bump, 2015; Dickerson & Saul, 2016; Dickey, 2016; Dreid & Najmabadi; Frosch & Audi, 2015; Kingkade, Workneh, & Grenoble, 2015; Hartocollis, 2016; Jaschik, 2016; Wong & Green, 2016).

In an analysis of the 51 colleges/universities with formal demands created by students, Libresco (2015) noted that 35 schools, or 69%, list mandatory diversity training for faculty and/or diversity-related classes for students as a top priority in hopes of improving campus race relations. Within this context, understanding the short- and long-term impact of race and social justice courses – courses that actively address the dynamics of power, privilege, and oppression in pursuit of a more equitable world – on student values and actions is essential.

4 Kristie A. Ford

As Nagda, Gurin, & Lopez (2003) stated, "universities and colleges serve as a pipeline, socializing and training prospective workers to fulfill economic interest. On the other hand, higher education institutions are also an arena for preparing citizens for a *public* democracy, for civic leadership and public service" (p. 165). Colleges and universities in the U.S. have a unique and multifaceted role in shaping the hearts and minds of students who enter their institutions (Nagda et al., 2003). From a functional perspective, they are tasked with the responsibility of instilling the skills that students will need to productively work in a global economy; from a more idealist perspective, they are also directly and indirectly preparing students to use their leadership abilities to make a difference in their communities (Nagda et al., 2003). In order to effectively teach students how to bridge content learning with hands-on experience, higher educational institutions are increasingly turning to applied social justice teaching practices including, but not limited to, service-learning, civic engagement, and inter-/intra-group dialogue (Diaz & Perrault, 2010; Engberg, 2004; Gurin, 1999; Mayhew & Fernandez, 2007). This book focuses specifically on inter-/intra-group dialogue (IGD) as one compelling form of social justice education (Ford, 2012; Ford & Malaney, 2012; Nagda et al., 2003; Nagda, Gurin, Sorensen, & Zúñiga, 2009; Nagda & Zúñiga, 2003; Nagda, Zúñiga, & Sevig, 1995; Sorensen, Nagda, Gurin, & Maxwell, 2009; Zúñiga, Nagda, Chesler, & Cytron, 2007). More concretely, in this book we explore how, if at all, 28 former IGD peer-facilitators are applying what they learned to their personal and professional lives three to five years post-college. We begin by providing an overview of relevant literature on social justice education and IGD; then, we outline the organization and objectives of our book.

Social Justice Education and Advocacy

Bell (1997) defined social justice in the following manner:
The goal of social justice education is full and equal participation of all groups in a society that is mutually shaped to meet their needs ... [T]he process for attaining the goal of social justice ... should be democratic and participatory, inclusive and affirming of human agency and human capacities for working collaboratively to create change (pp. 3–4).

Using Bell's (1997) definition as a framework, Hackman (2005) articulated five key components connected to social justice education: (1) content mastery, (2) tools for critical analysis, (3) tools for social change, (4) tools for personal reflection, and (5) an awareness of multicultural group dynamics (pp. 103–104). Moreover, Landreman, Edwards, Balon, & Anderson (2008) argued that social justice educators must possess four competencies: knowing ourselves, knowing learners, designing outcomes-based activities, and co-creating facilitation (p. 3). Expanding upon this general framework, Mayhew and Fernandez (2007) contended that social justice education "centers the intersections of theory and practice (i.e., praxis) to intentionally consider process (e.g., teaching) and product (e.g., content, community action) in concert" (p. 61). In sum, ideally, social justice education should result in a cohort of students who have a nuanced sense of how to become social justice allies by "working with others to deconstruct

Introduction: The Power of Dialogue 5

systems of inequity" (Waters, 2010, p. 7). In other words, this approach should foster student empowerment and engagement in change actions based upon their social justice-related awareness, knowledge, and skills (Bell, 1997; Hackman, 2005; Landreman et al., 2008; Mayhew & Fernandez, 2007; Waters, 2010).

In addition, this body of literature focuses on the different stages of social justice advocacy and/or ally identity development (Broido, 2000; Broido & Reason, 2005; Edwards, 2006; Reason & Broido, 2005; Waters 2010). Edwards (2006), for instance, outlined three types of allyhood – allies for self-interest, altruism, and social justice: (1) allies for self-interest maximize their own gains within a racially structured society through individual interventions rather than acknowledging how they are implicated with the larger structural system of racism; (2) allies for altruism work *for* members of target groups, whom they sees as victims, in a (sometimes) patronizing effort to do the 'right' thing; and (3) allies for social justice work *with* members of oppressed groups, acknowledge their role in the racist system, and connect with other agent group members (adapted from Ford & Orlandella, 2015, p. 290). In the first and second types of allyhood, the focus remains on the self ("me") or others ("them"); instead, when allying for social justice the organizing principle is around "us" and the need to empower and seek justice for everyone. Similarly, Waters' (2010) model highlighted the three-stage maturation process required of racial justice advocates on cognitive, intrapersonal, and interpersonal levels. Focusing on White allies, stage one (the "initial" stage) is characterized by attributes like racial naiveté, adherence to dominant narratives, and homogenous (White) social networks. Stage two (the "intermediate" stage) involves increased awareness of differing social identities and perspectives, acknowledgement of systemic racial oppression and privilege, and fear of cross-racial interactions. Finally, the third stage (the "mature" stage) is distinguished by a "multifaceted, contextual, and culturally informed" world view (Waters, 2010, p. 5). During this developmental phase, allies have meaningful relationships with people of color, engage in anti-racist dialogue with other White people, and take action (Waters, 2010).

When conceptualizing an ally or justice-focused identity, however, it is also important to recognize the non-linear, fluid, and aspirational nature of this work that further complicates the practice of social justice (Edwards, 2006; Waters, 2010). As such, for the purposes of this book, we define social justice advocacy as the intentional, lifelong developmental process that people embark on, both individually and collectively, in hopes of creating a more just and equitable world around a range of social issues such as racism and white supremacy, classism, and heteropatriarchy.

Program on Intergroup Relations (IGR) and Inter-/Intra-Group Dialogue (IGD)[1]

A form of social justice education, the Program on Intergroup Relations (IGR) is a nationally recognized academic, credit-bearing program that originated at the University of Michigan in 1988 as a means of addressing racial tension (for more, see: www.igr.umich.edu). Its primary goal is to support student learning

6 *Kristie A. Ford*

and competencies around inter- and intragroup relations, conflict, and social justice across a range of social identities, including race, gender, sexuality, social class, religion, and nationality. Since then, it has expanded to a number of other colleges and universities across the United States.

Under the umbrella of IGR, Intergroup Dialogue (IGD) is defined by Zúñiga, Nagda, Chesler, and Cytron (2007) as a facilitated, face-to-face encounter that aims to cultivate meaningful engagement between members of two or more social identity groups that have a history of conflict. A race dialogue, for instance, brings together People of Color and White People (POC/WHITE). The components that distinguish IGD from more traditional courses include (1) structured, small group interactions between two or more social identity groups, (2) engaged pedagogies that balance content and process knowledge, and (3) co-learning environment led by two trained peer-facilitators (Nagda, Gurin, Sorensen, & Zúñiga, 2009; Zúñiga et al., 2007). (Adapted and reprinted with permission of Taylor & Francis: Ford & Malaney, 2012.)

While IGD is the most common dialogue practice, Intragroup Dialogues, like the Multiracial Identity (MRID) or White Racial Identity (WRID), support the exploration of a single marginalized or privileged group identity (Adams, Bell, & Griffin, 2007). Structurally similar to POC/WHITE, in the MRID or WRID, students explore common experiences, issues of power, privilege, and oppression, and the meaning of their racial identities through an intersectional lens. While the curricula may slightly differ depending upon the focus of the dialogue, all the courses follow a four-stage pedagogical model,[2] incorporate engaged learning activities and assignments,[3] and contain foundational readings on key concepts. (Adapted and reprinted with permission of Taylor & Francis: Ford & Malaney, 2012.)

Research on IGD

There is a growing body of research on the positive content and process-related student learning outcomes associated with race and gender focused IGD courses (Ford, 2012; Ford & Malaney, 2012; Nagda et al., 1995; Nagda & Zúñiga, 2003; Nagda, Gurin, Sorensen, Gurin-Sands, & Osuna, 2009; Nagda et al., 2009; Sorensen et al., 2009; Zúñiga, Lopez, & Ford, 2014). Nagda, Gurin, Sorensen, & Zúñiga (2009), for instance, identified three key learning outcomes of IGD – it enables students to (1) explore their social identities and critically examine structural inequities, (2) develop meaningful cross-identity relationships, and (3) apply content and process learning to promote alliance building and social action.

Moreover, based on a multi-university study across nine different colleges/ universities (Gurin, Nagda, & Zúñiga, 2013), Sorensen et al. (2009) created a Critical-Dialogic Theoretical Model that informs IGD curricular practices; the model provides a concise way of summarizing the observed pedagogical, communicative, and psychological processes that contribute to positive intergroup outcomes for students in race and gender dialogues. (See Figure 1.1.) More

Introduction: The Power of Dialogue 7

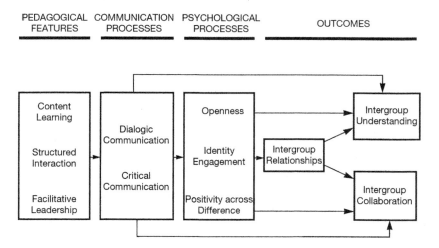

Figure 1.1 A Critical-Dialogic Theoretical Model of Intergroup Dialogue
Source: Sorensen et al., 2009

concretely, when controlling for selectivity, the quantitative and qualitative data indicated a number of attitudinal and behavioral changes in both White students and students of color, including (1) increased self-reflexivity about issues of power and privilege, (2) heightened awareness of the institutionalization of race and racism in the U.S., (3) improved cross-racial interaction, (4) diminished fear about race-related conflict, and (5) increased participation in social change actions during and after college. According to Nagda, Gurin, Sorensen, and Zúñiga (2009), students who participate in IGD experience these outcomes to a more significant extent than students in a control group or students enrolled in social science courses. Nagda et al. (2009) also theorized that there are two processes that mediate the influence of the IGD pedagogy on the related outcomes – communication processes which "occur between individuals" and psychological processes which "occur within individuals" (p. 4). In other words, content alone is not sufficient in fostering intergroup understanding, positive intergroup relationships, and intergroup collaboration; the dialogic process is also necessary (adapted with permission of APA: Ford, 2012).

Less, however, is understood about the long-term impact of inter-/intragroup pedagogies (Engberg, 2004; see Diaz & Perrault, 2010, and Vasques-Scalera, 2011 for exceptions). Highlighting this point, in his review of four different models for addressing racial bias, Engberg (2004) identified long-term assessment as necessary in order for scholars to better understand the promises and challenges of social justice educational interventions. In addition, most of the current literature focuses on student learning outcomes, not the skill sets

8   *Kristie A. Ford*

developed by the peer-facilitators who lead the IGD courses (Maxwell, Chesler, & Nagda, 2011; see Beale, Thompson, & Chesler, 2001; Nagda et al., 1995; Zúñiga et al., 2007 for exceptions).

Research on IGD Peer-Facilitators

In the Foreword to *Facilitating Intergroup Dialogues* (2011), Gurin emphasized the important role that IGD facilitators play in effectively guiding the group process by attending to the intellectual and emotional domains of social justice work (p. xix). Typically, IGD courses consist of 12–16 participants who meet weekly under the guidance of trained peer-facilitators representing the relevant social identities (Nagda & Maxwell, 2011). Unique to IGD, this model of critical-dialogic facilitation focuses on understanding oneself and others, as well as broader issues of power, privilege, and inequality (Nagda & Maxwell, 2011). In particular, Nagda and Maxwell (2011) outlined three central components of IGD facilitation: (1) "guiding, not just teaching," (2) "empowering, not just being empowered," and (3) "attending to processes, not just procedures" (pp. 7–18). The first principle recognizes, as Freire (1970) did, that this is a mindfully guided co-learning process in which facilitators and participants learn with and from each other. Second, this framework acknowledged that facilitators are continually learning through action and reflection, or "praxis" (Nagda & Maxwell, 2011, p. 10). The final principle emphasized that the communication processes of IGD are just as important as the structured activities and interactions. In sum, Nagda and Maxwell (2011) described IGD facilitators as "bring[ing] their learned expertise to guide the critical-dialogic process but do not reproduce a hierarchy of expert teachers and passive learners ... [They] use their selves and their own life standpoints ... in strategic ways, to generate the learning in the group" (pp. 17–18).

The training and support model for peer-facilitators centers on four components: (1) increasing facilitator knowledge of relevant theoretical frameworks, (2) encouraging facilitators to complicate their understanding of their own positionality and its societal implications, (3) building facilitator skill sets and competencies regarding social justice pedagogies, and (4) developing a nuanced understanding of group dynamics and inter-/intragroup interactions (Maxwell, Fisher, Thompson, & Behling, 2011). Informed by Jackson's (n.d.) "framework of multicultural competencies," IGD facilitators work to develop the Passion, Awareness, Skills, and Knowledge, or PASK, necessary to be successful in this demanding role (Maxwell, Fisher, Thompson, & Behling, p. 44). (See Chapter 2 for a description of the peer-facilitator training process.)

While we know that the role of peer-facilitators is crucial to student development in IGD, research on the short- and long-term outcomes of facilitators remains an under-explored area of scholarly inquiry (Engberg, 2004; Maxwell, Fisher, Thompson, & Behling, 2011). A few recent studies on the topic, however, emphasized the learning potential for this group of students, who were more aware of how to address power relationships within and across social identity groups (Maxwell, Fisher, Thompson, & Behling, 2011; Nagda, Timbang, Fulmer, & Tran, 2011), developed effective co-facilitator relationships, remained in alliances for social justice, and deepened their commitment to this work (Nagda et al., 2011). Moreover, we also know that the intensity of the IGD experience empowered peer-facilitators to engage in social justice actions once they graduated from college (Vasques-Scalera, 2011). Given that the unique position of peer-facilitators, as both teachers and learners in this process, can yield more significant and lasting outcomes than dialogue participants, IGD facilitators warrant more scholarly attention.

Objectives and Organization of Book

In order to better prepare for an increasingly diverse society, it is crucial that colleges/universities in the U.S. find innovative ways of integrating race and justice into the curricula. Highlighting this point, Nagda, Gurin, Sorensen, and Zúñiga (2009) argued: "Colleges and universities must create academic initiatives that engage students intellectually and foster an understanding of group-based inequalities and other dynamics that affect intergroup relationships" (p. 4). To address these concerns, many institutions of higher education have developed IGR programs to help students navigate diverse learning environments (Hurtado, 2005).

This book project highlights the collective efforts of faculty, staff, and peer-facilitators who delivered Skidmore College's IGD curricula over a five-year period, from 2009 to 2013. Specifically, through 28 in-depth qualitative interviews and five auto-ethnographies, *Facilitating Change through Intergroup Dialogue: Social Justice Advocacy in Practice* explores how, if at all, former IGD facilitators are applying what they learned to their personal and professional lives three to five years post-college. In particular, through a qualitative lens we examine the following questions: What are the short- and long-term implications of IGD on facilitators' personal and professional trajectory? How do IGD facilitators navigate race and social justice issues post-college? And, do IGD pedagogies help foster sustained racial identity and ally development?

This book is divided into three sections. First, it begins by summarizing the institutional context for this study and explaining the research methodology. Next, it presents the auto-ethnographies and unpacks emergent themes from the interview data – highlighting facilitators' learning outcomes. Finally, it ends with a discussion of suggested curricular and programmatic revisions that might strengthen IGD programs in hopes of furthering social justice advocacy and change within and beyond higher educational settings.

More concretely, Chapter 2 showcases Skidmore College as the context for this study – providing an overview of the institution, the pilot IGR program that eventually led to the first IGR minor in the United States, and the peer-facilitation training and instructor support model. It ends by outlining the methods of inquiry and the potential limitations of our chosen methodological approach.

10 *Kristie A. Ford*

After contextualizing the auto-ethnographies in a preface, the next five chapters feature former IGD facilitators' social justice pathways in their own words. Specifically, in Chapter 3, Malaney discusses her journey to becoming a social justice advocate. She begins with how she was introduced to IGR at Skidmore College and then considers her transition into the professional world, elaborating on how IGR informed her post-college job opportunities. Next, she reflects on her personal relationships and discusses how IGR contributed to her own self-growth. Malaney concludes by defining her commitment to social justice and why she will continually strive to be a social justice advocate both in her personal life and as an educational researcher and higher education administrator.

"Social Justice in Action and Inaction" explores the messy and nonlinear journey of a White IGD facilitator to sustain dedication to social justice and antiracism. In Chapter 4, Faude critically examines her experience as a White student in historically White institutional spaces, a White teacher in a predominately African American urban secondary school, and ultimately as a White researcher and teacher in a higher educational context.

Chapter 5 explores the complicated, and at times, uncomfortable lesson of advocacy through the work of the IGR program at Skidmore College. Through her own complex journey as a multiracial individual, IGR taught Hatch to force herself into uncomfortable situations, continuously challenging her surroundings and her own prejudices. By leaning into discomfort, confronting injustices, and empowering others, Hatch was able to gain the language and the tools to navigate the world through a social justice lens, guiding her to advocate for high school students in her post-college work.

In Chapter 6, Bajak discusses how Skidmore's IGR program forced her to reevaluate her understanding of her own identity as a half-Latina with the physical attributes of a White woman. It was, and continues to be, a productive struggle in her personal and professional life. As social justice advocates, she argues that we must not dismiss the constant interaction of race, class, language, and culture between ourselves and the different systems within which we all exist. As a social worker, by practicing empathy and challenging her own preconceptions, she strives to inspire change in those she can have impact on.

Concluding the auto-ethnographies, in Chapter 7, Bissonnette discusses how our identities are implicated in all that we do, especially in our work as social justice advocates. In "Toward a New Operational Paradigm for Social Justice," he argues that we must begin engaging with new ways of understanding the construction of our identity as well as the world around us in order to more effectively serve our communities.

Synthesizing patterns across the auto-ethnographies and interview data, Chapter 8, "Communicating Differently Post-College," focuses on the skills undergraduate students developed by co-facilitating IGD and highlights its related benefits in their post-college lives. Specifically, participants continued

Introduction: The Power of Dialogue   11

to hone their IGD practices, such as listening actively and with empathy, being attentive to group dynamics, balancing voice within a space, applying appropriate social justice terminology, and developing as effective leaders. Additionally, interviewees acknowledged the overarching benefits of IGD, including sureness in speaking about social justice topics, understanding systems of oppression, attention to racially diverse social networks, and programmatic support.

Next, to address the research question, "Do IGD pedagogies help foster sustained ally development and social justice advocacy?", Chapter 9 highlights four central themes, and related sub-themes, that inductively emerged in the data analysis process: (1) definitions of social justice advocacy, (2) how the facilitators have applied social justice to their personal and professional lives, (3) the challenges of engaging in this work, and (4) the motivation to continue working for change. It also unpacks the raced and gendered differences embedded in these patterns.

While most of the participants attempted to actively engage with issues of social justice post-college, it is also important to acknowledge the exceptions in hopes of better understanding the complexities of various personal and professional pathways. Using one participant, a White male, as a case study, Chapter 10 explores this facilitator's complicated and, sometimes, contradictory relationship to social justice. In doing so, the intricacies embedded in this individual counterexample may provide a window into broader sociological phenomenon worthy of further investigation.

In Chapter 11, we conclude by summarizing our findings and discussing the implications for how higher educational institutions might better support students in their social justice pursuits. We also offer research recommendations for furthering social justice advocacy and change both within and beyond higher educational institutions.

Finally, in the Afterword, "The Dialogue Continues: The Future of IGR," Bissonnette and Malaney discuss their collective vision for the future of IGR, which lies in both strengthening its presence in institutions of higher education as well as expanding beyond into the corporate sphere.

Ultimately, it is our hope that this book will be both functional and inspirational – providing concrete strategies for better supporting undergraduate students' justice efforts post-college as well as a vision for imagining what social justice advocacy might look like in the future.

In addition, as racial tensions and other inequities remain across the U.S., not just in college classrooms, we imagine that the themes highlighted in this book will also be relevant to K-12 educators, community settings, and within the corporate sphere (Dessel, Rogge, & Garlington, 2006; Groth, 2001; Walsh, 2006) (for more, see Chapter 12). More concretely, the data presented in *Facilitating Change* can extend beyond formal dialogue courses as it provides insight into broader social phenomenon related to cross-racial preconceptions, (mis)communication, and conflict.

12   *Kristie A. Ford*

Notes

1 In the remainder of the book, we use IGR to refer to the overarching Program on Intergroup Relations at Skidmore College and IGD to refer to the dialogue courses and related pedagogies.
2 For more explanation of the four stages, see: Zúñiga et al. (2007, pp. 27–28).
3 Adams et al. (2007) and Zúñiga et al. (2007) provide an overview of some of these activities.

References

Adams, M., Bell, L. A., and Griffin, P., eds. (2007). *Teaching for diversity and social justice: A sourcebook*. 2nd ed. New York, NY: Routledge.

Beale, R., Thompson, M., & Chesler, M. (2001). Training peer facilitators for intergroup dialogue leadership. In D. Schoem & S. Hurtado (Eds.), *Intergroup dialogue deliberative democracy in school, college, community, and workplace* (pp. 227–246). Ann Arbor, MI: University of Michigan Press.

Bell, L. A. (1997). Theoretical foundations for social justice education. In M. Adams, L. Bell, & P. Griffin (Eds.), *Teaching for diversity and social justice: A sourcebook* (pp. 3–15). New York, NY: Routledge.

Broido, E. M. (2000). The development of social justice allies during college: A phenomenological investigation. *Journal of College Student Development, 41*, 3–18.

Broido, E. M., & Reason, R. D. (2005). The development of social justice attitudes and actions: An overview of current understandings. In R. D. Reason, E. M. Broido, T. L. David, & N. J. Evans (Eds.), *Developing social justice allies: New directions for student services*, (pp. 17–28). San Francisco, CA: A Wiley Company.

Bump, P. (2015, Nov. 21). Why college student protesters are battling free speech, in 1 graph. *Washington Post*. Retrieved November 7, 2016 from https://www.washingtonpost.com/news/the-fix/wp/2015/11/21/why-protesters-on-college-campuses-are-battling-free-speech-in-1-graph/.

Dessel, A., Rogge, M. E., & Garlington, S. B. (2006). Using intergroup dialogue to promote social justice and change. *Social Work, 51*(4), 303–315.

Diaz, A., & Perrault, R. (2010). Sustained dialogue and civic life: Post-college impacts. *Michigan Journal of Community Service Learning*, Fall, 1–12.

Dickerson, C., & Saul, S. (2016, Nov. 10). Campuses confront hostile acts against minorities after Donald Trump's election. *New York Times*. Retrieved December 6, 2016 from http://www.nytimes.com/2016/11/11/us/police-investigate-attacks-on-muslim-students-at-universities.html?_r=0.

Dickey, J. (2016, May 31). The revolution on America's campuses. *Time*. Retrieved December 6, 2016 from http://time.com/4347099/college-campus-protests/.

Dreid, N., & Najmabadi, S. (2016, Nov. 15). Here's a rundown of the latest campus-climate incidents since Trump's election. *The Chronicle of Higher Education*. Retrieved December 6, 2016 from http://www.chronicle.com/blogs/ticker/heres-a-rundown-of-the-latest-campus-climate-incidents-since-trumps-election/115553?cid=at&utm_source=at&utm_medium=en&elqTrackId=a2dd9e8f94d54a07ace40be7cd274130&elq=6b06ea5ff9a74a08b8f7e13eda48f056&elqaid=11482&elqat=1&elqCampaignId=4497

Edwards, K. (2006). Aspiring social justice ally identity development: A conceptual model. *NASPA Journal, 43*(4), 39–60.

Engberg, M. E. (2004). Improving intergroup relations in higher education: A critical examination of the influence of educational interventions on racial bias. *Review of Educational Research, 45*(4), 473–524.

Ford, K. A. (2012). Shifting white ideological scripts: The educational benefits of inter- and intraracial curricular dialogues on the experiences of white college students. *Journal of Diversity in Higher Education, 5*(3), 138–158. Adapted with permission of APA.

Ford, K. A., & Malaney, V. K. (2012). I now harbor more pride in my race: The educational benefits of inter- and intraracial dialogues on the experiences of students of color and multiracial students. *Equity & Excellence in Education, 45*(1), 14–35. Reprinted by permission of Taylor & Francis, Ltd, http://www.tandfonline.com.

Ford, K. A., & Orlandella, J. (2015). The "Not So Final Remark": The journey to becoming white allies. *Sociology of Race and Ethnicity, 1*(2), 287–301.

Freire, P. (1970). *Pedagogy of the oppressed*. New York, NY: Seabury.

Frosch, D., & Audi, T. (2015, Nov. 13). Tolerance, free speech collide on campus. *Wall Street Journal*. Retrieved December 6, 2016 from http://www.wsj.com/articles/tolerance-free-speech-collide-on-campus-1447375073.

Groth, G. A. (2001). Dialogue in corporations. In D. Schoem & S. Hurtado (Eds.), *Intergroup dialogue: Deliberative democracy in school, in college, community, and the workplace* (pp. 195–209). Ann Arbor, MI: University of Michigan.

Gurin, P. (1999). Selections from the compelling need for diversity in higher education, expert reports in defense of the University of Michigan. *Equity & Excellence in Education, 32*(2), 36–62.

Gurin, P., Nagda, B. A., & Zúñiga, X. (Eds.). (2013). *Dialogue Across Difference: Practice, Theory, and Research on Intergroup Dialogue*. New York, NY: Russell Sage Foundation.

Hackman, H. W. (2005). Five essential components for social justice education. *Equity & Excellence in Education, 38*, 103–109.

Hartocollis, A. (2016, Aug. 4). College students protest, Alumni's fondness shrink. *New York Times*. Retrieved November 7, 2016 from http://www.nytimes.com/2016/08/05/us/college-protests-alumni-donations.html?_r=0.

Hunter, M. A. (2013). *Black Citymakers: How the Philadelphia Negro changed urban America*. Oxford, UK: Oxford University Press.

Hurtado, S. (2005). The next generation of diversity and intergroup relations research. *Journal of Social Issues, 61*(3), 595–610.

I, too, am, Harvard. Retrieved from http://itooamharvard.tumblr.com/

Jackson, B. W. (n.d.) *PASK: Framework for multicultural competency*. Amherst, MA: New Perspectives. Mimeograph.

Jaschik, S. (2016, Sept. 12). Taking a stand by refusing to stand. *Inside Higher Ed*. Retrieved November 6, 2016 from https://www.insidehighered.com/news/2016/09/12/debate-grows-over-national-anthem-college-events.

Kingkade, T., Workneh, L., & Grenoble, R. (2015). Campus racism protests didn't come out of nowhere, and they aren't going away quickly. *Huffington Post*. Retrieved November 6, 2016 from http://www.huffingtonpost.com/entry/campus-racism-protests-didnt-come-out-of-nowhere_us_56464a87e4b08cda3488bfb4.

Landreman, L, Edwards, K. E., Balon, D. G., & Anderson, G. (2008). Wait! It takes time to develop rich and relevant social justice curriculum. *About Campus, 13*(4), 2–10. Hoboken, NJ: John Wiley & Sons, Inc.

Libresco, L. (2015, Dec. 3). Here are the demands from students protesting racism at 51 colleges. *FiveThirtyEight*. Retrieved from http://fivethirtyeight.com/features/here-are-the-demands-from-students-protesting-racism-at-51-colleges/.

Maxwell, K. E., Chesler, M., & Nagda, B. A. (2011). Identity matters: Facilitators' struggles and empowered use of social identities in intergroup dialogue. In K. E. Maxwell, R. A. Nagda, & M. C. Thompson (Eds.), *Facilitating intergroup dialogues: Bridging differences, catalyzing change* (pp. 163–177). Sterling, VA: Stylus Publishing, Inc.

Maxwell, K. E., Fisher, R. B., Thompson, M. C., & Behling, C. (2011). Training peer facilitators as social justice educators. In K. E. Maxwell, R. A. Nagda, &

14 Kristie A. Ford

M. C. Thompson (Eds.), *Facilitating intergroup dialogues: Bridging differences, catalyzing change* (pp. 41–54). Sterling, VA: Stylus Publishing, Inc.

Mayhew, M. J., & Fernandez, S. D. (2007). Pedagogical practices that contribute to social justice outcomes. *The Review of Higher Education, 31*(1), 55–80.

Nagda, B. A., Gurin, P., & Lopez, G. (2003). Transformative pedagogy for democracy and social justice. *Race, Ethnicity, and Education, 6*(2), 165–191.

Nagda, B. A., Gurin, P., Sorensen, N., & Zúñiga, X. (2009). Evaluating intergroup dialogue: Engaging diversity for personal and social responsibility. *Diversity & Democracy, 12*(1), 1–5.

Nagda, B. A., Gurin, P., Sorensen, N., Gurin-Sands, C., & Osuna, S. M. (2009). From separate corners to dialogue and action. *Race and Social Problems, 1*(1), 45–55.

Nagda, B. A., & Maxwell, K. E. (2011). Deepening the layers of understanding and connection: A critical-dialogic approach to facilitating intergroup dialogues. In K. E. Maxwell, B. A. Nagda, & Thompson, M. C. (Eds.), *Facilitating intergroup dialogues: Bridging differences, catalyzing change* (pp. 1–22). Sterling, VA: Stylus Publishing, Inc.

Nagda, B. A., Timbang, N., Fulmer, N. G., & Tran, T. H. V. (2011). Not *for* others, but *with* others for all of us. In K. E. Maxwell, B. A. Nagda, & M. C. Thompson. (Eds.), *Facilitating intergroup dialogues: Bridging differences, catalyzing change* (pp. 179–199). Sterling, VA: Stylus Publishing, Inc.

Nagda, B. A., & Zúñiga, X. (2003). Fostering meaningful racial engagement through intergroup dialogues. *Group Processes and Intergroup Relations, 6*(1), 111–128.

Nagda, B. A., Zúñiga, X., & Sevig, T. D. (1995). Bridging difference through peer-facilitated intergroup dialogues. In S. Hatcher (Ed.), *Peer programs on the college campus: Theory, training, and 'voice of the peers'* (pp. 378–414). San Jose, CA: Resource Publications.

Natarajan, R. (2014, Dec. 15). Racial profiling has destroyed public trust in police. Cops are exploiting our weak laws against it. *Washington Post*. Retrieved November 7, 2016 from https://www.washingtonpost.com/posteverything/wp/2014/12/15/racial-profiling-has-destroyed-public-trust-in-police-cops-are-exploiting-our-weak-laws-against-it/.

Reason, R. D., & Broido, E. M. (2005). Issues and strategies for social justice allies (and the student affairs professionals who hope to encourage them). In R. D. Reason, E. M. Broido, T. L. David, & N. J. Evans (Eds.), *Developing social justice allies: New directions for student services* (pp. 81–89). San Francisco, CA: A Wiley Company.

Ross, L. (2015). *Blackballed: The black and white politics of race on America's campuses.* New York, NY: St. Martin's.

Sorensen, N., Nagda, B. A., Gurin, P., & Maxwell, K. E. (2009). Taking a "hands on" approach to diversity in higher education: A critical-dialogic model for effective intergroup interaction. *Analyses of Social Issues and Public Policy, 9*(1), 3–35. Figure 1.1 Reprinted by permission of John Wiley & Sons.

Sue, D. W., Capodilupo, C. M., Torino, G. C., Bucceri, J. M., Holder, A. M., Nadal, K. L., & Esquilin, M. (2007). Racial microaggressions in everyday life: implications for clinical practice. *The American Psychologist, 64*(4), 271–286.

University of Michigan, The Program on Intergroup Relations. Retrieved from www.igr.umich.edu.

Vasques-Scalera, C. (2011). Changing facilitators, facilitating change: The lives of intergroup dialogue facilitators post-college. In K. E. Maxwell, B. A. Nagda, & M. C. Thompson. (Eds.), *Facilitating intergroup dialogues: Bridging differences, catalyzing change* (pp. 201–212). Sterling, VA: Stylus Publishing, Inc.

Walsh, K. C. (2006). Communities, race, and talk: An analysis of the occurrence of civic intergroup dialogue programs. *The Journal of Politics, 68*(1), 22–33.

Waters, R. (2010). Understanding allyhood as a developmental process. *About Campus*, Nov–Dec., 1–8.

Wong, A., & Green, A. (2016, Apr. 4). Campus politics: A cheat sheet. *Atlantic*. Retrieved June 6, 2016 from http://www.theatlantic.com/education/archive/2016/04/campus-protest-roundup/417570/

Woo, J., & Al-Hlou, Y. (2016, Oct. 13). #thisis2016: Asian Americans respond. *Times Video*. Retrieved November 7, 2016 from http://www.nytimes.com/video/us/100000004706646/thisis2016-asian-americans-respond.html

Zúñiga, X., Lopez, G., & Ford, K. (Eds). (2014). *Intergroup dialogue: Engaging difference, social identities, and social justice: Research perspectives and new directions*. New York, NY: Routledge.

Zúñiga, X., Nagda, B. A., Chesler, M., & Cytron, A. (2007). Intergroup dialogue in higher education: Meaningful learning about social justice. *ASHE Higher Education Report Series, 32*(4). San Francisco, CA: Jossey-Bass.

2 Skidmore College as a National Leader
Institutional Context and Methods of Inquiry

Kristie A. Ford

I just think it was an awakening experience for me. I feel like connecting it back to Skidmore now, even though I only engaged in IGR during my senior year that is what my Skidmore experience was because it was the first time where I felt like I was doing what I needed to be doing ... I don't even know where I would be now or what I would be doing if it haven't been for that ... it's all due to the work I did in IGR. (Sophie)

This program needs to be everywhere. I wish it was everywhere, that I could just like do this forever. I'm so happy that it's still a part of Skidmore. (Beatriz)

Skidmore College

This research took at Skidmore College, a selective, small private liberal arts college in upstate New York. In accordance with national trends within higher education, women outnumber men on campus, 60% and 40% respectively. In terms of racial demographics, approximately 22% of students self-identify as domestic students of color[1] and 9% identify as International students (Skidmore College, Admissions and Financial Aid). While the College continues to recruit and enroll increasingly diverse cohorts of first-year students, significant diversity-related challenges are still present at this predominately and Historically White Institution (HWI). Like many comparable institutions, Skidmore continues to face a range of ongoing issues, including (1) marginalized social identity groups experience micro- (or macro)aggressions in and outside of the classroom; (2) biased incidents regarding race, social class, gender, religion, and sexuality remain prevalent occurrences on campus; and (3) campus climate challenges make it difficult to retain faculty and staff of color (adapted with permission of APA: Ford, 2012).

Given these identified issues, the College still struggles with how to best achieve an inclusive community; in hopes of making progress in this regard, it included a provision in the revised 2010 Strategic Plan, which focused on developing the diversity-related knowledge and skills of faculty, staff, and students (adapted with permission of APA: Ford, 2012). The plan also acknowledged the importance of IGR in achieving its overall mission, stating: "we also need to identify specific learning goals relating to these issues [intercultural and global understanding] and build upon the good work that has already been done, for example, by faculty members and students through the Intergroup Relations (IGR) Program" (Glotzbach, 2010, p. 8).

Intergroup Relations (IGR) Pilot Program

In 2008, Skidmore College supported the development of an Intergroup Relations (IGR) pilot program, adapted from the University of Michigan's (UM) model, to meet our Strategic Plan goals focused on intercultural and global understanding. In congruence with this curricular model (for more, see: Chapter 1), Skidmore's race-based social justice courses follow a similar structure, pedagogical style, and course content. Within a 10- to 12-person dialogue, the Intergroup/Intragroup Dialogues (IGD) merge theoretical knowledge on race and racism (the "head") with affective learning and communication skills (the "heart").

Concurrent with its foundation, Skidmore's IGR program engaged in pre- and post-test quantitative and qualitative assessment of the dialogue courses. Consistent with the multi-university study discussed in Chapter 1 (Gurin, Nagda, & Zúñiga, 2013; Nagda, Gurin, Sorensen, & Zúñiga, 2009; Sorenson, Nagda, Gurin, & Maxwell, 2009), we found that IGD pedagogies helped Skidmore students develop new competencies around issues of race, dialogic communication, and social justice work (for more, see: Ford & Malaney, 2012; Ford 2012; Ford & Orlandella, 2015). Given these findings, their alignment with Skidmore's Goals for Student Learning and Development,[2] and increased student interest, the program decided to move forward with the establishment of a minor in IGR. While other institutions offer IGR through co-curricular events and curricular courses (Sorensen et al., 2009), it was our hope that institutionalizing IGR as a minor would provide further legitimacy, via the transcript designation, for the race-related awareness, knowledge, and skills students develop by participating in the program. After a year and a half of consultation with Skidmore's Curriculum Committee, the Committee on Educational Policies and Planning, and other relevant faculty, staff, and administrators on campus, the IGR program submitted a proposal for the creation of an IGR minor in December 2011.

First IGR Minor in the United States

> I can't say any other class I've taken or any other experience in my education has been that visceral. (Renee)

In 2012, Skidmore became the first college/university in the U.S. to offer a minor in IGR. The IGR minor is designed for students with a curricular interest in race, social justice, and dialogic pedagogies. The courses specified within

18 *Kristie A. Ford*

the minor provide students with a foundation in understanding conceptual and theoretical knowledge related to race, racism, and racial identity development in the U.S. The program also helps students bridge theory (content) with practice (process) by applying communication and facilitation skills within intergroup and intragroup dialogue settings. In addition, skills learned in Intergroup Relations courses are applicable to the "real world" – including preparing students to enter graduate programs focused on social action, work in diverse workplaces, and successfully navigate a global society (www.skidmore.edu/igr).

Summarizing the value of the new IGR minor, Ford is quoted as saying, "I see this filling a necessary gap in the curriculum … It is cutting edge and is a path that many institutions are following. It requires an intentional teaching strategy to effectively and purposefully engage across identities." She continued: "Students have been our biggest supporters and allies in developing this minor … their interest brought us to this point" (Wise, 2012).

To complete the IGR minor at Skidmore College, students must demonstrate proficiency in five areas, which total 18 or 19 credits (Reproduced with permission: www.skidmore.edu/igr):

1　Intergroup/Intragroup Race Dialogue Course, either A, B, or C (2 credits)

 a. IGR 201A: People of Color/White People
 b. IGR 201B: Multiracial Identity
 c. IGR 201C: White Racial Identity
  In intergroup/intragroup race dialogue, students learn about racial identity, conflict, community, and social justice in the United States. Trained peer-facilitators encourage and guide dialogue about controversial social issues, such as affirmative action, immigration reform, and interracial relationships in a small classroom setting within the context of the relevant racial identity group(s). Working together with their peer-facilitators, student participants explore similarities and differences among and across groups and strive toward building a multicultural and democratic community. *Prerequisite*: Permission of the instructor.

2　Foundational Course in Race, Racism, and Dialogue (4 credits)

 a. Sociology 219C: Race and Power
  An analysis of U.S. race relations. How do people learn what it means to be "Black" or "White" within U.S. society? How will the changing demographics of the U.S. affect the traditional Black-White approach to race relations? How is race complicated by ethnicity, class, gender, sexuality, and other social identities? Students explore these questions by examining how race is constructed and reproduced within hierarchical structures of power and privilege, including educational inequalities, immigration policies, interracial relationships, and depictions of race in popular culture. *Prerequisites*: Introductory sociology course and permission of the instructor.

Skidmore College as a National Leader 19

3 Facilitator Training Application Course

  a. IG 361: Racial Identities: Theory and Praxis (4 credits)
An integration of sociological theory and praxis in a seminar that prepares students to facilitate dialogues on race. What factors hinder meaningful discourse about race? What skills promote interracial communication? How can we learn to engage more effectively in dialogue about race, power, and privilege in the United States? Through readings in racial identity theory, reflective and analytic writing, and experiential practice of dialogic communication skills, students learn to facilitate dialogues on controversial race-related topics, such as affirmative action, immigration reform, and interracial relationships. *Prerequisites*: Grade of B or better in Sociology 219C and permission of the instructor.

4 Capstone Course (5 credits total)

  a. IGR 364: Practicum in Facilitating (3 credits) taken concurrently with IGR 365
A course that helps students develop and improve their skills as dialogue facilitators. This will be done in the context of the belief that facilitation skills can be used throughout life to create social change. Good facilitators are social change agents. Moreover, by debriefing their actual dialogue experiences, facilitators can deepen their learning about racial identity, discrimination, privilege, and social justice. Must be taken concurrently with IGR 365. *Prerequisites*: Grade of B or better in IGR 361 and permission of the instructor.

  b. IGR 365: Dialogue Facilitation (2 credits) taken concurrently with IGR 364
An intergroup or intragroup dialogue course in which students facilitate dialogues about racial identity, conflict, community, and social justice. Must be taken concurrently with IGR 364. *Prerequisites*: Grade of B or better in IGR 361 and permission of the instructor.

5 At least one of the following elective courses (3 or 4 credits)

  a. Choice of courses that provide a theoretical foundation focused on a particular racial identity group and/or a race-focused topical area. Other courses with identity foci that demonstrate intersectionality with race will also be considered by the Program Director. Examples include:
a.1. American Studies 260J: Diversity in the U.S.
a.2. American Studies 331: Critical Whiteness in the U.S.
a.3. American Studies 376E: Disorderly Women
a.4. Anthropology 228: Queer Cultures: Sexual and Gender Identities in a Globalizing World
a.5. English 227: Intro to African American Literature
a.6. English 327: Special Studies in African American Literature
a.7. Music 205: Taiko and the Asian American Experience
a.8. Sociology 208: Social Inequalities
a.9. Social Work 212: Social Work Values and Populations at Risk

20 Kristie A. Ford

Peer-Facilitation Model and Training

One of the unique features of the Skidmore model is the intentional focus on peer-facilitation. Specifically, the Intergroup/Intragroup Dialogues are interdisciplinary, elective, letter-graded courses led by two trained undergraduate students with different (for the intergroup) or the same (for the intra-group) racial identities (Nagda & Maxwell, 2011). Peer-facilitators are trained by faculty/staff instructors at the College and are selected based on their academic performance, facilitation skills, developmental maturity, and leadership potential. As outlined in the previous sub-section, to be considered, peer-facilitators have to successfully complete a series of race-focused IGR/Sociology courses to adequately prepare them for this experience over at least a year-and-a-half period: (1) an introductory course which provides students with the opportunity to experience dialogue, (2) a 200-level course on theories of race and racism, and (3) a 300-level training course that helps facilitators develop and practice relevant skills. In addition, while facilitating a peer-led dialogue, students must enroll in a practicum course that provides ongoing support and supervision throughout their facilitation experience (also see: Maxwell, Fisher, Thompson, & Behling, 2011, pp. 43, 47).

Faculty/Staff Roles and Responsibilities

A collaborative initiative between Academic Affairs and Student Affairs, Skidmore's IGR program relies on the dedication of the instructor team. Over the years, approximately twenty rotating faculty/staff have been trained to teach one of the minor courses. In particular, facilitator oversight during the peer-led intergroup (People of Color/White People) and intragroup (White Racial Identity or Multiracial Identity) dialogues is crucial. Structurally, facilitators have two points of contact with faculty/staff instructors to enhance their Passion, Awareness, Skills, and Knowledge (PASK) toolkits (Maxwell et al., 2011): (1) Practicum in Facilitating, and (2) Dialogue Facilitation. The former is taught by a single instructor who meets weekly with all the peer-facilitators during a three-hour class period. Depending upon emergent issues in the various dialogue sections, the focus of the class may include debriefing the dialogues, brainstorming appropriate pedagogical strategies to address group dynamics, refining facilitation skills, increasing content knowledge, and engaging social identities at a deeper level. In addition, each co-facilitator team meets individually with a faculty/staff instructor or "coach" who provides more focused mentorship and support. Coach responsibilities include helping the facilitators adapt the dialogue curriculum to meet student needs, debriefing and problem-solving class-specific challenges, observing two of the dialogues and providing constructive feedback to the co-facilitation team, and grading all student and facilitator assignments.

It is within this institutional context that we launched our book project; next we outline our methods of inquiry.

Methodology

To gain an in-depth understanding of the long-term impact of IGD courses on facilitator development, we used a qualitative lens as we thought that this methodological approach would best capture the complexities of participants' post-college pathways (Berg, 2009).

Recruitment and Sample

We attempted to reach all Skidmore College IGD facilitators who were three to five years post-college at the time of the interview; this resulted in a cohort of 32 alumni from 2009 to 2013. Our sample consisted of 28 facilitators, or 88% of the population. Consistent with IGD enrollment trends, 9 self-identified as people of color, 5 as multiracial, and 14 as White; the majority, 18 participants, self-identified as women, and 10 identified as men. (See Table 2.1.) The participants also represented a range of other group and social identities, including differing nationalities, religious affiliations, sexualities, and social class backgrounds.

Table 2.1 Participant Demographics

Participant	Pseudonym	Race	Gender	Career Field
1	Talia	Multiracial	Woman	Higher Education
2	Sophie	White	Woman	Graduate School
3	Mia	Multiracial	Woman	K-12 Education
4	Vivian	Multiracial	Woman	Graduate School
5	Savannah	White	Woman	Nonprofit
6	Gabriel	Latino	Man	Higher Education
7	Frederick	Latino	Man	Higher Education
8	Leah	Multiracial	Woman	Graduate School
9	Elise	Latina	Woman	Social Work
10	Renee	White	Woman	Publishing
11	Julia	White	Woman	Social Work
12	Logan	Black	Man	Higher Education
13	Isabelle	Black	Woman	Graduate School
14	Beatriz	Latina	Woman	Social Work
15	Melissa	White	Woman	Graduate School

(continued)

22   Kristie A. Ford

Table 2.1 (continued)

Participant	Pseudonym	Race	Gender	Career Field
16	Seth	White	Man	K-12/Nonprofit
17	Evan	White	Man	K-12/Nonprofit
18	Laura	White	Woman	K-12 Education
19	Kiera	Multiracial	Woman	Business/K-12
20	Reese	White	Man	Business
21	Jennifer	Black	Woman	Higher Education
22	John	White	Man	Law
23	Samantha	White	Woman	Marketing
24	Reagan	White	Woman	Social Work
25	Katie	White	Woman	Business
26	Eliott	White	Man	K-12 Education
27	Jeremy	Latino	Man	Business
28	Devon	Black	Man	K-12 Education

Data Collection Procedures

Upon receiving IRB approval, Kristie Ford, the principle researcher, conducted semi-structured in-person or phone interviews, which ranged from 45 to 90 minutes, to understand each facilitator's experiences with and struggles around social justice. To explore facilitator growth in relation to the learning goals of the dialogues, the interview protocol included questions like the following: "What have you been doing post-college both personally and professionally? Reflecting on your IGD experience, what immediately comes to mind? Did you maintain the skill sets you developed as an IGD facilitator? Based on your experiences in IGD and beyond, what does it mean to you to be a social justice advocate? Do you consider yourself to be one? In what ways, if any, have you integrated social justice work into your personal or professional post-college life? Did your IGD experiences influence these decisions? What are the greatest challenges to continuing with social justice work after IGD?" As the director and an instructor for the program, Kristie knew all the participants from their IGD involvement at the College. In many cases, the interviewees' willingness to be honest and open in their responses may have enriched the findings of this study; social desirability and interviewer bias, however, could have also influenced participants' responses (Berg, 2009).

Data Analysis Procedures

The audio-recorded interviews were transcribed, assigned a number, and cleaned of any personally identifiable information; pseudonyms were used to protect participant identities. In hopes of enhancing credibility in the coding process by allowing for multiple racial lenses and interpretations of the data (Shenton, 2004), the interviews were read by Kristie, an African American woman, as well as four IGD research assistants of different racial identities. We employed an inductive analytical approach in an effort to remain open to the range of possible themes (Berg, 2009). Specifically, the research team used line-by-line hand-coding to identify the sociological phenomena that surfaced in the data. Then, through open and focused coding, the identified words or phrases were categorized into a list of themes and sub-themes. This enabled the research team to develop a coding scheme, which was subsequently entered into the QSR N-Vivo qualitative software program. Through N-Vivo the research team ran keyword and thematic searches, as well as numerical reports, which helped us refine previous schemata and focus on core emergent themes. Finally, by developing conceptual and theoretical memos, and examining relevant excerpts from the data, we compared themes to discern common patterns across the interviews (Berg, 2009; Emerson, Fretz, & Shaw, 1995). While the diversity of the research team was strategically employed to allow for various perspectives to surface, we nonetheless recognize that the identities of the team ultimately influenced the ways in which we co-created meaning in these analyses. In an effort to be attuned to potential subjectivities and biases in the collection and interpretation of the data, we regularly reflected on and debriefed the research process (Berg, 2009).

For this portion of the analysis, we were primarily interested in presenting themes that reflected group, rather than individual-level, differences, as it is the cross- and within-group patterns that might help researchers further elucidate the post-college pedagogical implications of IGD (adapted with permission of APA: Ford, 2012).

Auto-Ethnographies

In addition, this book includes auto-ethnographies from five of the interviewees, which "intentionally assumes a personal stance" through self-reflective writing, as the personal transformations evident in these data were also powerful (Babbie, 2011, p. 325; Berg, 2009). This unique approach provides an especially useful and provocative data source, as it allows facilitators to engage in self-reflexivity, which is paramount to the IGD process (Nagda & Maxwell, 2011). In doing so, through self-reflections, critical analysis, and engagement with the relevant literature, the authors showcase their social justice pathways, in their own words. Each chapter is thus distinct in format and voice.

The auto-ethnographies in this book emerged as an expanded version of remarks given during an IGR alumni panel at the inaugural Northeastern IGR Conference hosted by Skidmore College in June 2014. Based on their astute reflections, panelists were invited to submit a chapter that grappled with the

24 Kristie A. Ford

following questions: "What does being a social justice advocate mean to you? How have you achieved this ideal, in your various post-college roles? How have you failed to achieve this ideal? What are the moral and/or philosophical challenges you face when engaging in social justice work from a privileged social location? How do you know you are making a difference? How do you know when you might be reinforcing oppressive systems? What support do you need? What support are you getting? How do you stay focused on the goal despite the challenges? How did the IGR program help you navigate the complexities of social justice work? In what ways did IGR not fully prepare you for entering the work world and its challenges?" The included personal narratives provide insightful commentary into the individual struggles and successes of IGD alumni as they work to apply their social justice ideals to post-college life.

Limitations

Although this study has the potential to advance our understanding of IGD facilitators' sustained learning, it also has several limitations. First, given the small sample size, the results cannot be generalized to other programs or student populations. The benefit of qualitative research, however, is the nuance of empirical evidence that it provides – knowledge that can be subsequently adapted, expanded, and applied to future studies in the field (Berg, 2009). In addition, while we tried to reach out to all 2009–2013 facilitators, in a few cases, we were unable to locate current contact information. Finally, since the participants were located across the U.S. and abroad, phone interviews were often a more efficient option, but did not allow for documentation of body language. In spite of these shortcomings, the rich data presented in this book provide useful information as educators and practitioners continue to examine the best pedagogical practices to foster students' long-term commitment to and engagement with issues of equity and justice. These findings not only have significant implications for predominately White higher educational institutions, but can also potentially impact the way racially segregated secondary schools engage with issues of race and social justice in the classroom. Future research can build on these results by further exploring the nuances of student learning across institutional context, demographic setting, and time.

Turning to the study at hand, in the subsequent chapters, five former IGD facilitators write their own auto-ethnographies, reflecting on their social justice journeys during and after college.

Notes

1 The number of students of color at the College is based on student self-identifications, which reflects people of African, Asian, Latin American, and indigenous descent. While the number is not inclusive of International students, it is possible that some students might identify with both categories.
2 The four Goals for Student Learning and Development are (1) knowledge, (2) intellectual skills and practice, (3) personal and social values, and (4) transformation June 8, 2016 (https://www.skidmore.edu/assessment/goals-for-student-learning.php).

References

Babbie, E. (2011). *The basics of social research*. Belmont, CA: Wadsworth.

Berg, B. L. (2009). *Qualitative research methods for the social sciences*. Boston, MA: Pearson Education.

Emerson, R. M., Fretz, R. I., & Shaw, L. L. (1995). *Writing ethnographic fieldnotes*. Chicago, IL: University of Chicago Press.

Ford, K. A. (2012). Shifting white ideological scripts: The educational benefits of inter- and intraracial curricular dialogues on the experiences of white college students. *Journal of Diversity in Higher Education, 5*(3), 138–158. Adapted with permission from APA.

Ford, K. A., & Malaney, V. K. (2012). I now harbor more pride in my race: The educational benefits of inter- and intraracial dialogues on the experiences of students of color and multiracial students. *Equity & Excellence in Education, 45*(1), 14–35. Reprinted by permission of Taylor & Francis, Ltd, http://www.tandfonline.com.

Ford, K. A., & Orlandella, J. (2014). The "Not So Final Remark": The journey to becoming white allies. *Sociology of Race and Ethnicity, 1*(2), 287–301.

Glotzbach, P. (2010). Strategic renewal: Reframing Our priorities at the midpoint of the strategic plan. Retrieved June 8, 2016 from https://www.skidmore.edu/planning/documents/reports/Strategic-Renewal-PDF.pdf.

Gurin, P., Nagda, B. A., & Zúñiga, X. (Eds). (2013). *Dialogue across difference: Practice, theory, and research on intergroup dialogue*. New York, NY: Russell Sage Foundation.

Maxwell, K. E., Fisher, R. B., Thompson, M. C., & Behling, C. (2011). Training peer facilitators as social justice educators. In K. E. Maxwell, R. A. Nagda, & M. C. Thompson (Eds.), *Facilitating intergroup dialogues: Bridging differences, catalyzing change* (pp. 41–54). Sterling, VA: Stylus Publishing, Inc.

Nagda, B. A., Gurin, P., Sorensen, N., & Zúñiga, X. (2009). Evaluating intergroup dialogue: Engaging diversity for personal and social responsibility. *Diversity & Democracy, 12*(1), 1–5.

Nagda, B. A., & Maxwell, K. E. (2011). Deepening the layers of understanding and connection: A critical-dialogic approach to facilitating intergroup dialogues. In K. E. Maxwell, B. A. Nagda, & Thompson, M. C. (Eds.), *Facilitating intergroup dialogues: Bridging differences, catalyzing change* (pp. 1–22). Sterling, VA: Stylus Publishing, Inc.

Shenton, A. K. (2004). Strategies for ensuring trustworthiness in qualitative research projects. *Education for Information, 22*, 63–75.

Skidmore College, Admissions and Financial Aid. Retrieved June 8, 2016 from http://www.skidmore.edu/admissions/facts/.

Skidmore College, Goals for Student Learning and Development. Retrieved June 8, 2016 from https://www.skidmore.edu/assessment/goals-for-student-learning.php.

Skidmore College, Intergroup Relations. Retrieved from www.skidmore.edu/igr.

Sorensen, N., Nagda, B. A., Gurin, P., & Maxwell, K. E. (2009). Taking a "hands on" approach to diversity in higher education: A critical-dialogic model for effective intergroup interaction. *Analyses of Social Issues and Public Policy, 9*(1), 3–35.

Wise, A. (2012). New minor in intergroup relations now available. Retrieved June 8, 2016 from http://www.skidmore.edu/news/2012/3551.php.

Part II
IGD Facilitator Reflections

II A. Individual Narratives of Change

Preface to the Auto-Ethnographies

Kristie A. Ford

Northeastern IGR Conference at Skidmore College

In 2014, Skidmore College hosted the inaugural Northeastern Intergroup Relations (IGR) Conference, which brought together approximately 150 Intergroup Dialogue (IGD) scholars, practitioners, teachers, students, and activists from across 28 colleges and universities in the United States and abroad. In hopes of highlighting emergent research in the field, sharing best practices, and networking with colleagues, the conference schedule included keynote speakers, panels, break-out sessions, film screenings, and social events. (Skidmore College, 2015)

Alumni IGD Facilitator Panel[1]

When the call for proposals was announced, Victoria Malaney and Sarah Faude, two Skidmore graduates, wrote a successful proposal for an alumni panel of IGD facilitators. In soliciting volunteers, they were attentive to a range of representational factors, such as attempting to diversify based on class year, academic major, and career pathway; in addition, they were thoughtful about the composition of the group in terms of race, ethnicity, gender, sexual orientation, and social class. Victoria and Sarah hoped that the panel would provide an opportunity for alumni to reflect on how they were introduced to IGR, how their facilitation experiences affected their college experience, and how IGR influenced their post-graduate plans and career trajectories. More concretely, the following questions guided the panel: (1) What was your involvement with IGR at Skidmore?, (2) In what ways did IGR impact the rest of your time at Skidmore?, (3) How, if at all, did IGR influence your post-graduation ambitions and/or plans?, and (4) Does IGR continue to guide your current work?

The stories that the panelists told during the 75-minute conference session eventually became the basis for the auto-ethnographies that follow. As noted in Chapter 2, auto-ethnography "intentionally assumes a personal stance" through self-reflective writing (Babbie, 2011, p. 325; Berg, 2009). This distinctive approach yielded especially meaningful data, as it allowed these five former facilitators to practice self-reflexivity, which is crucial to the IGD process (Nagda & Maxwell, 2011).

30   *Kristie A. Ford*

Reading the Auto-Ethnographies

In Chapters 3–7, auto-ethnographies by Victoria Malaney, Sarah Faude, Teshika Hatch, Luna Bajak, and Stephen Bissonnette offer introspective self-analyses about how the IGR program shaped their post-college pathways and how it continues to frame their current social justice work in higher educational institutions (Chapters 3 and 4), nonprofit and community organizations (Chapters 5 and 7), social services (Chapter 6), and K-12 schools (Chapter 7).[2]

As the reader will note, the subsequent auto-ethnographies are distinct in format and voice, each different in style, quality, and level of richness, which is perhaps indicative of post-college educational status, career trajectory, and access to a social justice community.

As the editor, Kristie Ford gave critical feedback on the drafts throughout the process in an effort to ensure clarity and cohesion; the ideas and perspectives presented in these chapters, however, reflect the authors' personal narratives.

Despite the individualistic differences, the reader should be attentive to four salient themes, and related sub-themes, that emerged through an analysis of the auto-ethnographies: (1) racial awakening and the path towards social justice advocacy; (2) acquisition of IGD content knowledge and voice; (3) application of IGD process knowledge and skills; and (4) power, privilege, empowerment, and social change (See Table 3.1.). The subsequent sub-sections outline each in turn:

Table 3.1 Summary of Auto-Ethnography Themes

---

1. *Racial Awakening and the Path to Towards Social Justice Advocacy*

   a. Understanding social identities, intersectionality of identities, and the complexities of identity
   b. Navigating whiteness and its implications
   c. Grappling with being the target and/or perpetrator of oppression

2. *Acquisition of IGD Content Knowledge and Voice*

   a. Developing language around issues of identity and justice

3. *Application of IGD Process Knowledge and Skills*

   a. Listening actively and with empathy
   b. Honoring divergent perspectives and experiences
   c. Striving to foster anti-hierarchical interactional spaces

4. *Power, Privilege, Empowerment, and Social Change*

   a. Choosing to remain engaged with social justice issues
   b. Using knowledge, skills, and voice to challenge systems of oppression
   c. Empowering communities to collectively work towards equity and justice

      i Remaining attentive to the ways in which these strategies may reify oppressive systems (e.g., colonizing mentality, "helping" narratives, White "savior" complex)

Preface to the Auto-Ethnographies   31

Racial Awakening and the Path to Towards Social Justice Advocacy

For these five facilitators, the path towards racial awareness and a social justice mindset was complicated, challenging, and messy. In different ways, each
reflected on their unique journeys, as they navigated the intersections of race,
ethnicity, gender, sexuality, social class, religion, nationality, language, and
culture. For the White facilitators, Sarah and Stephen, they grappled with their
relationship to whiteness (Helms, 1990/1995), as it intersected with other agent
and target social identities, as well as the societal meaning and implications associated with it. Contextualizing his racial story from a historical and contempo-
rary vantage point, Stephen described how both have shaped his current identity
as a "queer, anti-racist, feminist IGD peer-facilitator." Sarah also reflected on her
early racial socialization (Harro, 2000b), focusing, in particular, on the ways her
family ignored or silenced conversations about race – including never discussing interracial relationships, access to private school, or the raced and classed
implications of in-home cleaning services and caretakers. As White individuals
embedded in an inherently racist system (Bonilla-Silva, 2014; Feagin, 2013),
Sarah and Stephen both struggled with how to appropriately use their white
privilege and power to create change. Accordingly, Sarah questioned: "When is
using privilege the strategic use of armor to name oppression without injury and
when does it silence those who are trying to tell their stories?"

In a slightly different way, IGD helped Luna, who described herself as "half-
Latina with the physical attributes of a White woman," figure out how to take
responsibility for her "own complicity with whiteness" (Jensen, 2005). Likewise,
the two other multiracial facilitators, Victoria (Indo-Caribbean American,
Spanish, and White) and Teshika (Japanese American and White), learned
to reconcile the complexity of their identities within a society that tried to
place them into boxes with questions like, "What are you?" According to Tatum
(2003), this question reinforces others' need to racially categorize, and assign
meaning, to different groups of people.

In addition, the multiracial participants reported negotiating their positionality as both targets of oppression and unintentional agents of oppression, even
as they worked to achieve greater equity in their workplaces and communities.
Through critical reflection, they were continuously working to examine their
own biases and adjust their actions accordingly. To that end, Teshika admitted
that she initially felt unsafe in her Oakland, California neighborhood, which
was much more racially diverse than her previous (primarily White) community.
This realization, however, reminded her that re-socialization and (eventually)
liberation (Harro, 2000a) is a continual, life-long process of reflection, development, and change.

Acquisition of IGD Content Knowledge and Voice

In accordance with the Critical-Dialogic Theoretical Model of Intergroup
Dialogue (Sorensen, Nagda, Gurin, & Maxwell, 2009), the next two themes
highlight the content knowledge and process-related skills that students, and

32   *Kristie A. Ford*

facilitators more profoundly, learned through participation in IGD (Ford, 2012; Ford & Malaney, 2012; Maxwell, Chesler, & Nagda, 2011; Nagda, Gurin, Sorensen, & Zúñiga, 2009; Nagda & Maxwell, 2011; Nagda & Zúñiga, 2003; Sorensen, Nagda, Gurin, & Maxwell, 2009; also see Chapter 8). Beginning with the former, all five facilitators discussed the foundational terminology they acquired to discuss identity and justice issues. Throughout Teshika's narrative, for instance, she highlighted how she "learned the language" to constructively "verbalize what I had been feeling" and to promote social change:

> Without IGR I would have felt voiceless and powerless – I would never have learned the language to name what I had been feeling and I wouldn't have known that my experience was not unusual. Because of the experiences in IGR, I not only understand the world better but I feel empowered to be an advocate for others who are struggling to understand the world themselves. With the tools that I gained through facilitation, I have been able to recognize the process it takes to develop one's own social identity and have acquired the language to speak up when others are silenced.

For Teshika, as well as the other contributors, understanding and properly applying social justice-oriented theoretical frameworks, empowered her not only to speak up, but also to act.

Application of IGD Process Knowledge and Skills

Moreover, the facilitators underscored the process-focused communication and facilitation skills – including listening actively and empathetically, honoring divergent perspectives and experiences, and striving to foster anti-hierarchical interactional spaces (Freire, 1970; McCormick, 1999; Schoem, Hurtado, Sevig, Chesler, & Sumida, 2001) – that they continued to use in their post-college lives (also see Chapter 8). For example, in her work with mentally ill and chemically addicted homeless adult women, Luna employed her active listening skills to establish a "trusting and safe environment," which allowed her to better support their transition from homelessness to supportive housing. For Sarah, "critical dialogue and listening with empathy" were crucial IGD skills she used to more effectively teach, and learn from, a class of 12-year-old African American girls.

Power, Privilege, Empowerment, and Social Change

Finally, the facilitators discussed how to acknowledge their own power and privilege, empower others as well as themselves, and collectively work towards equity and justice. As they elaborated in their respective stories, these idealistic principles can be difficult to fully achieve in practice. Although they all wanted to use their knowledge, skills, and power to interrupt systems of oppression, they also questioned how to responsibly do so. For instance, when mentoring women who were incarcerated, Victoria asked: "Was I actually reifying the

Preface to the Auto-Ethnographies 33

subordinate experiences of women because I had the freedom of walking in and out of the jail? Like Victoria, Stephen and Sarah also grappled with the privilege of entering and exiting under-served communities and the consequences of their actions.

Wary of problematic "helping" narratives, colonizing mentalities, and the White "savior" complex (Edwards, 2006; Ford & Orlandella, 2015; Hughley, 2010; Kendall, 2006), Stephen pondered, "How do White Americans then advocate for social justice without overpowering the oppressed and perpetuating the White missionary complex?" Similarly, the remaining facilitators also worried about whether the social justice choices they made might have unintentionally reified oppressive systems. Sarah and Luna, for instance, both discussed the hierarchical and unjust approaches to discipline and control they observed in the K-12 schools where they were placed. Each facilitator, therefore, had to decide how to reconcile the cognitive dissonance they experienced between their social justice values and the day-to-day realities of their work environments. For some, this meant seeking alternate forms of employment; for others this meant re-defining their role and approach to working within a fundamentally oppressive, and broken, system. To that end, Teshika noted:

> I have come to see my role as a true advocate and ally – my job was not to *help* the youth or to fix their problems, but instead to empower them to recognize their own strengths and their own abilities, and in turn to give them the skills to navigate the systems of inequality. (Freire, 1970)

Moreover, Stephen reflected on the following: "If our traditional paradigms inherently house institutionalized systems of privilege and oppression, how do we operate outside of these paradigms and systems?" In response, he suggested that we need to envision a co-participatory model of engagement that would function outside of the traditional confines of power, privilege, and inequality. Victoria, Sarah, Teshika, and Luna, like Stephen, were also committed to disrupting the status quo, challenging dominant narratives, and exploring new, more socially just ways of existing in the world. Despite the complexities and uncertainties along the way, they were (and are) actively choosing to remain engaged. According to Teshika, "After two semesters of IGD, there was absolutely no turning back for me." Their journeys, in their own words, are recounted in the next five chapters of this book.

References

Babbie, E. (2011). *The basics of social research.* Belmont, CA: Wadsworth.

Berg, B. L. (2009). *Qualitative research methods for the social sciences.* Boston, MA: Pearson Education, Inc.

Bonilla-Silva, E. (2014). *Racism without racists: Color-blind racism and the persistence of racial inequality in America.* Lanham, MD: Rowman & Littlefield.

Edwards, K. (2006). Aspiring social justice ally identity development: A conceptual model. *NASPA Journal, 43*(4), 39–60.

34 Kristie A. Ford

Feagin, J.R. (2013). *The white racial frame: Centuries of racial framing and counter-framing*. New York, NY: Taylor & Francis.

Ford, K. A. (2012). Shifting white ideological scripts: The educational benefits of inter- and intraracial curricular dialogues on the experiences of white college students. *Journal of Diversity in Higher Education*, 5(3), 138–158. Adapted with permission of APA.

Ford, K. A., & Malaney, V. K. (2012). I now harbor more pride in my race: The educational benefits of inter- and intraracial dialogues on the experiences of students of color and multiracial students. *Equity & Excellence in Education*, 45(1), 14–35. Reprinted by permission of Taylor & Francis, Ltd, http://www.tandfonline.com.

Ford, K. A., & Orlandella, J. (2015). The "not so final remark": The journey to becoming white allies. *Sociology of Race and Ethnicity*, 1(2), 287–301.

Freire, P. (1970). *Pedagogy of the oppressed*. New York, NY: The Continuum International Publishing Group Inc.

Harro, B. (2000a). The cycle of liberation. In M. Adams, W. J. Blumenfeld, R. Castañeda, H. W. Hackman, M. L. Peters, & X. Zúñiga (Eds.), *Reading for diversity and social justice* (pp. 463–469). New York, NY: Routledge.

Harro, B. (2000b). The cycle of socialization. In M. Adams, W. J. Blumenfeld, R. Castañeda, H. W. Hackman, M. L. Peters, & X. Zúñiga (Eds.), *Reading for diversity and social justice* (pp. 15–20). New York, NY: Routledge.

Helms, J. E. (1990). *Black and white racial identity: Theory, research, and practice*. Westport, CT: Greenwood.

Helms, J. E. (1995). An update of Helm's white and people of color racial identity models. In J. G. Ponterotto, J. M. Casas, L. A. Suzuka, & C. M. Alexander (Eds.), *Handbook of Multicultural Counseling* (pp. 181–98). Thousand Oaks, CA: Sage.

Hughey, M. (2010). The white savior film and reviewers' reception. *Symbolic Interaction*, 33(3), 475–496.

Jensen, R. (2005) *The heart of whiteness: Confronting race racism and white privilege*. San Francisco, CA: City Lights Publication.

Kendall, F. (2006). *Understanding white privilege*. New York, NY: Routledge.

Maxwell, K. E., Chesler, M., & Nagda, B. A. (2011). Identity matters: Facilitators' struggles an empowered use of social identities in intergroup dialogue. In K. E. Maxwell, R. A. Nagda, & M. C. Thompson (Eds.), *Facilitating intergroup dialogues: Bridging differences, catalyzing change* (pp. 163–177). Sterling, VA: Stylus Publishing, Inc.

McCormick, D. (1999). Listening with empathy: Taking the other person's perspective. In A. L. Cooke, M. Brazzel, A. S., Craig, & B. Greig (Eds.), *Reading book for human relations' training* 8th edition (pp. 57–60). Alexandria, VA: NTL Institute for Applied Behavioral Science.

Nagda, B. A., Gurin, P., Sorensen, N., & Zúñiga, X. (2009). Evaluating intergroup dialogue: Engaging diversity for personal and social responsibility. *Diversity & Democracy*, 12(1), 1–5.

Nagda, B. A., & Maxwell, K. E. (2011). Deepening the layers of understanding and connection: A critical-dialogic approach to facilitating intergroup dialogues. In K. E. Maxwell, B. A. Nagda, & Thompson, M. C. (Eds.), *Facilitating intergroup dialogues: Bridging differences, catalyzing change* (pp. 1–22). Sterling, VA: Stylus Publishing, Inc.

Nagda, B. A., & Zúñiga, X. (2003). Fostering meaningful racial engagement through intergroup dialogues. *Group Processes and Intergroup Relations*, 6(1), 111–128.

Schoem, D., Hurtado, S., Sevig, T., Chesler, M., & Sumida, S. H. (2001). Intergroup dialogue: Democracy at work in theory and practice. In D. Schoem & S. Hurtado (Eds.), *Intergroup dialogue: Deliberative democracy in school, college, community, and workplace* (pp. 1–21). Ann Arbor, MI: University of Michigan Press.

Skidmore College (2015). 2015 Northeastern IGR Conference. Retrieved on December 6, 2016 from https://www.skidmore.edu/igr/northeast-conference/index.php.

Sorensen, N., Nagda, B. A., Gurin, P., & Maxwell, K. E. (2009). Taking a "hands on" approach to diversity in higher education: A critical-dialogic model for effective intergroup interaction. *Analyses of Social Issues and Public Policy*, 9(1), 3–35.

Tatum, B. (2003). *"Why are all the black kids sitting together in the cafeteria?": And other conversations about race*. New York, NY: Basic Books.

Notes

1 Since they organized the alumni panel, Victoria Malaney and Sarah Faude co-authored this section of the preface.

2 While some of the facilitators' post-college pathways included jobs in several of these areas, for organizational purposes the chapters are delineated based on their existing professions at the time the auto-ethnographies were written.

3 On Becoming a Social Justice Advocate

Victoria K. Malaney

In high school my favorite quote was, "Be the change you wish to see in the world," by Mahatma Gandhi. While this quote still resonates with me, I have found that my understanding of Gandhi's meaning has since evolved. Intergroup Dialogue (IGD) made me self-aware of my social identities by providing me the opportunity to critically examine my power and privileges. As a result, I have committed to creating social change, and thereby becoming a social justice advocate who uses my spheres of influence to encourage others to do the same (Goodman & Shapiro, 1997).

Reflecting on my experiences with IGD at Skidmore College, I can now clearly see that IGD was pivotal in influencing the choices I have made thus far in my post-college life. Throughout this chapter, I highlight both the successes and challenges of my ongoing professional and personal social justice journey.

Entering College

When I entered college, I left my family for the first time to come to an entirely new state to pursue higher education. As a first-generation student, I was nervous about going to school in the Northeast when I had grown up in a multiracial[1] (Indo-Caribbean American, Spanish, and White) family in the South. As I began my first year at Skidmore, I wrestled with understanding my mixed-race identity against the background of a predominately and historically White institution (Moore, 2007). Commonly, peers asked, "What are you?" and although I had heard this question many times growing up, it was in the college environment that I began to notice how it bothered me even more than before and made me feel annoyed each time I was asked. I would later learn that the question, "What are you?" is actually a multiracial microaggression (Johnston & Nadal, 2010), because the question objectifies a multiracial person and reduces his or her mere existence to being "treated like an object" or even further dehumanizes the person as being a symbol of the racialized ideal. Repeatedly, hearing this same question also transmits the message, "You are not normal, and it is okay for me to ask you about it" (Johnston & Nadal, 2010, p. 133). In sum, racial microaggressions are common "daily verbal, behavioral or environmental indignities, whether intentional or unintentional, that communicate hostile, derogatory or negative racial slights and insults toward people of color" (Sue, Capodilupo, Torino, Bucceri, Holder, Nadal, & Esquilin, 2007, p. 271). Though I now know about racial microaggressions, prior to my introduction to IGD, I did not have the ability to conceptualize questions about my multiple races and understand racism in critical way. Moreover, while I had experienced uncomfortable moments related to my racial ambiguity as a mixed-race woman of color and based on my middle-class status, it was not until I took a course in the Intergroup Relations (IGR) program at Skidmore College that I started to comprehend the relationship between intersecting social identities. I also learned that depending on a person's ascribed social identities, an individual possesses different levels of power, privilege, and oppression (Johnson, 2005).

My Introduction to the IGR Program

I was a rising sophomore at Skidmore and 19 years old when I met Professor Kristie Ford at the National Conference on Race and Ethnicity in American Higher Education (NCORE) in San Francisco, California. I was selected to attend the NCORE conference because I was involved in the executive board of a student organization focusing on the cultural heritage of African/African American/Caribbean American students. It was my first national conference and I attended a session on being multiracial, which helped me to further reflect on race and encouraged me to claim a multiracial identity. While I knew what it meant to have parents from different racial backgrounds, I was not familiar with using the term "multiracial," and prior to NCORE, I did not engage in critically thinking about my mixed-race heritage or racial identity. It was in the multiracial conference session that I became conscious of the fact that I was not alone in having experienced the question, "What are you?" (Fulbeck, 2006). The NCORE conference catalyzed my ability to start thinking more intentionally about my own racial identity and issues of social justice in ways I had not thought of before.

Upon my return to Skidmore in the Fall of 2007, my racial awakening at NCORE conference motivated me to continue learning more about racial identity, oppression, and power. At the time I still did not have the language to articulate how race, power, and privilege connected to living in a socially just world. When I returned to campus, I was hired to work as a student assistant for Professor Ford. As a student assistant, I started conceptually learning about IGD, as much of my assigned tasks were to support the development of the IGR program. I also read research focused on social inequality in the U.S. to support Professor Ford's research agenda. After spending my sophomore year and part of my junior year working on the research side of the IGR program, I heard from other students about how IGD courses had changed their perspectives and that the dialogue class was, in their opinion, one of the best classes they had taken at Skidmore. Intrigued by my peers' recommendations and the research I read, I was encouraged by Professor Ford to experience IGD for myself, and I enrolled in the training course.

38 Victoria K. Malaney

Skidmore's IGD Training and Co-Facilitation of the People of Color/White People Dialogue

The IGD facilitator training course, Racial Identities: Theory and Praxis, gave me the chance to question how I viewed the world. Specifically, the course challenged me to reflect on my own socialization and how systems of oppression are operationalized in everyday life. I began to notice how power is organized and relates to the dominant order within various social institutions, like the media (Brookfield, 2004). I appreciated reading articles that allowed me to critically learn more about social justice issues and view the underpinnings of racial and other forms of social inequality (Gurin, Nagda, & Zúñiga, 2013). For instance, prior to IGD, I was unaware of terms like "ableism" or "religious oppression," and I could not fathom that privilege could be so hegemonic (Adams, 2007; Blumenfeld, 2006). As I reflected on my own experiences of being seen as the racial "other," I began to understand the nuances of structural and racial inequality and how each of our social identities interconnect and influence how we present ourselves and how we are viewed in society (Adams, Bell, & Griffin, 2007). After finishing the training course, I was excited to be selected to co-facilitate an IGD and that I could continue learning about social justice and racial inequalities.

Having the opportunity to facilitate a People of Color/White People race dialogue at the conclusion of my undergraduate career was a transformative experience for me, because it challenged me to understand the complexities of social identities and racial stereotypes. In one of our sessions, for instance, a participant mentioned that one of the weekly readings made her reflect on her education in high school to the point that she became emotional. The student said, "I finally understand why I was told by my teacher why I would never amount to anything." She made the connection that coming from an under-resourced school and being a student of color impacted why her teacher discouraged her from attending college. She realized that her teacher was socialized to believe in the ideologies of the culture of poverty and in turn made false assumptions about this student's experience and future self-worth (Gorski, 2008).

Another rewarding aspect of being a co-facilitator was hearing how IGD participants were able to articulate a distinct shift in their perspective-taking, empathy, and active listening at the end of semester (Ford & Malaney, 2012). Seeing this transformation occur over the course of the semester made me want to figure out how I could translate the experience I had with IGR to my professional life post-Skidmore. The conclusion of IGD also coincided with my graduation, and I was, like most seniors, unsure of what to do next with my life. I struggled because I wanted to find a job that allowed me to contribute explicitly to disrupting oppression and shifting the perspectives of those around me. The IGR program set the foundation for me to commit myself to a lifelong process of enhancing my skills in the pursuit of social justice (Griffin & Ouellett, 2007). I never thought I would be a social justice advocate, and I did not know what being a social justice advocate actually meant until I graduated and entered the workplace.

AmeriCorps VISTA

After graduating from Skidmore College with a Bachelor of Arts in English-Spanish and minors in Dance and Latin American Studies, I was approached by an AmeriCorps recruiter to become a Volunteer in Service to America (VISTA) member in the Albany, New York, region. The national service program VISTA was created in 1965 by President Johnson in an effort to eradicate domestic poverty. AmeriCorps members live and serve in some of our nation's poorest urban and rural areas, and they create or expand programs designed to bring individuals and communities out of poverty (AmeriCorps, 2016). I faced criticism from some family members for considering AmeriCorps because they thought I worked too hard in college to settle for such a low-paying job. As a first-generation college graduate, my family expected me to earn above the poverty guidelines. They were also surprised that I decided to work with VISTA in a religious nonprofit in Upstate New York. Despite my family's initial concerns, AmeriCorps VISTA appealed to me because of its social justice focus and its mission to support low-income communities in the United States. Retrospectively, I can now say that I came to the job with more privilege than I admitted. As a college-educated young woman, each day I entered my program site knowing that being part of the staff was very different than being a client receiving support services. The main clients we served were women transitioning back into the community after spending significant time in prison or in jail. I was a fresh-faced college graduate in my first job who was completely unaware of how difficult life could be.

Transitioning into the Professional World

My stomach was in knots as the sound of the heavy iron door locked behind me during my visits to the local jail. Although I knew I was safe walking with the case manager and the nun into the women's unit of the Rensselaer County Jail, I tightly gripped pamphlets I had printed the day before. I was in my second month as a VISTA, working for Catholic Charities of the Diocese of Albany as a grant writer and a Life Coach Coordinator. The Life Coach mentoring program was developed to support and empower women reentering their communities after completing their jail or prison sentences. Over the course of the year, each of those women were encouraged to join the new mentoring program that they helped me design. During my first visits to jail, I spoke with each of the women to find out their specific concerns and needs. We would discuss the importance of making connections and developing support from family, friends, and a Life Coach. Together, we focused not on their past, but on building a successful transition plan to reintegrate them back into their community. I found the skills I developed in IGD, like perspective-taking, active listening, and empathy, helped me in each conversation to build trust with the women coming out of incarceration. At the end of each visit, I had the privilege of walking out of that jail. This was not a privilege they shared, and it always gave me cause

40 Victoria K. Malaney

for reflection on my social identities as an upwardly mobile multiracial woman of color (Johnson, 2005).

Many of these women hadn't finished high school and here I was, a recent college graduate, coming to talk to them about mentoring. I faced pointed questions by the women about my intentions. Sometimes I wondered why I was even coming into the jail. I doubted I was making a difference. Was I actually reifying the subordinate experiences of women because I had the freedom of walking in and out of the jail? In spite of these concerns, many of the women respected the nonprofit organization I worked for and saw that receiving our center's support services had helped other women in the community successfully reintegrate without recidivating back to jail or prison. I knew I had to work on building their trust each time I went into jail, so they would continue to visit the center and continue their engagement in the mentoring Life Coach program after they were released from incarceration.

Despite my own self-doubts about whether the mentoring program would work, where I found the most reassurance in my social justice work was in the deeper conversations I had with the women mentees in jail. One of the mentees, whom I will call Rita, was encouraged to try out the Life Coach program. She was matched with a mentor and found that after being out of jail for three months and attending weekly meetings with her Life Coach, she had a new perspective on her life. After receiving consistent and positive encouragement from her Life Coach, Rita found her Life Coach to be an important source of confidence for her. Her Life Coach was able to put into perspective how far she had come since getting released from jail, and she was an outside person from Rita's family and friends who could see her growth and help her reflect and set benchmarks to achieve her personal and professional goals.

While I could see the mentoring program working for the mentees and the Life Coaches, the challenge was knowing that there was nothing I could do or say to ensure that the women I built a relationship with in jail would not recidivate back into the criminal justice system. However, I discovered that the more I listened to the women mentees in jail, the more we mutually contributed to our dialogue and built trust, while creating a foundation for our working relationship (McCoy & Scully, 2002). My ability to critically self-reflect began through the experiential and dialogic methods of IGD (Zúñiga, Nagda, Chesler, & Cytron-Walker, 2007). Reflection allowed us to curiously explore the differences that make us unique and commonalities that make us the same. Unlike the majority of the community members I served in AmeriCorps, who were living in poverty and had experiences with the criminal justice system, I knew that my vow of poverty had a contracted end date. To me, earning a low wage taught me a lot about myself and the resiliency of the human spirit, especially as I got to know the community members I served.

After working with Catholic Charities, my next job as a VISTA Leader at Siena College focused on mentoring VISTA members who were placed in various nonprofit sites fighting poverty across Albany, New York. The facilitation skills I learned in IGD helped prepare me for my second job, as I would listen to my team struggle with facing challenges at their program sites. Some of the members would talk about not knowing what to do when they saw power enacting itself in their low-income community work sites. For example, one of the directors of a nonprofit organization made a quick decision to eliminate a community program without consulting with the members who regularly attended events. In response to their concerns, I relied on my IGD facilitator training to help provide another lens to view this situation by examining how power operates within a hierarchical system (Freire, 2008). I also offered them advice on how to communicate with coworkers, ask deeper questions to understand what was going on in their work site, and build trust with the community they served. Working for VISTA was a great learning experience where I found my jobs directly applied social justice values, but when my two national service years were completed, I was ready to return to Skidmore College, this time as a full-time staff member.

It was surreal to be back at Skidmore working in Student Affairs for the Office of Student Diversity Programs (OSDP). It had been only two years since I graduated. I loved this job because I was able to translate my passion for social justice to the field of higher education. I organized and facilitated social justice programming for undergraduate students. Being back at Skidmore was both exciting and eye-opening. While I knew what it was like to be a student, being employed by Skidmore was an adjustment. Power, oppression, and privilege is inherent in the structure of academia (Maher & Tetreault, 2009). While I read about this in IGD classes, I was now able to see how power and privilege operationalizes itself within my professional interactions. I found power and privilege to be the most challenging in meetings with administrators and faculty when the status of the person voicing her/his opinion would influence funding decisions. In one specific instance, for example, a faculty member's voice on a Student Affairs Committee overpowered the voice of a student affairs professional who had a keener understanding of how the funding could impact student life outside the classroom.

The job, however, was rewarding because many students were eager to engage in co-curricular programs that focused on structural and systemic inequalities. Drawing from IGD pedagogies, I helped create Skidmore's first cocurricular student group, "So What Are You Anyways?" that focused on the multiracial and transracial adoptee student experience (OSDP Blogspot, 2012). The group provided a space for multiracial students to openly discuss the complexity of their racial identities and the impact of monoracism, while at the same raising the consciousness of the campus community about how oppression also effects multiracial individuals (Johnston & Nadal, 2010; Malaney & Danowski, 2015).

Together, my post-college professional experiences – both the challenging and rewarding moments – compelled me to continue my education at the University of Massachusetts (UMass) Amherst to earn a Master's in Higher Education Administration. I chose this school because of its public commitment to social change and because their graduate social justice education program is led by one of IGR's seminal researchers, Dr. Ximena Zúñiga.

42 Victoria K. Malaney

During my first semester at UMass Amherst, I took an Intergroup Dialogue course with Dr. Zúñiga and was able to learn from her expertise; it was rewarding and reinvigorating for me to stay connected to IGD research and pedagogy while I further enhanced my dialogue and facilitation skills. One of my biggest learning outcomes from the course was realizing that self-reflection is an ongoing and constant process (Buber, 2010) and that being dedicated to social justice work is a lifelong commitment. As I progressed through my program, I gravitated towards taking courses that would help expand my knowledge of social justice issues and problem-posing education (Freire, 2008). For example, inspired initially by my college experiences with IGD, my master's thesis focused on understanding the experiences of multiracial students with race-based support services at a large predominately White research university. More concretely, I wanted to know if multiracial students participated in culturally based student organizations on campus and, if so, did these groups meet their needs (Renn, 2004). One of my primary findings was that multiracial students at this institution needed tailored race-based support services to best encourage their racial identity development. As I look back now, I realize that IGD was the main reason that I was even pushed to think about my multiracial identity, and it was because I had the space as an undergraduate student to critically self-reflect and grapple with my personal experiences with oppression. Completing the IGR program at Skidmore directly impacted my journey to becoming a social justice advocate in the field of higher education.

Currently, I am a doctoral student in the Educational Policy, Research and Administration program concentrating in Higher Education at UMass Amherst. In my program of study, I plan to continue studying race, multiracial identity, student activism, and intergroup dialogue. I credit Skidmore's IGR program for providing me with a transformative learning experience, which has helped me build a strong foundation to guide my professional career and personal life both now and in the future. I envision myself continuing my career as a scholar-practitioner in higher education who focuses on inequality and social justice. In addition to shaping my professional career, IGR has also impacted many of my personal life choices.

Personal Reflections with IGR

Social justice is an ongoing conversation in my relationships with family, friends, and my partner. Prior to my involvement with IGR, I had a neutral or less critical approach to issues of inequality. It was only after I was trained in IGD that I began to speak up and engage my family and friends in difficult dialogues related to power, privilege, and oppression. Within my interracial family, we now more frequently hold in-depth family conversations about how we are racialized as individuals, but also as a multiracial family in a monoracial world. Prior to college, we did not have many dialogues about topics like race relations, immigration policy, or socioeconomic inequities. However, as we grow older and are able to bring different perspectives to understand how social justice manifests in our lives, we have increased our ability to engage in sustained conversations. By actively listening to one another's opinions, even if we disagree, we now have a better understanding of how our unique social identities contribute to our group dynamics as a family.

Moreover, it was very important to me that my life partner, a White male, also has a commitment to understanding social justice issues. While we were dating, many of our conversations focused on discussing our cultural heritages, white privilege, power, and oppression. While we are both educators, we still have a lot to learn and experience as we grow as a couple. As such, we challenge ourselves daily to think about how we integrate social justice values into our educational practice and work. For instance, my partner is a music educator who serves students from a highly privileged socioeconomic background. In an effort to engage these students with justice issues, we have had many conversations about how he can incorporate lessons on how music can contribute to social change.

Although my partner experiences the world differently from me based on his privileged social identities, he understands white supremacy as well as other intersecting oppressions, and can empathize with my experiences from his perspective as a white ally. This is especially important to me when discussing our future family, since our children will likely face questions as multiracial individuals of color. Being on the same page about inequality is therefore very important to us when we teach our future children how to understand racism, power, and privilege. Additionally, it is comforting to know that while he might not understand every oppressive experience I have and will face, at least I know I am not alone in the struggle for equality. Together, as a team, I am confident that my partner and I will continue developing our learning edges by expanding our understanding of social justice and inequality.

Final Thoughts

Reflecting on my IGD training, I know that my professional and personal commitment to social justice will only continue to increase over time. As I am disheartened by seeing more reports of racial tension on college campuses, police brutality, and global injustices, I ask myself, how can I better understand these issues? Can I dedicate intentional space to social justice as part of my research interests? I know as a scholar-practitioner, I will continue to grapple with these questions and question how I can contribute more fully to the fight for justice through practicing humanizing research practices in my scholarly work (Paris & Winn, 2014). I will also remain focused on my personal commitment to social justice because I am hopeful for change. By continuing to engage in these difficult conversations with my family and friends, I hope that we can deepen our understanding of our social identities and related privileges together as we attempt to create change in our individual spheres of influence (Goodman & Shapiro, 1997).

44 *Victoria K. Malaney*

Although I am invested in working towards becoming a stronger social justice advocate, I recognize that this work can sometimes be mentally draining and exhausting, so I need to ensure that I do not become overwhelmed, anxious, or burned out (Chen & Gorski, 2015; McClellan, 2012). As such, I have developed a network of personal and academic connections – mentors, friends, family, and colleagues – who keep me energized and motivated to continue to understand and challenge racial inequities and other forms of injustice (American College Personnel Association, 2016). I find some balance by spending time with my family and close friends so I can recharge and remind myself of the moments where love, hope, and humanity occur in this world. Additionally, I carve out intentional time for self-care by doing healthy activities like practicing yoga and meditation, which help me remember the reason why I entered the field of education – to help create social change. By keeping myself personally and professionally motivated to do social justice work, I can hopefully make an impact in a more sustained way.

In sum, as I reflect on what I have learned after graduating from Skidmore, I can confidently say that IGR was a life-changing experience for me. I do not think I would be where I am personally and professionally today without the consciousness-raising and social justice awakening I received from IGD (Freire, 2008; Zúñiga, Nagda, Chesler, & Cytron-Walker, 2007). Although I consider myself a work in progress, I am striving to become a social justice advocate who can productively use my power and privileges to improve the communities in which I live and work. Ultimately, I hope to influence the people around me "to be the change" in their communities while encouraging all of us to live in a safer, more socially just world.

Note

1 I use the terms "multiracial" and "mixed-race" interchangeably to describe an individual with two or more racial heritages and whose parents are from different ethnic backgrounds (Pew Research Center, 2015).

References

Adams, M. (2007). Overview: Religious oppression. In M. Adams, L. A. Bell, & P. Griffin (Eds.), *Teaching for diversity and social justice*, (pp. 245–254). New York, NY: Routledge.

Adams, M., Bell, L. A., & Griffin, P. (2007). *Teaching for diversity and social justice*. New York, NY: Routledge.

American College Personnel Association (2016). Multiracial network about us. Retrieved June 2, 2016 from http://www.myacpa.org/scma-multiracial-network-mrn-about-us.

AmeriCorps (2016). AmeriCorps VISTA. Retrieved from http://www.nationalservice.gov/programs/americorps/americorps-vista/what-vista-members-do.

Blumenfeld, W. J. (2006). Christian privilege and the promotion of "secular" and not-so "secular" mainline Christianity in public schooling. *Equity and Excellence in Education*, 39, 195–210.

Brookfield, S. D. (2004). *The power of critical theory: Liberating adult learning and teaching*. San Francisco, CA: Jossey-Bass.

On Becoming a Social Justice Advocate   45

Buber, M. (2010). *I and thou*. Mansfield Centre, CT: Martino Publishing.

Chen, C. W., & Gorski, P. (2015). Burnout in social justice and human rights activists: Symptoms, causes, and implications. *Journal of Human Rights Practice, 7*(3), 1–24.

Ford, K. A., & Malaney, V. K. (2012). "I now harbor more pride in my race": The educational benefits of inter- and intra-racial dialogues on the experiences of students of color and multiracial students. *Equity and Excellence in Education, 45*(1), 14–35.

Freire, P. (2008). *Pedagogy of the oppressed*. New York, NY: Continuum International.

Fulbeck, K. (2006). *Part Asian, 100% Hapa*. San Francisco, CA: Chronicle Books.

Goodman, D., & Shapiro, S. (1997). Sexism curriculum design. In M. Adams, L. A. Bell, & G. P. Griffin (Eds.). *Teaching for diversity and social justice: A sourcebook* (pp. 89–113). New York, NY: Routledge.

Gorski, P. (2008). The myth of the "culture of poverty." *Educational Leadership, 65*(7), 4–9.

Griffin, P., & Ouellett, M. L. (2007). Facilitating social justice education courses. In M. Adams, L.A. Bell, & P. Griffin (Eds.), *Teaching for diversity and social justice* (pp. 89–113). New York, NY: Routledge.

Gurin, P., Nagda, R.A., & Zúñiga, X. (2013). *Dialogue across difference: Practice, theory, and research on intergroup dialogue*. Troy, NY: Russell Sage Foundation.

Johnson, A. (2005). *Privilege, power, and difference*. New York, NY: McGraw Hill.

Johnston, M. P. & Nadal, K. (2010). Multiracial microaggressions: Exposing monoracism in everyday life and clinical practice. In D. W. Sue (Ed.), *Microaggressions and marginality: Manifestation, dynamics, and impact* (pp. 123–144). New York, NY: Wiley & Sons.

Maher, F. A., & Tetreault, M. K. (2009). Diversity and privilege. American Association of University Professors. Retrieved June 16, 2016 from http://www.aaup.org/article/diversity-and-privilege#.VtUe9MdUdFI.

Malaney, V. K. & Danowski, K. (2015). Mixed foundations: Supporting and empowering multiracial student organizations. *Journal Committed to Social Change on Race and Ethnicity, 1*, 55–85.

McClellan, G. S. (2012). Maintaining your passion for the job. *Chronicle of Higher Education*. Retrieved June 12, 2016 from http://chronicle.com/article/Maintaining-Your-Passion-for/132905/.

McCoy, M. L., & Scully, P. L. (2002). Deliberative dialogue to expand civic engagement: What kind of talk does democracy need? *National Civic Review, 91*(2), 117–135.

Moore, W. L. (2007). *Reproducing racism: White space, elite law schools, and racial inequality*. Lanham, MD: Rowman and Littlefield.

OSDP Blogspot (2012). Student highlight: Jomack Miranda '16 of SWAYA? Office of Student Diversity Programs Blog, Retrieved July 2, 2016 from http://skidmorecollegeosdp.blogspot.com/2013/12/student-highlight-jomack-miranda-16-of.html.

Paris, D., & Winn, M. (Eds.). (2014). *Humanizing research: Decolonizing qualitative inquiry with youth and communities*. Thousand Oaks, CA: Sage.

Pew Research Center (2015). Multiracial in America: Proud, diverse, and growing in numbers. Washington, D.C. Retrieved from http://www.pewsocialtrends.org/files/2015/06/2015-06-11_multiracial-in- america_final-updated.pdf.

Renn, K. (2004). *Mixed race students in college: The ecology of race, identity, and community on campus*. Albany, NY: State University of New York Press.

Sue, D. W., Capodilupo, C. M., Torino, G. C., Bucceri, J. M., Holder, A. M., Nadal, K. L., & Esquilin, M. (2007). Racial microaggressions in everyday life: implications for clinical practice. *American Psychologist, 64*(4), 271–286.

Zúñiga, X., Nagda, B., Chesler, M., & Cytron-Walker, A. (2007). *Intergroup dialogue in higher education: Meaningful learning about social justice* (ASHE-ERIC Higher Education Report 32, No. 4). San Francisco, CA: Jossey-Bass.

4 Social Justice in Action and Inaction

Sarah Faude

I did not participate in the Intergroup Relations (IGR) program at Skidmore College until my senior year. I entered the program as a Sociology major who was still reeling off my realization that not only was "meritocracy" a myth in the United States, but that the premise of such a model had real implications that disproportionately benefitted me because of my many privileged identities. Despite an interest in inequality broadly, I was very good at summarizing and synthesizing different experiences in an academic context but quite inexperienced at listening critically in any context. On the topic of race in particular, I was adept at navigating content in exactly the distanced, intellectualized manner that I was trained for in my elite education. This was particularly clear in one of the first activities I remember participating in during the Skidmore IGR program: an assignment to write our racial-autobiography. In my best liberal, colorblind (Bonilla-Silva, 2010), well-intentioned efforts to fulfill the requirements of the assignment, I did what my whiteness had taught me to do: see the world through a lens of "otherness" (specifically racial otherness) instead of through a racial lens that was both reflexive and accounted for power disparities. I successfully ignored the racial dynamics of my family, which includes two interracial marriages and several biracial cousins; I ignored the racialized and classed dynamics of my household in which a dark-skinned Jamaican woman cleaned my home each Thursday; I ignored my own path of privilege with live-in nannies, private schooling, and debt-free college. My whiteness was powerful in part because of its silence.

IGR was a foundational step in my struggle to recognize and name my whiteness. It was the first and, perhaps, one of the only spaces in which I was simultaneously supported, challenged, confronted, and loved for my non-linear path towards social justice advocacy. I am fortunate because my experience in IGR was also incredibly disruptive of a meritocratic world view I had grown up learning to be true. Before IGR (and arguably within it), my conception of my role as a social justice advocate was located firmly within the frame of abstract liberalism as defined by Bonilla-Silva (2010, p. 28), particularly in the ways that I saw opportunity and inequality as individualized rather than structural phenomenon. I grew up hearing family members say, "It's a can-do household," where hard work was explicitly valued, named, and used to explain the root of

Social Justice in Action and Inaction 47

all achievements. The unearned, cumulative advantage of the White family I was born into was never named as a contributor to success.

Even throughout the process of IGR, I never fully realized the structural nature of inequality and did not have the tools and language to name how the intersection of my different identities complicated and humanized those who are otherwise "rendered partial, unrecognizable, something apart from standard claims of [...] discrimination" (Cho, Crenshaw, ... McCall, 2013, pp. 790–791). While we spent a lot of time examining privilege, power, and positionality through the lenses of target and agent[1] identities, I failed to see how my identities intersected or how on their own they were almost exclusively agentic and dominant identity markers. Instead, each week I named my identity in a specific category (be it sexual orientation, religion, or ability-status), unpacked some of its components and features in society, and then discarded that knowledge as something isolated and separate from my "full humanity" (Tatum, 1997, p. 27). I misunderstood identity as fragmented and because of my privilege I also misunderstood identity as something I could choose to wear publically (or not). I chose to understand identity as both colorblind and power-neutral in the service of my own privilege.

However, the activities, discussions, and reflective spaces within the IGR program all pushed me to see and hear the embedded racism and inequalities in all spaces. Although I was first introduced to Critical Race Theory (CRT) in this context, it took me many years to fully realize its premise that racism is endemic to American life (Matsuda, Lawrence, Delgado, ... Crenshaw, 1993). In college, I wanted to believe this but simply had not yet seen the world enough through this framework to know it to be so.

Making Sense of White Institutional Spaces

Much of my experience from my senior year in college through today has been an iterative process of coming to realize what it means to embrace a social justice and activist frame. I have been struggling to know when to listen and value the experiential knowledge of individuals of color, as well as when to speak up and use my privilege to say what otherwise goes silent. I'm still working on the balance, particularly as I increasingly find myself situated in all-White professional spaces within academia. This, however, has been a really messy path. While still in college, for instance, I abruptly began my role as a social justice advocate by berating my close friends and family. I fought with them in an effort to get them to feel the guilt, shame, and confusion that I was navigating as I came to terms with my whiteness. Within the same year I challenged the language of close friends, accused my family of racist traditions, *and* attended a Mexican-themed birthday party for a close (White) friend without realizing how that was problematic, hypocritical, and racist. IGR helped me moderate my efforts by giving me the space to name my challenges of feeling inarticulate, awkward, and uneasy. IGR managed to both hold me accountable for my missteps and support me as I worked to do better. The most important thing that

48 *Sarah Faude*

IGR reminded me, however, was that I had the privilege to walk away from this work at any time; it is unquestionably this lesson that keeps me embedded in this fight for social justice.

Part of not walking away has been my own efforts to relearn my own autobiography (racial and otherwise) through an explicit racial lens. When I began to do so I realized that the IGD process at Skidmore was perhaps my first time engaging in explicit conversations on race, and was certainly one of the only integrated classrooms of my educational experience. While most, if not all, of my K-12 educational experiences included sharing a school or classroom with students of color, my inability to articulate to what extent we shared school spaces highlights the ways that my peers of color were not given, empowered to, or even allowed to fully share in that educational space. I later understood this through critical race scholarship like that of Moore (2008), where through an ethnography of law schools she examined and named the contours of white institutional space, stating explicitly that there "exists no historically or legally supported right to be free from racism in education for students of color" (p. 12). By retracing my own autobiography as occupying a series of linked white spaces, I came to see the ways in which I had not learned to recognize my own racial identity but instead was taught to see racial otherness. Through reflection and dialogue I realized that I have memories of my protection within white institutional spaces as far back as kindergarten. I remember Black students from neighboring Hartford, Connecticut, being bussed into my White, affluent, suburban elementary school classroom specifically as a result of a voluntary desegregation program Project Concern (now known as Project Choice or Open Choice).

My professional path after college led me back to public K-12 education, and I worked for three years with middle and high school students as an English Language Arts teacher in two different schools in North Philadelphia. I went from all-White social and professional spaces to a professional space in which I was one of the only White people (my social spaces remained largely White ones). My first two years out of college were spent teaching in an Afrocentric charter school, which I had hoped would be an opportunity to finally work as a social justice educator. However, I entered into my experience with Teach For America believing the meritocratic argument that optimistically and problematically asserted, "Poverty is not destiny" (Teach for America, n.d.) and then began working within a social context that vehemently argued otherwise. The school I worked with operated within a broader crisis of chronic disparities in school funding that sustained race and class educational gaps (Anyon, 1997; Bell, 2004) and the increased spatial segregation of neighborhoods and schools (Orfield, 2009, 2013; Orfield & Lee, 2005; Rothwell, 2012) in the wake of neoliberal "choice" movements (Linn & Welner, 2007; Roda & Wells, 2013; Saporito & Hanley, 2014; Saporito & Lareau, 1999; Saporito & Sohoni, 2007) and the dismantling of 1954's *Brown v. Board of Education* through legislative cases like Seattle's *Parents Involved*. During my two years there, the public charter school in which I worked served students who were 99% African American, 98% eligible for *free* lunch[2], and 25% of the school was identified as requiring special education services (National Council for Education Statistics, 2012); the school mirrored the demographic composition of many other chronically underperforming schools in Philadelphia (and indeed in many cities across the United States).

Despite how overwhelmingly different this school was from any context in which I had ever worked, I spent much of my first year teaching returning to the safety of abstract liberalism. Given my work differed widely from that of many of my elite college peers, I hid behind the identity of my new role as an urban teacher and failed to work on my own privilege. It was not until several months into teaching that I distinctly remember that my ability to drive away from the blighted, segregated neighborhoods was an explicit extension of my privilege. Additionally, the violent and academically troubled environment of the school became personal, and I misread its structural roots. I implicitly assumed that because the people within that space were almost entirely African American, that the space could not also be a "white institutional space." Given that I had learned, in the words of Peggy McIntosh (1989), "to see racism only in individual acts of meanness, not in invisible systems conferring dominance on my group." I was looking for villains, particularly White ones, to explain the problems within my school. However, there were few White individuals in the school space, and I did not know how to explain the pain and injustice I was witnessing without a clear perpetrator. I also never looked reflexively, or at least not for a while, at how my presence as an inexperienced, White privileged young woman was a symptom of white supremacy in urban institutional spaces, no matter my intentions at disrupting that same system of oppression.

One thing that IGR did not prepare me for was how to be a social justice advocate in a diverse space in which allies were not visible. My racial awakening was so abrupt (although certainly not complete), that I assumed that there were those who were part of the fight and those who were barriers. However, within the school, many, if not most, of the problematic statements wielded towards our African American students were by staff and faculty of color. I left college prepared to understand and challenge white racism, but had never even considered how I might challenge an African American peer. It has taken me several years and many academic and personal writing opportunities to unpack that what I witnessed and heard in the school is an example of the pervasiveness of white supremacy. In particular, I came to see the ways in which racism is structural, instead of just a cumulative effect of individual bad (or white) apples. This finding is substantiated in works like Lewis's (2003) book *Race in the Schoolyard*, in which she demonstrated that even demographically non-white schools are embedded with white norms that result from broader institutionalized racism in education (see also Bettie, 2003; Ferguson, 2001). These two years of teaching were incredibly isolating, as I felt as though I lacked the tools and the community to unpack the work environment I experienced each day. During most of my time there, I was not an effective teacher. I was not what my students deserved or desperately needed. If I'm honest, I know that I spent many hours of classroom instruction yelling at students because I was

50   Sarah Faude

ineffective and out of control and woefully underprepared to teach. Worst of all, I felt as if I did not know how to get any better without the safe, supportive communities I was so used to. By the end I knew that my ability to physically drive out of North Philadelphia each evening was a privilege, but I constantly struggled to know how to use that privilege to do more than protect myself.

Intersectionality, Voice, and Listening: Qualitative Research as a Return to IGR Basics

Fortunately, in graduate school, I had explicit opportunities to return to the foundational components of both IGR and CRT through qualitative research opportunities. For my Master's thesis in Education, we conducted practitioner inquiries in which we had the opportunity to ask a question and then explore what it might mean in the context of our classrooms. I decided to conduct a project in which I answered Freire's (1982) call for education to center otherwise marginalized individuals as "the masters of inquiry into the underlying causes of the events in their world" (p. 30). With my all-girls homeroom, we co-constructed a unit on a book of their choice, and they chose Sharon Flake's (1998) *The Skin I'm In*, a young adult novel with a dark-skinned African American protagonist who struggled to accept her identity. Through this project I started listening to the students in my class, and realized that what they wanted was a chance to talk through and navigate their identities and experiences; they wanted an educational space that had room for who they were to be at the center.

But listening was hard and painful, for both the students and myself. I more than once had to schedule these co-planned lessons when key administrators were outside the building or tied up in meetings simply because disregarding the banking model of education[3] also meant allowing things to be messy and loud sometimes. Most importantly, however, I stepped back from my position of authority in order to listen and value the experiences of my students and help them unpack the ways in which their identities intersected and unraveled in their everyday experiences. In one activity a student wrote in her class journal, "Since I'm Black I have to be treated different." Not "I am treated different" but "I *have* to be treated different." She was twelve, and already had begun to name the ways that structural racism subsumes her identity, normalizes difference, and others her in the process.

The students in my class helped me to realize that although the school was 99% African American, this did not mean that their lives and identities were not complex in other ways. A classroom of twelve-year-old girls taught me intersectionality, and showed me how the politics and processes of naming identity includes "some degree of agency" despite "unequal power" (Crenshaw, 1991, p. 1297). Building off of the momentum of this project, my next unit focused on the role of children in the Civil Rights Movement, in an effort to allow all the students to picture themselves as powerful contributors to history. This was the most successful unit I taught in Philadelphia, even though my world-class education and white privilege had explicitly and purposefully not prepared me for any context in which I would need to be fluent in the histories or experiences of communities of color.

This collaborative project, in the spring of my second year teaching, helped me realize that I could create a supportive community to discuss race. It also helped me realize that without courageous conversations, and room for those conversations to occur, there was no way to create community that authentically engaged in critical dialogue. Further, I learned that my role in that space was partially to facilitate, but most importantly to listen with empathy. Relearning how to really listen and connect with experiences different from one's own has transformed my professional experiences. I've always been drawn to qualitative methods for its potential to use narrative as a tool to deconstruct and decolonize power and space through efforts to "center the experiences and voices" of individuals, particularly of color and from other target identities (Moore, 2008, p. 163). Since reentering graduate school in pursuit of a Ph.D. in Sociology, I have returned to what I learned in the classroom as well as what I learned in IGR: critical dialogue and listening with empathy.

Both methodologically and thematically, the lessons of IGR return again and again. In semi-structured interviews, I focus on presenting my interviewer role akin to that of my IGD facilitator role; focus on listening, transitioning, and finding ways to privilege the experiences that my respondents share; and guide them to share and explain more without my own biases, experiences, and assumptions interrupting their ideas. Thematically, my research projects unpack the causes of school segregation, explore White middle-class perceptions and conceptions of diversity in the classroom, and examine the ways that educational institutional spaces structurally disadvantage families (disproportionately mothers) of color. I also find myself using my whiteness strategically alongside my IGD training, particularly to gain entry and trust with White respondents whose racially guarded and coded language can be probed for a clearer sense of who they mean when they describe "disruptive" students in a classroom.

Continuing Challenges of Social Justice Advocacy

The ideal of a social justice advocate is slippery, particularly when constructed with an intersectional lens. In any given context, we are performing and misrecognizing the ways in which our multiplicative identities influence and are interpreted by others just as much as we are shaped by broader social structures. The potential and challenges of social justice advocacy also varies based on individual positionality. Hughey (2012) emphasizes this complexity for Whites (although not speaking to White social justice advocates exclusively) by articulating that "the meaning of whiteness varies spatially (by location), temporally (by historical eras and within the individual life span), contextually (by the relative culture), differentially (by power), and intersectionally (by combination with class, gender, sexual orientation, and so on" (p. 12). Despite these variations, whiteness remains bound together as "a singular dominant and racially

52   *Sarah Faude*

privileged group" (p. 12). It is in this balance between structural power and individual identity that the challenge of effective advocacy lays.

Given this complexity, I have found that the first and most critical step in my own engagement with social justice advocacy is to always choose *not* to walk away even when my privilege affords me the option to do so. It's trying both personally and professionally to be sure, but my privilege protects me from the cumulative day-to-day injuries that so many others do not have the option of avoiding. Once I've reaffirmed my commitment, the challenges of course continue. The one I struggle with the most, as a privileged extrovert, is how to speak up and name injustice without silencing the voices of others. This is an issue I've struggled with and have been working on since co-facilitating the White Racial Identity Dialogue; in our efforts to co-facilitate and navigate our whiteness, my white privilege sometimes silenced and injured my co-facilitator who self-identified as both White Latina and White Non-Latina. If it is challenging to balance speaking up and listening during explicit conversations about inequality and oppression, how can one successfully embody the ideals of social justice advocacy in everyday contexts? When is using privilege the strategic use of armor to name oppression without injury, and when does it silence those who are trying to tell their stories?

Notes

1   Target identities are identities that are structurally disadvantaged in a particular context, while agent identities are those identities for which we receive structural advantage or privilege. For example, my whiteness is an agentic identity while my gender as a woman is a target identity.
2   While public schools collect data on both free and reduced lunch, this school had so many students falling below the poverty line that almost all students qualified for "free lunch." For example, for a family of four to qualify for free lunch in the 2009–2010 school year, students' families had to prove that they were making under $29,000 a year. If they were to qualify for "reduced lunch," a family of four would be making under $41,000 (USDA FNS, 2009).
3   Freire's (1970) concept of traditional education characterizes students as empty vessels waiting to be filled with the knowledge provided by teachers, similar to a bank account waiting to be filled with money.

References

Anyon, J. (1997). *Ghetto schooling: A political economy of urban educational reform.* New York, NY: Teachers College Press.
Bell, D. (2004). *Silent covenants: Brown vs Board of Education and the unfulfilled hopes for racial reform.* New York, NY: Oxford University Press.
Bettie, J. (2003). *Women without class: Girls, race, and identity.* Berkeley, CA: University of California Press.
Bonilla-Silva, E. (2010). *Racism without racists: Color-blind racism and the persistence of racial inequality in America.* Lanham, MD: Rowman & Littlefield.
Brown v. Board of Education, 347 U.S. 483 (1954).
Cho, S., Crenshaw, K. W., & McCall, L. (2013). Toward a field of intersectional studies: Theory, applications, and praxis. *Signs, 38*(4), 785–810.

Crenshaw, K. (1991). Mapping the margins: Intersectionality, identity politics, and violence against women of color. *Stanford Law Review, 43*(6), 1241–1299.

Ferguson, A. A. (2001). *Bad boys: Public schools in the making of black masculinity.* Ann Arbor, MI: University of Michigan Press.

Flake, S. (1998). *The skin I'm in.* New York, NY: Hyperion Books for Children.

Freire, P. (1970). *Pedagogy of the oppressed.* New York, NY: Seabury.

Freire, P. (1982). Creating alternative research methods: Learning to do it by doing it. In B. Hall, A. Gillette, & R. Tandon (Eds.), *Creating knowledge: A monopoly* (pp. 29–37). New Delhi, India: Society for Participatory Research in Asia.

Hughey, M. W. (2012). *White bound: Nationalists, antiracists, and the shared meanings of race.* Stanford, CA: Stanford University Press.

Lewis, A. E. (2003). *Race in the schoolyard: Negotiating the color line in classrooms and communities.* New Brunswick, NJ: Rutgers University Press.

Linn, R. L., & Welner, K. G. (2007). Race-conscious policies for assigning students to schools: Social science research and the Supreme Court cases. Retrieved October 15, 2015 from: http://nepc.colorado.edu/files/Brief-NAE.pdf.

Matsuda, M. J., Lawrence, C. R., Delgado, R., & Crenshaw K. W. (1993). *Words that wound: Critical race theory, assaultive speech, and the First Amendment.* Boulder, CO: Westview Press.

McIntosh, P. (1989). White privilege: Unpacking the invisible knapsack. *Peace and Freedom Magazine,* July/August, 10–12.

Moore, W. L. (2008). *Reproducing racism: White space, elite law schools, and racial inequality.* New York, NY: Rowman & Littlefield.

National Center for Education Statistics (2012). *CCD public school data.* Retrieved October 15, 2015 from: http://nces.ed.gov/ccd/schoolsearch/index.asp.

Orfield, G. (2009). Reviving the goal of an integrated society: A 21st century challenge. Los Angeles, CA: The Civil Rights Project/Proyecto Derechos Civiles at UCLA.

Orfield, G. (2013). Choice theories and Schools. In G. Orfield, E. Frankenberg & Associates (Eds.), *Educational delusions?: Why choice can deepen inequality and how to make schools fair* (pp. 37–66). Berkeley, CA: University of California Press.

Orfield, G. & Lee, C. (2005). *Why segregation matters.* Cambridge, MA: The Civil Rights Project at Harvard University.

Roda, A. & Wells, A. S. (2013). School choice policies and racial segregation: Where white parents' good intentions, anxiety, and privilege collide. *American Journal of Education. 119*(2), 261–293.

Rothwell, J. (2012, April 19). *Housing costs, zoning, and access to high-scoring schools.* Retrieved October 15, 2015 from https://www.brookings.edu/research/housing-costs-zoning-and-access-to-high-scoring-schools/.

Saporito, S. & Hanley, C. (2014). Declining significance of race? In A. Lareau & K. Goyette (Eds.), *Choosing homes, choosing schools,* (pp. 64–96). New York, NY: Russell Sage Foundation.

Saporito, S. & Lareau, A. (1999). School selection as a process: The multiple dimensions of race in framing educational choice. *Social Problems, 46*(3), 418–439.

Saporito, S. & Sohoni, D. (2007). Mapping educational inequality: Concentrations of poverty among poor and minority students in public schools. *Social Forces, 85*(3), 1227–1253.

Tatum, B. D. (1997). *"Why are all the black kids sitting together in the cafeteria?": And other conversations about race.* New York, NY: Basic Books.

Teach For America. (n.d.). Retrieved October 15, 2015 from https://www.teachforamerica .org/get-involved/ways-to-give/annual-giving%20.

USDA FNS (United States Department of Agriculture, Food and Nutrition Services). (2009). Retrieved October 15, 2015 from http://www.fns.usda.gov/sites/default/files/IEGs09-10.pdf.

5 Learning the True Meaning of Advocacy

Teshika R. Hatch

Working in the field of college access now, I often look back on my own college search process and wonder how I found myself at a predominately White, small, liberal arts school on the other side of the country. I was raised in a multiracial, multicultural, multilingual household where race and identity were constant topics of conversation. My White father, raised in one of the wealthiest (and Whitest) parts of Seattle, was a journalist for much of my childhood and always questioned the status quo. My Japanese mother was naturally skeptical of almost everything White and American (apparently not of my dad – at least then) and early on encouraged my siblings and I to understand our own mixed-race identity. My childhood was spent in part in one of the most diverse neighborhoods in Seattle, then the incredibly homogenous country of Japan for four years, and later back in the States – to the more segregated and homogenous parts of White Seattle. This back and forth of culture shock, assimilation, and reverse culture shock forced us to confront our own understanding of our racial identity and challenged us to answer the typical pigeonholing question: "What are you?" As Tatum (1997) explained, the question may be innocent, but "the insistence with which the question is often asked represents society's need to classify its members racially" (p. 175).

My mother was the adventurous and nontraditional parent, who at the age of 19 had decided to leave Japan for France for the sake of getting out of her comfort zone. She instilled the belief of always "leaving your comfort zone," which quickly became my personal mantra. My father, much more rational and calculated, raised me to be proud of my intellect and to seek out academic opportunities where I would thrive. When it came to the college search process, my father encouraged small liberal arts schools; my mother, an immigrant to this country and less knowledgeable about the college admission and financial aid processes, encouraged something different. She wanted me to attend the local public university, the University of Washington, for its lower cost and the safety of being around people who would look like me. The combination of my mother's idea of stepping out of your comfort zone and my father's knowledge of small private schools led me to the East Coast, and eventually, Skidmore College. Although I knew that my lived experiences would be somewhat different from my peers simply because of my geographic upbringing, I was not prepared for race and class to be such a big part of that feeling of otherness.

Adjusting to Change: Growth through IGR

My first year at Skidmore was filled with frustrating arguments and overwhelming discomfort. At the time I could not seem to put this discomfort into words. I felt like I was always the angry one – the one who always seemed to engage in heated debates about race, the "PC (politically correct) police," or the one who was found always calling out the racist jokes or the unintentional-yet-deeply-offensive microaggressions, defined by Davis (1989), as "stunning, automatic acts of disregard that stem from unconscious attitudes of White superiority and constitute a verification of Black inferiority" (p. 1576). In addition to growing up in an outspoken household in a racially progressive city, I had also attended an incredibly diverse and socially active high school, well known for its Martin Luther King Jr. rallies, its budget-cut walkouts, its testing boycotts, and its political history as a hotspot for Black Panther activities. No one had prepared me for how much my identity and my cultural understanding of the world would be challenged.

Outside the classroom I found some comfort in becoming active in the Office of Student Diversity Programs (OSDP) and taking part in various cultural clubs where I could be around others who also expressed feeling like an outsider. Being a White and Asian mixed-raced student from the West Coast, however, I didn't fit into the polarized community divided along racial and socioeconomic lines. Many of the White students were full-pay and from wealthy suburbs, while many of the students of color were Black and Latino/a students from New York City's outer boroughs. To many people in the Skidmore community, Asian seemed to mean first-generation immigrants in the country. Knowledge or awareness of Asian American culture and history of oppression seemed limited, and even more so, the understanding of the experience of a mixed-race individual was minimal.

Browsing through the course catalog my first year and discovering Race & Power, the Intergroup Relations (IGR) program's first course in the three-step process, there was no doubt I would enroll in the course. I jumped on the opportunity to talk about race in a school culture that seemed to treat it as a taboo subject. It was in this class with Professor Kristie Ford that I finally learned the language to verbalize what I had been feeling and to connect with others who were also frustrated by the defensive majority of the campus. I began to understand that what I was feeling was normal, and much of my anger and discomfort had to do with the fact that I *was* in a completely different cultural environment than the one I had grown up in.

Never having been exposed to the Intergroup Dialogue (IGD) process before, it seemed as though we were unknowingly being introduced to the many stages of Harro's (2000a) Cycle of Liberation, moving through the processes of "waking up," "getting ready," "reaching out," and "building community." Eventually the concept of IGR – a pilot program at the time – was introduced and eight of us decided to continue on to the next course, Racial Identity Theory and Praxis (Racial ID). If Race & Power was about reaffirming my experiences and teaching me the language to explain what I had been going through all my

56   Teshika R. Hatch

life, Racial ID was a class that forced us all to dig deeper and to truly sit in the uncomfortable. We quickly learned Professor Ford's motto, "lean into discomfort," a concept that resonated with me so well. It was during this class that the first interpersonal conflicts began to appear and instead of trying to smooth things over, we were taught to sit with those emotions and process how and why we think and feel the way we do. Explained by Zúñiga, Nagada, Chesler, and Cytron-Walker (2011), "intergroup dialogue is marked by its critical-dialogic approach to exploring commonalities and differences in and between social identity groups, its reliance on sustained communication and involvement to bridge differences and move participants to deeper and more meaningful levels of engagement, and its intergroup focus" (p. 3). In a sense, we had entered the stage of becoming our own mediators – using the skills we had learned to be active listeners, to be hyperaware of group dynamics, and to confront our emotions, all while moving toward group solidarity.

After two semesters of IGD, there was absolutely no turning back for me. When we were prepped on the next step in the process, I assumed I would be facilitating the interracial dialogue with White students and students of color. Although I identify as multiracial and have always been very proud of my mixed-race heritage, it never occurred to me that I could be a good candidate to facilitate the intragroup, Multiracial Dialogue. I had spent so much time in the previous two semesters identifying with the experience of being "the other" – being a person of color in a predominately White college and a predominantly White society – that a part of me was still not entirely sure what it meant to be mixed. I was worried I wasn't qualified to lead a class on an identity that had been talked about so little.

Being involved with IGR meant that even as a facilitator, I was continuing to grow and learn about my own racial identity. In our Multiracial dialogue course, we began to see challenges and issues appear that had not been present (or at least not so obvious) in our own interracial classes from the previous two semesters: moments of internalized oppression among some participants, conflict between students who didn't fall along the Black–White binary, and confusion with individual struggles that led to intense introspective experiences. In a classroom full of students who either identified as mixed race, Latino/a, or transracially adopted, there were so many gray areas that limited us from intimately connecting for much of the first half of the semester. Through our Multiracial dialogue course, we experienced firsthand how binary thinking can "conceal the checkerboard of racial progress and retrenchment and hide the way dominant society often casts minority groups against one another to the detriment of both" (Delgado & Stefancic, 2001, p. 71).

Beyond the experience of facilitating our own dialogues, the main reason the third and final semester of IGD was so powerful was because of our weekly Practicum course, where all the facilitators had the opportunity to get together and support one another. This was a place where we could discuss challenges and successes in our own classrooms, but it was also a place where we continued to challenge one another and grow individually and as a group. Although our

Learning the True Meaning of Advocacy   57

class was scheduled from 6:00–9:00 p.m., there were nights we chose to stay until past 10:00 p.m. because of the deeply emotional classes that could include crying, yelling, and laughing all in one session. When I look back on college, those Wednesdays night sessions still stand out as the best memories from my Skidmore days.

Struggling to Stay Connected: Post-IGR Life at Skidmore

After IGD, I struggled to find my grounding and sense of belonging. Although I always knew IGR was an amazing experience and opportunity, it wasn't until after the IGD sequence was over that I really began to understand how big of an impact it had made in changing my life. Luckily, I spent the next semester studying abroad through a program titled Culture, Development, and Social Justice, and was able to incorporate my understanding of social justice through my own research on discrimination in the Chilean media. Because of this semester away, my sense of loss and confusion didn't really hit until after I returned to campus. I struggled to find the sense of community and family established during the two years in the IGR program.

I began to look for ways to stay connected to the Skidmore community. At times I felt I didn't have the safe space to air out my frustrations or discuss racial injustices, but I continued to speak up because I knew the alternative would further continue the cycle of oppression. More than once I heard people say, "There's Teshika talking about race again …" but I reminded myself what I was taught in IGR: being an "innocent bystander" to even small incidents of unintentional racism is equivalent to standing still on the moving walkway towards systemic racism (Tatum, 1997, p. 11). Thanks to my heightened understanding of social justice and my greater understanding of my own racial identity, I was no longer angry all the time, but instead had learned the language and gained the patience to combat racist incidents. I could process my emotions more clearly and began to see each individual on her/his own path toward racial identity development – which meant communicating with each of my peers differently, depending on where they were in that process (Helms, 1990). For some of my peers, my part-White identity appeared to give them the permission to be more honest and blunt with their ignorant comments, since I didn't fully fit into their definition of the "other." At times, this actually led to more fruitful conversations in intent versus impact, sociohistorical contexts, and how it all fits into the larger systems of oppression.

As campus climate issues began to emerge, the anonymous space of the internet became a hotspot for hateful language and the exposure of many students' true racist colors. The *Skidmore News* published editorials and op-ed pieces drenched in subtly racist undertones. The comments that followed were full of similarly racist sentiments, no longer clouded in politically correct language. Without the proper space for dialogue, comments sections escalated quickly into personal attacks, with outspoken members of the community being at the target. Although I was often happy to speak up publicly, there were times when

58   Teshika R. Hatch

I feared for my own safety and either chose to hide behind anonymity or turn away altogether. In their findings on racial microaggressions on college campuses, Solórzano, Ceja, and Yosso (2000) reported that the racial incidents and feelings of discomfort that students of color experience on campus contribute to the development of a negative racial climate and discourage some students from taking advantage of student services.

In the midst of this tension, individuals experienced in conflict mediation were contacted by campus leaders to help lead discussions about campus climate. Because of my experience with IGR, I was skilled at addressing issues of identity, but I hadn't truly realized how difficult it could be with participants who didn't voluntarily sign up to be a part of these discussions. Unlike a semester-long course where we could spend hours intentionally creating a safe and confidential space, smaller and shorter workshops were a challenge in itself to try to establish community guidelines and prepare for discussions that could be so deeply emotional. Although we were successful in having dialogues with various groups, with professors leading teach-ins and lectures to address issues of racism, I found that two years later, the same issues were still being brought up. In just three years, I felt I had witnessed the full cycle of disengagement: how the campus initially reacts, attempts but struggles to fully address, and then ultimately fades away from actively engaging in community improvement.

With senior year approaching, I felt that the deeply emotional work I had done with IGR during my sophomore year had not been properly expanded upon. I felt I had put in so much effort actively engaging with issues of social justice during my first couple of years, but other than some community discussions, conference attendance, and on-campus jobs as the student assistant for diversity offices, I felt disconnected. I decided to try to reengage with IGR my senior year by applying to be the Peer Mentor for Professor Ford's First-Year seminar course, Race in the Obama Era.

Becoming the peer mentor for Race in the Obama Era seemed to turn everything around. I was able to connect with the first-year students on a more deeply emotional level outside of class, while assisting Professor Ford in teaching the concepts of privilege, power, and oppression during class time. The class was structured like an IGD, so much of the first part of the course focused on working through the process, setting up the class so that students could speak honestly, and creating a safe and trusting space for students inside and outside the classroom. As Washington and Evans (2000) explained in "Becoming an Ally," my role was to model advocacy, remain a supportive figure, and to consistently confront any type of inappropriate behavior.

During orientation, I decided to lead an ice breaker activity to bring the class together and help us get to know one another on a deeper level. Activities meant to strengthen community and build trust had become so commonplace that I hadn't realized how meaningful this activity was in setting the tone for the semester. I asked all the students to find one artifact from their dorm rooms and share the importance of that artifact with the group. Before giving the first-years time to return to their dorms, I explained the activity and shared with the group the significance of a ring I wore every day and how it was a representation of the highs and lows of a tumultuous relationship with my mother. Following this, students shared stories ranging from experiences of being the victim of bullying to struggles with body image and suicide attempts. Later a student thanked me for being so honest with the group and creating that space where others also felt comfortable opening up. Although I understood that my vulnerability helped to create that space, I knew that it was my experience with IGD that taught me to be intentional about setting the tone and to always dig deeper. As explained by Zúñiga et al. (2011), it was the facilitator's responsibility "to be on the alert to move the group beyond surface and trite conversation by asking questions, probing deeper, and expanding the conversation" (p. 54).

The next year was full of moments of joy and reflection on my own journey through IGD. I was able to watch 16 first-year students engage with a topic I had become so passionate about and had the opportunity to witness their own progress through their racial identity development (Helms, 1990). During this year, I began to truly realize what it meant to be an advocate and a mentor for younger students. I engaged in conversations around social justice during class time, but more importantly I was able to support the first-year students outside of class when things became difficult and they needed a space to process their emotions. In many ways I felt I had become an older sister to the students and it was my role to provide guidance and understanding without further creating a division in power. Beyond the actual teachings of social justice through IGD and engaging in conversations around privilege and oppression, IGD had given me the tools to recognize how power dynamics come into play and how the youngest members of the Skidmore community could benefit from my support.

Skidmore Admissions Office

As my college days were coming to a close, I decided to move forward and apply to become a multicultural recruiter for Skidmore's admissions office, while simultaneously applying to other urban education-related positions and working as a research assistant for IGR. Although I wasn't exactly sure where I was headed, I knew I wanted to take my experience with social justice into the education sector, and thought that working as a multicultural recruiter would be a step in the right direction by being a liaison for the prospective students of color. For the next two-and-a-half years, I struggled with my own privilege as a staff member working for a predominantly White institution and the challenges in trying to confront a system of selective admissions that has been firmly established to benefit upper-class White students.

The first year working in admissions was full of lessons on how the college admissions world was set up, and understanding the painful reality of college access for low-income, first-generation students. As a multicultural recruiter, I became one of the two voices in the admissions office constantly speaking up for students of color, confronting questionable language and tactics, and became the face of "diversity" for the office. I felt like it was my responsibility to

60 *Teshika R. Hatch*

challenge the dominant narrative of the office – to advocate for the individuals who had more complicated life circumstances, question the way we looked at students' racial identities, and to support the conversations around diversity for many administrative offices.

The biggest challenge in the admissions office came when I started to see my own role in furthering the cycle of discrimination and marginalization for students of color. As a staff member responsible for increasing the number of students of color on campus, I knew how important preview visits and "diversity" weekends were for not only students who could not afford to visit on their own, but also for the institutional goal of increasing diversity. The challenge was how to be realistic and transparent for the prospective students, while also working to try and enroll as many students of color as possible. From my own experience as a student, I knew that having more students of color on campus was important, but I also knew that diversity visits were notorious for painting a false picture of a predominantly White campus as being much more diverse.

An even bigger challenge was the ways in which race and class intersected and how I had unknowingly become a catalyst in the campus divide along race and class lines. Working for a financially aware school meant we were forced to make some admissions decisions based on whether students were applying for financial aid and how much. Because we needed to meet our strategic goals of increasing racial diversity, White students who needed financial aid were less of a priority and the White students that we were able to admit were majority full-pay students. Although it took me some time to really recognize the ways in which we were impacting campus culture, it was devastating once I connected the dots as to how and why our campus was made up primarily of wealthy White students and students of color with high financial need.

In the midst of adjusting to the challenges of being a multicultural recruiter for a predominantly White college, I was faced with the bigger challenge and adjustment of being among an even more predominantly White staff. Having been a student, I had noticed the makeup of the faculty and staff being fairly homogenous but had put very little thought into what that experience was like for the few staff and faculty of color. As a student, I had felt supported by my mentors and advisors of color and allies, but it wasn't until I entered the role of an admissions officer that I realized how difficult it was to be one of the very few staff of color. I continued my ways of speaking up and challenging subtle microaggressions, but found there were suddenly so many more power dynamics at play from when I was a student. As one of the youngest members of the admissions office, let alone the college, I felt more powerless and voiceless than ever.

Because of IGR, however, I knew there were outlets for processing my frustrations. As soon as I could, I found ways to connect with the IGR program as a staff member, and participated in a diversity training workshop for the Admissions and Advancement offices. In a room of over 100 staff members, I looked around and noticed less than four of us identified as people of color. Immediately I was reminded of how difficult it can be to challenge firmly established systems of hierarchy and power, especially with a very small minority.

I remembered, however, that I was experienced in being a part of the minority and that in many ways, I was an expert at diversity conversations. I took advantage of my experience and attempted to step forward confidently in every way as a diversity trainer. I ended up leading diversity trainings for new tour guides and tried to remain an ally for students who felt a sense of discomfort because of their identity on campus.

Although there were several areas of my role as a multicultural recruiter that proved to be challenging, my favorite moments were when I was able to actually connect with students – particularly those of color and those in lower-resourced areas. Every travel season I was thrilled to be able to visit several community-based organizations and to individually meet many of the students whose parents had not gone to college themselves. My goal in the admissions office instantly became about finding allies in other institutions and organizations and together collaborate on ways to improve the landscape of higher education and educational inequality. I signed up to become a mentor for the College For Every Student (CFES) summer program for first-generation students and attended every conference I could that had any type of emphasis on college access and college success for low-income students.

After three summers of working for CFES and numerous conversations about the college access landscape with colleagues in the nonprofit sector, I realized I was unhappy because the end goal of my job was about institutional diversity, as opposed to supporting the needs of first-generation students. I was also engaging with difficult conversations around race so much less and seemed to become immune to the sometimes racist, sexist, and homophobic attitudes found in a small town like Saratoga Springs, New York. I began to question my own uneasiness when I would walk into a bar or restaurant and feel all eyes turn on me. I was struggling to find comfort in such a homogenous small town and was constantly craving the presence of people of color.

Rediscovering Community: Moving Back West

Knowing how unhappy I was, I reminded myself of Professor Ford's words, "lean into discomfort." I decided it was time for me to finally return to the West Coast and to truly pursue my passion for social justice education. I quit my job, packed up my apartment, and loaded all of my belongings into my car. Driving through conservative states as a young woman of color with an Obama bumper magnet felt terrifying at times, but I felt incredibly privileged to be in a place where I could take time off and live carefree, exposing myself to parts of the country that were so drastically different than anywhere I had lived before. I was overjoyed with the prospect of living among people of color again in a large city, and to hopefully work in an organization with like-minded social justice activists. At the core of the cycle of liberation remains the knowledge and confidence that we are not alone. In order to believe once again in my ability to take part in this work, it was necessary to seek out my own support network and community of activists that were committed to the same liberation (Harro, 2000a).

62 Teshika R. Hatch

After a whirlwind ten day adventure, I arrived to Oakland, California, and was immediately shocked at how anxious I felt living in an urban environment. I found myself having to confront my own prejudicial feelings of safety in my own neighborhood and became acutely aware of the efforts many Black men would take to avoid being seen as "dangerous": purposefully moving far out of the way to avoid walking too close, crossing the street so as not to be seen as a disturbance to many White females, or letting out very casual yet confident greetings while passing by. I had realized that living in a very White town for over six years had reinforced society's stereotypical messages, and I was furious that I could hold such prejudiced feelings and still call myself a social justice advocate. I needed to remind myself of my privileges as a light-skinned female, and attempt to interrupt the cycle of socialization (Harro, 2000b).

Soon enough I fell right back into feeling a part of a community and appreciated so much of what I had missed for so many years: diversity in grocery stores, public transportation, street festivals with live music and art, graffiti in alleyways, Ethiopian restaurants, Asian food markets, protests and marches in the streets. I also found a community of educators who were passionate about social justice and discovered a space where I felt completely at home. Through these networks, I was able to land a role as a case manager and youth development advocate for a college access organization whose students are all first in their family to attend college.

Because of my background working in college admissions, I was falsely under the impression that my role would be primarily to support students in finding the right fit for college and helping them through the college application process. Although these were important end goals, it was clear that my experience in IGR would help support me in so many other ways. Being an advocate for low-income students meant there were so many psychosocial and emotional needs that had to be addressed before talking about college. It was important to recognize the variety of trauma the youth had gone through and to support them through issues such as homelessness, domestic violence, neighborhood crime, teenage pregnancy, depression, and thoughts of suicide. As one of the five faces of oppression, Young (2000) argued that violence "is systemic because it is directed at members of a group simply because they are members of that group" (p. 46). Our young people face varying levels of violence either at home, their communities, or at school, but oftentimes the violence is normalized by society and individuals are not often given the tools to cope with the trauma they have faced (Young, 2000). Because of this, I have come to see my role as a true advocate and ally – my job was not to *help* the youth or to fix their problems, but instead to empower them to recognize their own strengths and their own abilities, and in turn to give them the skills to navigate the systems of inequality (Freire, 1970).

In addition to understanding the needs of seeing youth holistically and empowering them to become their own self-advocates, I have used my skills of facilitation and lesson planning that I gained from IGD in this new role. Meeting with students on a biweekly basis, I am able to build curriculum and lead workshops, while also recognizing the underlying group dynamics and processes. Because of IGD, I know when to remain flexible, when to stay on task, and have several tools for addressing varying group dynamics. As explained by Zúñiga et al. (2011), "practitioners using the IGR design at times need to adjust the topics covered in each stage to match specific group dynamics or participants' needs" (p. 31).

When I first decided to take on the role, I had no idea how much of an influence my IGD training would have. Because of the dialogues around power and privilege in college, I am also more aware of how nonprofit organizations themselves can represent hierarchical systems. The struggle of working at a nonprofit organization within a capitalistic and White-dominated society means the youth often end up being seen merely as service recipients as opposed to our future leaders, and those who work directly with the youth end up just being expendable service-deliverers, rather than experts in youth empowerment and youth development. Young (2000) defined the powerless as "those who lack authority or power even in the mediated sense, those over whom power is exercised without their exercising it" (p. 43). Although we work to empower young people, the organization implicitly reminds us that as direct-service staff members, we are powerless. For example, an ongoing tension is felt between departments needing to raise money and youth advocates who hesitate to share their students' success stories for the fear of exploitation, the romanticization of poverty, or the glorification of "making it out."

The challenge with working in youth advocacy is also the conflict of wanting to be a good role model for youth while also not falling into the savior complex (Cole, 2012). As Cole (2012) argued, anyone can become a godlike savior, have his or her emotional needs satisfied, and do it "under the banner of 'making a difference.'" If IGR taught me anything, it was to constantly be critical of the intentions of myself and others and to challenge situations when they further the cycle of oppression for marginalized people (Young, 2000). In addition, in an attempt to support young people in escaping poverty and gaining the skills to be successful young adults, we often engage in respectability politics (Young, 2000), encouraging students to dress, act, speak, and present themselves a certain way, in order to assimilate into White America.

Although I face these challenges on a near-daily basis, I try to remind myself the reason for doing the work that I do. As a part-White woman, I do have the privilege to opt out of the struggle against many forms of oppression and exercise my privilege by staying silent (Wildman & Davis, 2000). Because of my experience with IGR, however, it is impossible for me to remain silent. IGR opened my eyes to the systems of power and privilege and has transformed me into a social justice advocate who will not condone any form of injustice. My personal and professional relationships have been influenced by my commitment to activism, and the types of conversations I have with family, friends, and significant others are guided by my understanding of oppression. Although some of my family members seem to get fed up with my attempts at confronting racist, homophobic, classist, or misogynistic comments, I can no longer ignore these attitudes.

64 *Teshika R. Hatch*

There is no doubt in my mind today that IGR changed my life and the lives of so many other individuals. Without IGR I would have felt voiceless and powerless – I would never have learned the language to name what I had been feeling, and I wouldn't have known that my experience was not unusual. Because of the experiences in IGR, I not only understand the world better but also I feel empowered to be an advocate for others who are struggling to understand the world themselves. With the tools that I gained through facilitation, I have been able to recognize the process it takes to develop one's own social identity and have acquired the language to speak up when others are silenced. Although IGR taught me that the struggle always continues, I am confident in the importance of leaning into discomfort and love being able to witness young people doing the same.

References

Cole, T. (2012, March 21). The White-savior industrial complex. *Atlantic*. Retrieved from http://www.theatlantic.com/international/archive/2012/03/the-white-savior-industrial-complex/254843/.

Davis, P. C. (1989). Law as microaggression. *Yale Law Journal*, 98, 1559–1577.

Delgado, R., & Stefancic, J. (2001). *Critical race theory*. New York, NY: New York University Press.

Freire, P. (1970). *Pedagogy of the oppressed*. New York: The Continuum International Publishing Group.

Harro, B. (2000a). The cycle of liberation. In M. Adams, W. J. Blumenfeld, R. Castañeda, H. W. Hackman, M. L. Peters, & X. Zúñiga (Eds.), *Readings for diversity and social justice* (pp. 463–469). New York, NY: Routledge.

Harro, B. (2000b). The cycle of socialization. In M. Adams, W. J. Blumenfeld, R. Castañeda, H. W. Hackman, M. L. Peters, & X. Zúñiga (Eds.), *Readings for diversity and social justice* (pp. 15–21). New York, NY: Routledge.

Helms, J. (1990). *Black and white racial identity: Theory, research, and practice*. Westport, CT: Praeger.

Solórzano, D., Ceja, M., & Yosso, T. (2000). Critical race theory, racial microaggressions, and campus racial climate: The experiences of African American college students." *Journal of Negro Education*, 69(1/2), 60–73.

Tatum, B. (1997). *"Why are all the Black kids sitting together in the cafeteria?": And other conversations about race*. New York, NY: Basic Books.

Young, I. M. (2000). Five faces of oppression. In M. Adams, W. J. Blumenfeld, R. Castañeda, H. W. Hackman, M. L. Peters, & X. Zúñiga (Eds.), *Readings for diversity and social justice* (pp. 35–49). New York, NY: Routledge.

Washington, J., & Evans, N. J. (2000). Becoming an ally. In M. Adams, W. J. Blumenfeld, R. Castañeda, H. W. Hackman, M. L. Peters, & X. Zúñiga (Eds.), *Readings for diversity and social justice* (pp. 312–318). New York, NY: Routledge.

Wildman, S. M., & Davis, A. D. (2000). Language and silence: Making systems of privilege visible. In M. Adams, W. J. Blumenfeld, R. Castañeda, H. W. Hackman, M. L. Peters, & X. Zúñiga (Eds.), *Readings for diversity and social justice* (pp. 50–60). New York, NY: Routledge.

Zúñiga, X., Nagda, B. A., Chesler, M., & Cytron-Walker, A. (2011). *Intergroup dialogue in higher education: Meaningful learning about social justice*. K. Ward & L. E. Wolf-Wendel (Eds). Hoboken, NJ: Wiley Periodicals.

6 Interrogating Privilege

Luna Malachowski Bajak

My commitment to social justice started at an early age. I was raised in Colombia and Germany, the daughter of a Peruvian artist and a New York-born foreign correspondent. I believe this unique upbringing exposed me to an array of differences and the plight of others, particularly people of other nationalities and identities historically underrepresented in the United States. As a half-Latina, I was raised to embrace my Peruvian heritage as a strength, and use my fluency in Spanish as a tool to help others. Racially, however, I am of European origin and was raised among the economic elite. Growing up I rarely questioned the complexity of my social identities. Not until I found the Intergroup Relations (IGR) program as a senior at Skidmore College did I begin to admit the extent of my privileged identities, and did I start to take real accountability for my own complicity with whiteness (Jensen, 2005, p. xvii).

Prior to finding IGR, I thought of myself as a social justice advocate without knowing what exactly that embodied. I had spent the previous summer interning for a Brooklyn-based social services center, where I helped train recent Latino immigrants in job-finding skills, as well as designing and launching a workers' cooperative owned and run by women. Although helping empower and advocate for individuals in this way was tremendously satisfying, I also found myself immensely frustrated and saddened by the oppressive narratives I witnessed. I realized I could be a good advocate for others, and help name the unrecognized experiences of marginalized populations as a means for social justice, but I did not have the tools or self-awareness to best navigate these individual and structural systems of oppression (Bohmer & Briggs, 1991).

When Oppression Is Structural

The Intergroup Dialogue (IGD) courses brought a group of us together who shared and differed in social identities to engage intellectually through dialogue as opposed to discussion or debate (Yankelovich, 1999). This was my first exposure to the power and importance of dialogue as a means for productive social justice work. IGD asked that we name, and reflect, on a personal and deep level, on the social identities we were born into and how they relate to the dynamic system of oppression within which we all exist (Harro, 2000). IGD required

66 *Luna Malachowski Bajak*

us to harness trust and create a safe space to share subjugated experiences and acknowledge our individual privileges. As trust between the group grew, and was tested, we felt "freer to probe issues, [as well as] challenge self and others" (Hurtado & Schoem, 2001, p. 6). I recall moments of conflict, particularly when individuals with agent social identities (i.e., men, White) felt attacked and would bring up the topic of "reverse oppression" (Bohmer & Briggs, 1991, p. 158). While women may express hatred toward men or people of color may despise White people, we quickly learned that this hatred manifests only in the form of prejudice (Bohmer & Briggs, 1991). Oppression, however, is more than prejudice and discrimination (Bohmer & Briggs, 1991). In the context of society at large, oppression is structurally embedded in institutions and "operates only in one direction, with the oppressed group as the target of exploitation" (Bohmer & Briggs, 1991, p. 158). At that time, it was much easier for me to understand and accept acts of oppression on an individual level, but dissecting and acknowledging the harsh reality of oppression on an institutional level stirred up a lot of emotions. I could actively make changes on a micro level, but how would I begin to address the issues on a macro level? I felt guilt and anger. Fortunately IGD was also a supportive environment. My feelings of discomfort and resistance were never devalued, but rather encouraged as part of the process.

IGD encouraged me to reevaluate my understanding of my own identity as a half-Latina with the physical attributes of a White woman. It was, and continues to be, a productive struggle. Classroom activities that forced me to identify racially still resonate with me as moments of clarified self-identity. When the class was asked to divide into caucus groups based on how we self-identified racially, I experienced inner turmoil. Yes, my skin is white, but what about my ethnic and cultural heritage? What about the fact that while I grew up there were times my family struggled socioeconomically? I hated being placed in a box, but the discomfort and struggle I felt were part of the process. I hadn't previously understood how much I benefit from privilege. I am a member of the dominant racial group, and as a result I benefit both unconsciously and consciously in that whiteness and superiority (Jensen, 2005). IGD asked me to not only visualize my white privilege but also to name it. Even though my upbringing included some financial strain, my father's whiteness gave him an advantage in securing jobs and opportunities. I also had to admit the different ways in which I had used my Peruvian American identity to my advantage. There were instances in which I manipulated my half-Latina identity as leverage such as checking the "non-White" box on my college application.

White Teacher, Marginalized Student

As I entered the workforce, I was committed to the ongoing acknowledgement and examination of my privilege. I also wanted to hone my empathetic nature, and exercise it in a productive manner. Empathy allows for privileged

Interrogating Privilege   67

individuals to begin seeing oppressed groups who deal with dominance on a daily basis in "their own light rather than through [our White and dominant] projection of them in our light" (Howard, 2006, p. 79). As a white ally I strived to "create an empathetic environment in which [the stories and experiences of marginalized people] can be acknowledged and shared" (Howard, 2006, p. 79). Within that environment I could continue to engage in productive dialogue, interrupt racism, and ultimately strive for social justice.

Upon graduating, I worked briefly as a volunteer in special education classrooms for primary school students in an underprivileged district of Holyoke, Massachusetts. The environment was rough, resources were limited, and funding was sparse. The student population was diverse, primarily students of color, whereas the teachers and staff were predominantly White. The teachers appeared to be exhausted and overworked. The classrooms were also staffed with paraprofessionals who were instructed to physically contain and discipline the children if they acted out (Bessette & Wills, 2007). When the students arrived in the morning, they were asked to line up to enter the building, and were scolded when they strayed off course. The students were also provided with breakfast and lunch because it was accurately assumed that the students were not being fed at home.

I recall teachers discussing one particular student who had noticeably been losing weight, and kept acting out. I witnessed him being kicked out of the class on multiple occasions for being disruptive. The teachers would shake their heads, and tell me that this was an example of a child who will never be "mainstreamed" and placed in a "regular school," but instead would remain in a special education classroom. Later I learned that this student's father had been in and out of prison for some time and had recently returned home. This factor had not been considered in responding to his behavior. This surprised me. Paulo Freire (1970) discussed the dynamic between teacher and student as similar to that of the oppressor and the oppressed. Freire (1970) argued that the oppressor (who considers her/himself more knowledgeable) will often "project an absolute ignorance upon [the oppressed] whom they consider to know nothing" (p. 72). I was disappointed and frustrated that these White educators were not acknowledging the experience of these marginalized students, and taking into account environmental or social factors outside the school setting. Instead, prejudices were dictating intervention, and dominant groups were exercising an "assumption of rightness" about the "other" whom they knew very little about (Howard, 2006, p. 61).

It was evident to me that many of these teachers also looked at their work as a job and not as a "calling for change" (Howard, 2006, p. 125). I assumed I would find empathic educators that shared my same idealism, and ideology, to work on undoing the "tragic impact of White dominance, and thereby free [students] to enjoy the full fruits of their own intelligence and success" (Howard, 2006, p. 125). Unfortunately, I was wrong. The students needed more trauma-informed support, and an empathic environment in order for them to exercise their potential.

Navigating a Broken System

I have now spent the past five years working in New York City in social services and public health. My focus has been specifically with people living with HIV/AIDS and people who struggle with addiction and have been diagnosed with mental health and/or chronic illnesses. I worked in a women's mental health shelter for nearly four years and am now a supervisor at a supportive housing site. I work every day within a broken system. I work together with staff and clients to best navigate the system-based disparities that continue to oppress an already targeted population.

The shelter houses 43 women from an array of social identities. I had a caseload of between 10 and 12 severely and persistently mentally ill (SPMI) and often mentally ill and chemically addicted (MICA) homeless adult women. I was responsible for advocating and empowering these women to pursue sobriety and psychiatric and physical stability in preparation for a transition from street homelessness to supportive housing within a four- to six-month period. I engaged in daily dialogues, both in individual and/or group sessions, where it was crucial to foster a trusting and safe environment, and practiced skills I had honed through IGD such as active listening to help the women discuss history, hardships, and explore whatever barriers may exist when finding housing.

The shelter was a fast-paced milieu setting with on-site medical and psychiatric services, along with 24-hour social services. The learning curve was steep. The program was expected to house a certain number of women every year. If the target was met, the program was fully funded. Unfortunately, for every target not met, the program was subject to budget cuts. In addition, for every woman who was housed but returned to the shelter system within six months, the program was penalized for recidivism. It was a numbers game. I struggled with the thought of the women as numbers, and not individuals. There were countless instances where I was forced to house women, knowing they were not fully prepared and that they may or may not relapse, decompensate medically or psychiatrically, and subsequently run the risk of returning to the shelter system.

I realized I must not dismiss the constant interaction of race, class, language, and culture among our clients, ourselves, and the different systems within which we all exist. All the women in the shelter had endured some level of oppression, abuse, and/or trauma in their lives. The camaraderie between these women, across differences and similarities, was contagious. However, these variations and connections also triggered verbal and physical altercations. Emotions and racial tension ran high. The women of color often argued that the White women were favored by staff and housing agencies. I did often question why women of color appeared to be hospitalized more often. Even if our program strived to be racially unbiased and competent, I witnessed firsthand how the women were often swimming upstream against individuals, institutions, and structures that oppress them.

I was also one of two Spanish-speakers on staff. My Peruvian heritage, years of living in Colombia, and language skills strengthened my dynamic with others.

My own "whiteness" had been transmuted by my "multiethnic identity" (Samuels, 2014). This complicated everyone's views of whiteness for both staff and clients. I realized that I could productively use my racial identity in this context. I built a strong rapport with my clients. I realized that I am no expert; rather, they are the experts of their own experience. Freire (1970) spoke to this premise and argued that, "the oppressed mustn't strive to be integrated into this structural oppression [they face in a setting such as the shelter, but rather] transform that structure to become beings for themselves" (p. 74).

Classroom as Solutions Lab

After two years working in the shelter, I was awarded a scholarship to pursue a Master's in Social Work at Hunter College in Manhattan while working full-time. This provided me the opportunity to put theory into immediate practice. As social work practitioners, we are trained to assist and empower the people we serve on a micro level, that is, case management. What we are not trained to do is assist and empower the people we serve on a macro level. Fortunately, a lot of our coursework focused on closing this gap. We learned how to consider the interdependence and interrelatedness of the systems in which we worked and how they affect our clients (Smith, Chambers, & Bratini, 2009). We were asked to approach our personal and professional lives through an "anti-oppressive lens" (Smith et al., 2009). We dialogued in ways similar to IGD at Skidmore. Together we explored, and strived to be cognizant of micro-aggressions, common and subtle exchanges that "communicate demeaning messages to people of color" or any marginalized individuals, and worked on different ways to interrupt these instances in our everyday lives (Smith et al., 2009, p. 161).

As a result of a graduate school requirement, I also had the opportunity to co-lead a group at a shelter called Seeking Safety, an evidence based practice group focusing on clients who have histories of trauma. Once again, I was provided an opportunity to tap into skills I had learned from IGD and facilitate a dialogue. As a group we worked to find safety from within to help battle targeted identities. The women were often triggered, and struggled to regulate their emotions. I often had to redirect, refocus the group, and remind the participants of the importance of staying committed to the process, albeit difficult.

Working full-time while in graduate school proved to be emotionally and physically draining, but also incredibly enlightening. I strengthened my knowledge of social policy, psychopharmacology, counseling, and advocacy. I honed my communication skills and became more self-aware. I was able to draw parallels between the theory I was learning in the classroom and the practical work I was doing in the field. I also realized I had a growing interest in the problematic intersection of mental health and medical care. Research shows that individuals with serious mental illness receive inadequate medical care when compared to the general population (Lester, Tritter, & Sorohan, 2005). There is not one explicable reason for this. Different factors contribute to this disparity;

70 Luna Malachowski Bajak

however, stigma is a prominent one. Individuals with a severe mental illness are in the minority, and often oppressed. Frequently, the process of stigmatization occurs when there is a power differential. Individuals have argued that "only powerful groups can create social inequities" (Arboleda-Flórez & Stuart, 2012, p. 458). Fortunately, the mental illness stigma discourse has been moving towards "a human rights model that views stigma as a form of social oppression" (Aborleda-Flórez & Stuart, 2012, p. 457).

With that said, stigma associated with mental illness can be both a self-imposed as well as a perceived stigma. Individuals with a mental health diagnosis often internalize the stigma projected by others, and believe that they are deserving of being treated differently because of their diagnosis and label (Aborleda-Flórez & Stuart, 2012). For example, I witnessed firsthand how individuals diagnosed with a mental illness would resort to emergency services, such as a hospital emergency room, rather than attend primary care appointments that could improve their health by means of more preventative care. A lot of factors, including fear of judgment or psychiatric instability, could contribute to these circumstances. Accordingly, research has shown that individuals with a mental illness feel "negatively judged and often ignored" by systems that are meant to assist them (Liggins & Hatcher, 2005, p. 363). In my role, I am often a liaison between the clients I work with and their medical providers. I have also gone in ambulances with clients, and followed up with doctors upon arrival to the emergency room to ensure clients are treated with respect, and not discriminated or mocked. My continued interest in the social work field, and as a social justice advocate, is to interrupt this process of stigmatization. Every day I hope to empower the population I work with to develop skills to cope, manage, and challenge the negative associations tied to their marginalized identities (Aborleda-Flórez & Stuart, 2012).

Staying Active and Committed

After completing my Master's in Social Work, I was promoted to supervisor at one of my agency's permanent housing sites. Our site houses 167 tenants, the majority of whom were formerly homeless. Tenants struggle with mental health, chronic illness, and/or substance use. I coordinate care and am responsible for assessing tenants for psychiatric and physical stability. As a social work supervisor, I also determine whether or not a tenant is a danger to her/himself or others and if the police need to be called, or hospitalization is required. Individuals with a mental illness are frequently stereotyped to be incompetent, and are often perceived to be violent, or involved in crime (Cummings, Lucas, & Druss, 2013). I bore witness to many outbursts that "may be seen as dysfunctional from a dominant perspective," but in reality these moments entail "survival strategies and resistance to institutional barriers" that have historically oppressed them (Bohmer & Briggs, 1991, p. 157). For that reason, I tend to err on the side of not involving force when possible. In my experience, the police rarely understand how best to interact with the mentally ill. I have witnessed police exacerbating the situation by silencing my clients with physical or verbal violence. In some instances, however, police involvement is necessary, and I must navigate the situation to my best ability. This is an instance where I am reminded by IGR to use my whiteness productively by engaging the police in a respectful manner with the sole intention of advocating for my tenant. I have also previously built a rapport with tenants so in moments of crisis, they trust me and maintain the ability to de-escalate their emotions. Social work practitioners should aim to make an impact, and educate others both in their professional and personal circles. I am committed to raising awareness and challenging the stigma and prejudice that so many people attach to the homeless and the mentally ill. For example, sharing information widely about physical health risks in persons with severe mental illness will encourage awareness and advocacy. Sensitizing the public to their humanity can help society's equilibrium. It has been my experience that knowledge is key to change. Education is vital. In educating the public, myths and misinformation about the "nature and prevalence of mental illnesses" can be replaced with truth and facts – thereby improving "mental health knowledge and overall mental health literacy" (Aborleda-Flórez & Stuart, 2012, p. 461).

As I continue to develop as a clinician and social worker, I must always remain mindful of the interdependence and interrelatedness of the oppressive systems in which we work (Smith et al., 2009). The population I work with is vulnerable, and relies on social welfare policies and programs that are often unavailable, misleading, and discriminatory. The United States government originally adopted social welfare policies as a way to enhance the welfare of their citizens (Levin, MacInnis, Carroll, Bourne, & Fanning, 2000). However, it is evident from academic research and firsthand experience that the way in which our welfare system distributes resources and benefits is arbitrary, biased, and discriminatory (Levin et al., 2000). Annual budget cuts continue to deplete access to care. We are in danger of losing resources. If state and federal government allocated more funding for mental health, more programs and research could be performed to start shifting and rewriting policies.

Looking back at who I was at the start of my involvement in the IGR program, and who I am today, I am astounded. The impact the IGR program has had on my personal and professional self cannot be measured. IGR provided me the foundation and tools to navigate the different forms of oppression the population I serve endures from our White-dominated society, and the power struggle between human agency and the structures that continue to oppress them (Bohmer & Briggs, 1991). If my goal as a social justice advocate is to strive for justice, and progressive social change, it requires ongoing commitment for what "one is fighting for, while at the same time being realistic about just how much one really understands a complex world" (Jensen, 2005, p. 85). I started to address this issue in my own life, beginning with my involvement with IGR, by not only working continuously to name and challenge my own privileges, but also by inspiring change in those whom I have an impact on.

72 Luna Malachowski Bajak

References

Arboleda-Flórez, J., & Stuart, H. (2012). From sin to science: Fighting the stigmatization of mental illnesses. *Canadian Journal of Psychiatry*, *57*(8), 457–463.

Bessette, K., Wills, H. (2007). An example of an elementary school paraprofessional-implemented functional analysis and intervention. *Behavioral Disorders*, *32*(3), 192–210.

Bohmer, S., Briggs, J. (1991). Teaching privileged students about gender, race, and class oppression. *Teaching Sociology*, *19*(2), 154–163.

Cummings, J. R., Lucas, S. M., & Druss, B. G. (2013). Addressing public stigma and disparities among persons with mental illness: The role of federal policy. *American Journal of Public Health*, *103*(5), e1–e5.

Freire, P. (1970). *Pedagogy of the oppressed*. New York, NY: Continuum International Publishing Group.

Harro, B. (2000). The cycle of socialization. In M. Adams, W. J. Blumenfeld, R. Castañeda, H. W. Hackman, M. L. Peters, & X. Zúñiga (Eds.), *Reading for diversity and social justice* (pp. 15–20). New York, NY: Routledge.

Howard, G. (2006). *We can't teach what we don't know: White teachers, multiracial schools*. 2nd edition. New York, NY: Teachers College Press.

Hurtado, S., & Schoem, D. L. (2001). *Intergroup dialogue: Deliberative democracy in school, college, community, and workplace*. Ann Arbor, MI: University of Michigan Press.

Jensen, R. (2005). *The heart of whiteness: Confronting race, racism, and white privilege*. San Francisco, CA: City Lights Publication.

Lester, H., Tritter, J. Q., & Sorohan, H. (2005). Patients' and health professionals' views on primary care for people with serious mental illness: Focus group study. *British Medical Journal*, *330*(7500), 1122.

Levin, J., MacInnis, K., Carroll, W. F., Bourne, R., & Fanning, J. P. (2000). Gender inequality. In *Social Problems: Causes, Consequences, Interventions* (pp. 82–104). Los Angeles, CA: Oxford University Press.

Liggins, J., & Hatcher, S. (2005). Stigma toward the mentally ill in the general hospital: A qualitative study. *General Hospital Psychiatry*, *27*, 359–364.

Samuels, G. (2014). Multiethnic and multiracialism. *Encyclopedia of Social Work*. Retrieved January 15, 2016 from http://socialwork.oxfordre.com/view/10.1093/acrefore/9780199975839.001.0001/acrefore-9780199975839-e-991.

Smith, L., Chambers, D., & Bratini, L. (2009). When oppression is the pathogen: The participatory development of socially just mental health practice. *American Journal of Orthopsychiatry*, *79*(2), 159–168.

Yankelovich, D. (1999). *The magic of dialogue: Transforming conflict into cooperation*. New York, NY: Simon & Schuster.

7 Toward a New Operational Paradigm for Social Justice

Stephen A. Bissonnette

My relationship with social justice advocacy began at a young and highly impressionable age. The intersection of my various social identities evolved within a context of structural and institutionalized subordination in a way that helped to manifest my current perspective and passion for social justice advocacy. As Delgado and Stefancic (2001) stated in *Critical Race Theory*, "'intersectionality' means the examination of race, sex, class, national origin, and sexual orientation, and how their combination plays out in various settings" (p. 51). The manner in which my education and professional work connects to social justice relies heavily upon my own social identities and how their unique intersectionality impacted my own socialization and development as a social agent. The intersectionality of my identities also exists within a larger sociohistorical context that is worth identifying explicitly in order to more fully understand the greater implications for my work as an agent of social justice and before exploring more deeply the arch of this work thus far.

Contextualizing My Origins

I was born to a mother descended from farmers from the Açores and a father descended from Québécois hunters and beekeepers. Such specific knowledge of my own ancestry is demonstrative of my level of racial privilege as a White individual and national privilege as a U.S. citizen. Both the paternal and maternal sides of my family were early 20th-century Catholic immigrants, who moved to the United States and settled in rural towns and postindustrial ports along the South Coast of Massachusetts. My father achieved a working-class socioeconomic status after growing up in an impoverished urban neighborhood and, with my mother, purchased almost 20 acres of woodland atop a hill surrounded by wetland conservation, cranberry bogs, and farms in the same small town that my great-grandfather moved to when he arrived in the United States. This region was once the heart, and last stronghold, of the vast Wampanoag Nation of the Algonquian people (Conkey, Boissevain, & Goddard, 1978). My parents both utilized their access to an immense reservoir of skill-based capital that outweighed any lack of monetary capital in the family and used the land to build the house that my younger brother and I were raised in. I attended the

74   *Stephen A. Bissonnette*

same Catholic school system in the neighboring city that my father's family had attended for two generations and later the public regional high school in my hometown.

It is also necessary to contextualize my identity and experience within the modern narrative –within which we all exist – that is responsible for the current oppressive vestigial structural forces of European colonization, the genocide of indigenous peoples, the enslavement of the global South, the rise of industrialization and capitalism via environmental exploitation, immigration and displacement, Judeo-Christian religious dominance, the (in)accessibility of White privilege, and racism (Delgado & Stefancic, 2001; Maathai, 2009; Zinn, 2005). All these realities are functionally responsible for the circumstances that have created my very existence, including my ethnic and national identities. These realities have played integral roles in the creation of my socioeconomic reality and have perpetuated cycles of poverty and oppression both domestically and globally. I am the direct product, as a White Québécois-Açoriano-American, of the culminating interaction of these systems thus far.

Cultivating a New Perspective

Most pertinent to the beginning of my socialization and development of a social justice consciousness is an institution interwoven throughout our history's narrative: that of (hetero)sexism and homophobia. Attending a highly conservative Catholic school in the 1990s during the second decade of the HIV/AIDS epidemic and within the hypermasculine space of a Portuguese inner-city community resulted in highly misinformed perceptions of and violent reactions toward my own femininity, flamboyance, and unyielding proclivity for same-gender attraction. It was here that I began to understand the importance and challenges of advocating for social justice. It was because of these experiences at such a young age that I began working toward deconstructing antiquated systems of oppression to co-develop meaningful equitability.

Skidmore College shone as a beacon from my standpoint as a queer adolescent in high school. More than anything I sought out a safe haven for unapologetic and genuine self-expression. Before even being able to identify sites of my own privilege in society and work toward advocating for a multitude of marginalized identities, I first needed to cultivate my own self-discovery. Social consciousness and awareness are not possible until one truly expresses, deconstructs, and reflects upon one's own identity and socialization (Nagda, Gurin, & Lopez, 2003). Skidmore provided the opportunity for such work to begin, and it was here that I found the Intergroup Relations (IGR) program. After enrolling in a First-Year Seminar on Human Dilemmas, my professor announced the piloting of the IGR program and encouraged us to participate in the upcoming semester.

Through both the seminar and my experience in IGR, I was able to begin deconstructing my own paradigm of understanding social identities and institutions. This allowed me to deconstruct my own socialization while engaging with queer theory, Critical Race Theory (CRT), and feminist theories and methodologies for the first time. My perspective shifted after being exposed to the concept of racism as an institutionalized system "by which society allocates privilege and status" (Delgado & Stefancic, 2001, p. 17) for a specific socially constructed group. Interrogations with CRT helped me understand that "racial hierarchies determine who gets tangible benefits, including the best jobs, the best schools, and invitations to parties in people's homes" (Delgado & Stefancic, 2001, p. 17). I confronted my inherent racism, which had been completely normalized and made invisible in my hometown insofar as it had never been addressed, considered, critiqued, or questioned.

Racism had been an integral component of my upbringing through the very absence of racial diversity due to historical and structural planning of White spaces. As Delgado and Stefancic (2001) stated:

> Real estate steering, redlining, and denial of loans and mortgages, especially after the end of World War II, prevented Blacks from owning homes, particularly in desirable neighborhoods. It also excluded them from sharing in the phenomenal appreciation in real estate property values that the last few decades have brought. Confinement to certain neighborhoods, in turn, limits where Black parents may send their children to school and so perpetuates the cycle of exclusion from opportunities for upward mobility that have enabled many poor Whites to rise (pp. 107–108).

Diversity where I grew up was reduced to differentiating shades of European ethnicities, which simultaneously and consequently resulted in an "ethnicism" that mirrored institutionalized racism by privileging light-skinned English-speaking individuals, since "Whiteness, it turns out, is not only valuable, it is shifting and malleable" (Delgado & Stefancic, 2001, p. 77). The malleability of Whiteness, which consequently exposes its fragility and socially constructed nature, is imbedded within my own familial narrative. Because "the legal definition of Whiteness took shape in the context of immigration law, as courts decided who was to have the privilege of living in the United States," even immigrant groups from Europe could not immediately access White privilege (Delgado & Stefancic, 2001, p. 77). The fact that my mother and I are not fluent in Portuguese, for instance, is a direct result of my grandmother's conscious efforts to assist in our (successful) access to White privilege.

Nationalist and fascist concepts of ethnic "purity" (i.e. being able to trace ancestry to include only Portuguese nationals expressed as being "pure" Portuguese) also informed my racial identity development. Identifying ethnic "purity" was a way to unequivocally dismiss any relation to local family lineages, mostly descended from earlier British and German immigrants, who were referred to as "jucket." This marginalized group of impoverished families was highly stigmatized in our town. Families labeled "jucket" lacked the social, educational, and economic capital that had been inherited by the historically privileged upper-class and elite "WASPS," who were also descended from early Northern European immigrants (Schworm, 2009).

76 Stephen A. Bissonnette

Claims of ethnic purity were a source of pride for descendants of more recent immigrants from Southern Europe and Ireland, who were also marginalized compared to WASPS, because it differentiated them from those labeled 'jucket.' Even individuals descended from more than one newly immigrated ethnic group resisted identifying with the "impure" label of a "mutt" for as many generations as possible, until holding on to "pure-hybrid" ethnicities (i.e. French-Italian) became too unwieldy. As I grew up, between rural and postindustrial New England, there was a highly scrutinizing focus on constructing ethnic identity and its relation to socioeconomic class identity. Therefore, I did not become aware of my broader White racial identity and its accompanying privilege until I went to college.

Negotiating Theory with Praxis

Racial identity and institutionalized racism were both key topics in my education at Skidmore, both within and outside of the IGR program. First, the thematic focus of my graduating class's first-year experience centered on the sociohistorical context, political implications, and humanitarian effects of Hurricane Katrina, as well as the history and culture of the Gulf Coast. Study of this topic resonated with me deeply, as it provided insight on my own privilege, both racially and regionally, through exposure of a reality in our own country that I had not previously witnessed – a further testament to my own privilege – that also deeply disturbed me. Consequently, I was inspired to participate in a volunteer rebuilding effort along the Gulf Coast in the spring of my first year in college. My study of Hurricane Katrina and the Gulf region, as well as my experience volunteering, would later influence my postcollegiate work as a social justice advocate.

Second, through participation with the IGR program in different capacities – participant, researcher, and facilitator – I was able to develop an appreciation for not only the content of our dialogues, but also the process associated with their implementation. Integration of auto-ethnographic narratives, central to the Intergroup Dialogue (IGD) pedagogy, creates a valuable moment for reflection and resocialization. Presentation of experiential knowledge and auto-ethnography as legitimate methods for self-discovery, learning, and research, in conjunction with more traditional objective data, establishes a value of individual perspective and an evolved method for examination. As Freire (1970) proposed in *Pedagogy of the Oppressed*, "The teacher is no longer merely the-one-who-teaches, but one who is himself taught in dialogue with the students, who in turn while being taught also teach. They become jointly responsible for a process in which all grow" (p. 80). Participatory methods radically deconstruct more commonly used antiquated and oppressive notions of truth that traditionally privilege the experience and perspective of the ruling hegemonic class (the oppressors) and undervalue and silence the experiences and perspectives of marginalized communities and individuals (the oppressed). Freire (1970) reminded us that "those who have been denied their primordial right to speak

Toward a New Operational Paradigm   77

their word must first reclaim this right and prevent the continuation of this dehumanizing aggression" (p. 88). It is not enough, to impart knowledge and perpetuate hierarchical systems, which are oppressive; instead we must develop new systems that function in a way that we all contribute to and learn from.

The new operational paradigm I experienced at Skidmore that legitimized subjective perspectives and anti-hierarchical, cooperative structures and methods empowered me to work toward enacting change in the world with others operating within a similar paradigm. Since "the master's tools will never dismantle the master's house" (Lorde, 1984, p. 2), we must find new modes of operating if we are to enact truly fundamental and transformational change to shift our current systems to become more equitable. In order to enact such change, the process of this shift must incorporate as many perspectives and lived experiences as there are individual social agents. My undergraduate coursework of study provided the theoretical framework for such aspirations. In addition to IGR, my Sociology and Gender Studies majors, as well as my study-abroad work in Amsterdam, led me to pursue a future in social justice advocacy.

In my senior year I was accepted as a Teach For America (TFA) corps member and was serendipitously placed in Memphis, Tennessee. Located in the Mississippi Delta, the history, culture, and economy of this region is directly linked to that of New Orleans and the Gulf Coast. I would later come to find this placement to be more deeply connected to my thematic topic of study in college than I had initially anticipated. I saw this experience as an ideal synthesis of my interests in social justice and education as well as an opportunity to place the theoretical frame I had interrogated, navigated through, and critiqued in college into a more realistic and impactful practice. While my experience with TFA did in fact become a practical manifestation of the theoretical worlds I explored at Skidmore, the operational paradigm of the schools I worked in did not match the anti-hierarchical ideals I had aspired to in college as a queer, anti-racist, feminist IGD peer-facilitator.

Soon after relocating from the Hudson Valley to the Mississippi Delta I found myself in a mass of well intentioned, predominantly Northern and White, surprisingly Christian, middle- or upper-class, cisgender, and mostly heterosexual recently graduated college students. While I most assuredly shared many aspects of this conglomerated identity, I also belonged to what could have been considered the tokenized gay male squadron of the Memphis corps and may have also been an unconscious participant in the diversifying of the corps along with a few other tokenized corps members of color.

Our work could be accurately located within the sociohistorical narrative of the White Savior Complex (Denzin, 2014). As Freire (1970) suggested, "we simply cannot go to the laborers – urban or peasant ... to give them 'knowledge' or to impose upon them the model of the 'good man' contained in a program whose content we have ourselves organized" (p. 94). We were about to do precisely this as corps members. We rode in myriad caravans of yellow school buses donning well-pressed dresses and freshly starched shirts buttoned with sweat-soaked collars over silk ties. Moving through infinite cotton fields

78 Stephen A. Bissonnette

toward dilapidated and tornado-battered school houses, we were offering up salvation to thousands of impoverished, underserved, under-resourced, forsaken American children almost entirely descended from enslaved Africans. This road was paved with good intentions, but over earth stained with the all too recent ancient horrors that are cemented into our country's foundation.

Fluid Social Identities and Rigid Social Institutions

Within the context of the Mississippi Delta, I began to more deeply understand the vast complexity of my privileged social identities. While in the Northeast and at Skidmore, I had felt strongly connected to a working-class and queer identity and had only begun to see my own Whiteness. In Memphis, my socioeconomic status was soon elevated to one of seemingly elite wealth compared to the desolate conditions of the rural impoverished South. My working-class status existed only in a space juxtaposed to the extreme luxury class of the urban and suburban Northeast, and so in Memphis I began to identify with a middle-class background.

I also became increasingly aware of my Whiteness and how it privileged me in ways I had never experienced before. In encounters with law enforcement and in most social transactions I would always be given the benefit of the doubt with overzealous courtesy. Friends I made in Memphis, who identify as African American, would tell me how shocked they were at the ease with which I approached police officers, for example. In their experience the police, especially White officers, were to be avoided at all costs for risk of provoking a potentially highly negative, or even fatal, reaction. I had never experienced this before, since in my hometown most of the police officers were old family friends. This is a further testament to my privilege as a White male. While in Memphis, I began to feel as though I were reinforcing existing systems of privilege and oppression instead of working against them.

In the Northeast I was a working-class queer, and in the South I was a wealthy Northern White man. Even my queer identity was outweighed and masked by my regional status and Whiteness. Conversely, however, it was through my queer identity – which at times did in fact prove to be a legible and problematic reality in the South – that I was able to form close relationships with individuals who were not White. Before my living in Memphis, all my close relationships had been with other White-identified individuals. In the South – and particularly in Memphis, which has a historically dominant African American and politically liberal community – almost all of my close relationships were with African American identified individuals who were also queer identified.

Thoughts of my thematic course of study at Skidmore related to Hurricane Katrina, structures of institutionalized racism, and the history that preceded and followed pervaded every aspect of my work and life in the Mississippi Delta. The plantation society of West Tennessee and Northern Mississippi was alive and well and manifested itself in a haunting physical reality that dominated the infrastructural landscape of the region. Functionally, the same wealthy White individuals descended from the slave-owning class still owned most

Toward a New Operational Paradigm   79

of the capital and property, while the same people descended from enslaved Africans lived in squalor with little to no access to equitable services and opportunities. In some instances, these individuals still farmed the same fields of cotton, corn, and soy as their enslaved ancestors. This was visible simply during a short drive through the countryside and painfully juxtaposed the region's natural beauty, once home to the Chickasaw and Choctaw Nations, before the U.S. government decimated and forcibly displaced their people along the Trail of Tears to Oklahoma (Zinn, 2005).

Within Shelby County and the City of Memphis, even the intangible sociopolitical infrastructure maintained malignant vestiges of slavery and the Jim Crow era. Despite the building momentum of progress to revitalize the city as the rich historical and cultural center that it is, a segregated past persisted in the organization of the city. The political system still operated with a White county mayor and county school system and an African American city mayor and city school system. During the time I lived there, an attempt was made in futility to merge and desegregate the two districts. County schools ceded from the merger or White families transferred their children to private schools, and the segregated division persisted (Zubrzycki, 2013).

While I worked in the city schools, I did not work in public schools and instead was placed through TFA into non-union privatized schools: first, a school within a national-charter network, and later a school that was taken over by the state of Tennessee as a result of failing to meet strictures established under the No Child Left Behind Act (Klein, 2015). It was here that I began to critique the authoritarian and inherently oppressive paradigm of the schools that I worked for. The curriculum, pedagogy, and school culture were ethnocentric, corporate, and punitive. There was a lack of cultural competency and no space for collective collaboration, student-centered learning, subjectivity, or self-expression. Students were expected to adhere to highly rigid and archaic standards of behavior, which included complete silence for the entire day, perfect posture while sitting in every class, and perfectly formed lines measured to the degree of individual body positioning of students' head, arms, and legs.

Additionally, the culture of the schools relied on antiquated behaviorist disciplinarian systems that incorporated a highly authoritarian paradigm wherein students were expected to listen and comply with sometimes meaningless direction, such as repeatedly sitting and standing in order to practice this routine. I learned that such systems represented a critical theory I had not witnessed before described as a School to Prison Pipeline. As the New York Civil Liberties Union (2007) stated:

> The School to Prison Pipeline is a nationwide system of local, state and federal education and public safety policies that pushes students out of school and into the criminal justice system. This system disproportionately targets youth of color and youth with disabilities. Inequities in areas such as school discipline, policing practices, high-stakes testing and the prison industry contribute to the pipeline (p. 3).

80 Stephen A. Bissonnette

As part of a credit and debit method of behavior tracking, students were constantly awarded and deducted "money" from their weekly "paychecks" through a digital platform and app that aligned to school-based celebrations and prizes for students based on a minimum threshold on their "paycheck." This system was framed negatively, for the most part, with a focus on giving deductions for minor infractions linked to obedience.

My experience using this system is representative of Wald & Losen's (2003) research on defining and redirecting the School to Prison Pipeline:

> Despite the seeming objective neutrality of a policy titled "Zero Tolerance," the actual operations of school discipline and related systems reveal a host of subjective factors that appear to be a breeding medium for disparities and discrimination. For example, one study found that Black students are punished more severely for lesser offenses, such as "disrespect, excessive noise, threat or loitering" than their White peers" (p. 3).

The rigid standards of these schools did not empower students with the skills and knowledge to express themselves and raise up their voices in order to advocate for their communities and achieve their greatest potential in spite of severe obstacles. Instead, the negative effects of oppression were perpetuated, including "self-depreciation," which Freire (1970) described as

> another characteristic of the oppressed, which derives from their internalization of the opinion the oppressors hold of them. So often do they hear that they are good for nothing, know nothing and are incapable of learning anything – that they are sick, lazy, and unproductive – that in the end they become convinced of their own unfitness (p. 63).

The culture of these schools silenced students and prepared them to follow inane instruction without critique or analysis, which accurately describes the statistical reality a majority of students in this demographic would face in prison.

Not only were students held to inappropriate standards, but also teachers were expected with great pressure to uphold the rigidity of the school's cultural structure, which caused there to be, at times, more effort expended upon student compliance to direction than actual learning. I did not anticipate such a reality when I joined the corps. I was now experiencing a grim internal conflict between continuing to serve my students, albeit via oppressive systems, or forsake them in order to pursue other work that more closely aligned with the pedagogical approach of the IGR program and the perspectives and practices of my other coursework at Skidmore College.

In Search of a New Way

I sought out an educational institution that would practice a more engaged and critical pedagogy and a more student-centered and empowering curriculum where "the method ceases to be an instrument by which the teachers (in this

Toward a New Operational Paradigm 81

instance, the revolutionary leadership) can manipulate the students (in this instance, the oppressed), because it expresses the consciousness of the students themselves" (Freire, 1970, pp. 68–69). In pursuit of a different educational experience, I accepted a teaching position at a private Montessori school in Boston, and I moved back to the Northeast. Now cemented into a rigidly working-class role again and living among the luxury class, my identities evolved and shifted once more.

I was teaching with a curriculum more closely aligned with aspects of my pedagogical approach to student learning, but within a space completely inaccessible to children from lower economic backgrounds, as most Montessori schools are independent and private and require extremely high costs for tuition with very little financial aid. I was relieved, however, to be in a space that housed radically different pedagogical philosophies than the schools I had worked with in Memphis. The pedagogical approach, based on Maria Montessori's philosophy, is deeply respectful of co-participatory methods, and as she states, "there is – so to speak – in every child a painstaking teacher" (Montessori, 1949, p. 6). This perspective resembles Freire's philosophy, although not explicitly, and agrees that "the teacher's thinking is authenticated only by the authenticity of the students' thinking. The teacher cannot think for her students, nor can she impose her thought on them" (Freire, 1970, p. 77). The inaccessibility of a private school, however, and its persistence to operate its organizational structure within an authoritarian paradigm, still did not align with the aspirations I had as a student of the IGR program at Skidmore College. In order to remedy this imbalance and in hopes of accessing a more socially just role, I also accepted a position to work simultaneously for a college-access nonprofit serving students at a charter high school in a deeply impoverished neighborhood of the city.

My experience working at a charter school in the Northeast, however, only confirmed my critique of charter schools in Memphis. A specific incident that exemplifies the ineffective and problematic punitive system of the school, and locates it along the School to Prison Pipeline, occurred when a student, who was tardy, was denied the federal-and-state-funded breakfast offered every morning – also necessary in order to take his medication – as a method of instilling punctuality. Leveraging food with an adolescent of any economic status or ability is not an ethical policy to address tardiness and truancy. As an employee of the nonprofit, I had to constantly navigate between the mission of our program to prepare students for college and the highly authoritarian policies of the school in which we served students. Ultimately, I observed many successes with the students I served in their development toward being more aptly prepared for college admittance, despite the discordant practices of the school and myself.

Ultimately, I was able to find two opportunities that closely aligned with my passion for social and environmental justice as well as my own operational paradigm that started to evolve during my experience in the IGR program at Skidmore College. I began providing consulting and editing services for an environmental start-up and serving as manager for a different college-access nonprofit. The environmental start-up works to steward human and ecological systems through community development and dialogue, research and

82　Stephen A. Bissonnette

publishing, and sustainable urban design projects. The start-up is a practice collaborative that functions outside traditional antiquated concepts of power, authority, and hierarchy. Instead, the collaborative values a multitude of perspectives, cooperative development, and co-participatory methods that partner with preexisting community leadership. This allows the collaborative to work toward its mission of stewarding community resilience that ultimately supports the health and resiliency of the larger bioregion and planet.

The college-access nonprofit maintains a unique model wherein it fosters partnerships with communities across New England that leverage and strengthen preexisting networks among local organizations, high schools, colleges, and universities. Its programs operate using a peer leadership model with current college students, many of whom are first-generation college students themselves, who then work directly with first-generation, low-income, college-bound high school students. The operational paradigm of both organizations seeks to deconstruct and reform oppressive social institutions in innovative ways that respond to each individual community partnership without imposing an external, prescribed agenda. In this way, meaningful equitability can become realized.

Shifting the Paradigm

Social justice advocates must work as social agents who are conscious of their own privilege and locus in society. Only after deconstructing oppressive paradigms within themselves can social agents then work with others to dismantle these very systems. This must be done in order to foster effective co-development of new equitable and just systems, because "a revolutionary leadership must accordingly practice *co-intentional* education" (Freire, 1970, p. 69). IGD helped me navigate the complexities of social justice work through providing the theoretical framework, method, practice, and experience with these issues as well as the tools necessary to deconstruct oppressive paradigms within myself. The world outside a private institution of higher education, however, is incredibly more complex, subtle, and bureaucratic than I anticipated.

My experience leaves me wondering: How do we, as social justice advocates, create equitable access to foundational resources and opportunities, such as education, for all people? If our traditional paradigms inherently house institutionalized systems of privilege and oppression, how do we operate outside these paradigms and systems? How do we continue to enact real, meaningful, and transformative social change that benefits all human and ecological systems? Freire (1970) argued that, "the oppressed must be their own example in the struggle for their redemption" (p. 54). How do White Americans, then, advocate for social justice without overpowering the oppressed and perpetuating the White Savior Complex (Denzin, 2014)?

As a White male, I constantly, inadvertently, and passively perpetuate oppressive societal systems unless I consciously stand in opposition to such systems. Structural oppression and systems of privilege are continuous so long as they are not being actively disrupted. A component of this active disruption

Toward a New Operational Paradigm 83

includes engaging in meaningful dialogue and collaborative social justice work in various capacities. I am forever a student of social justice advocacy, since "it is not our role to speak to the people about our own view of the world, nor to attempt to impose that view on them, but rather to dialogue with the people about their view and ours" (Freire, 1970, p. 96). The challenges and obstacles faced in advocating for social justice must not be deterrents, but must be channeled constructively as inspiration for emboldened passion to deconstruct antiquated systems of oppression.

We all live within a context that inextricably ties us to sociohistorical narratives and realities of oppressive relationships in all that we do. I exist only because systems such as European imperialism, the transatlantic slave trade, and Manifest Destiny existed. We all live and interact under the shadow and atop the foundation of European colonization, the genocide of indigenous peoples, enslavement of the global South, industrial exploitation of the environment, and socioeconomic class division (Delgado & Stefancic, 2001; Maathai, 2009; Zinn, 2005). We must either actively oppose such systems or willingly accept our implicit support of these systems. We need new models for social justice advocacy in order for social justice to be equitable. The problems we address are as complex as the history responsible for their existence and, therefore, have no easy solutions. Yet, the method for generating these solutions is unequivocal: it must be co-participatory. Our journey must begin within a new paradigm of understanding how our social world has formed and how our existence is implicated in this world based upon our own unique intersection of social identities.

References

Conkey, L. E., Boissevain, E., & Goddard, I. (1978). Indians of Southern New England and Long Island: Late period. In B. G. Trigger (Ed.), *Handbook of North American Indians: Northeast* (pp. 177–189). Washington, D.C.: Smithsonian Institution.

Delgado, R. & Stefancic, J. (2001). *Critical race theory.* New York, NY: New York University Press.

Denzin, N. (2014). The savior trope and the modern meanings of whiteness. In M. W. Hughey (Ed.), *The white savior film: Content, critics, and consumption,* (pp. 1–17). Philadelphia, PA: Temple University Press.

Freire, P. (1970). *Pedagogy of the oppressed.* New York, NY: Continuum International Publishing Group.

Klein, A. (2015). No child left behind: An overview. *Education Week.* Retrieved on August 5, 2016 from http://www.edweek.org/ew/section/multimedia/no-child-left-behind-overview-definition-summary.html.

Lorde, A. (1984). The master's tools will never dismantle the master's house. In A. Lorde (Ed.), *Sister outsider: Essays and speeches* (pp. 110–114). Berkeley, CA: Crossing Press.

Maathai, W. (2009). The challenge for Africa. New York, NY: Pantheon Books.

Montessori, M. (1949). *The absorbent mind.* Madras, India: Theosophical Publishing House.

Nagda, B., Gurin, P., & Lopez, G. (2003). Transformative pedagogy for democracy and social justice. *Race Ethnicity and Education,* 6(2), 165–191.

New York Civil Liberties Union. (2007). *School to prison pipeline toolkit.* Retrieved on November 8, 2015 from http://www.nyclu.org/publications/booklet-school-prison-pipeline-toolkit-2007.

84   Stephen A. Bissonnette

Schworm, P. (2009). Massachusetts' ethnic mosaic. *Boston.com*. Retrieved August 3, 2016 from http://archive.boston.com/news/local/massachusetts/graphics/12_26_10_mass_roots/.

Wald, J., & Losen, D. J. (2003). Defining and redirecting a school-to-prison pipeline. *New Directions for Youth Development, 99*, 9–15.

Zinn, H. (2005). *A people's history of the United States*. New York, NY: Harper Perennial Modern Classics.

Zubrzycki, J. (2013). Memphis-Shelby schools merge, amid uncertainty. *Education Week*. Retrieved on August 4, 2016 from http://www.edweek.org/ew/articles/2013/07/10/36memphis.h32.html.

II B. Synthesizing Change Patterns Across the Interview Data

8 Communicating Differently Post-College

An Analysis of IGD Skills and Outcomes

Heather J. Lipkin and Kristie A. Ford

As the auto-ethnographies in Chapters 3–7 indicate, IGD had a sustained impact on these five facilitators, influencing their personal and professional trajectories after graduating from Skidmore College. The next two chapters synthesize patterns across the auto-ethnographies and 28 qualitative interviews with former IGD facilitators.

In particular, Chapter 8 focuses on six transferrable communication and leadership skills facilitators developed from IGD, outlined in the next section, as well as four additional benefits of the program, including increasing confidence with social justice issues, thinking critically and recognizing systems of oppression, building cross-racial social networks, and gaining a community of support. (See Table 8.1.) First, we begin by elaborating on facilitators' IGD-acquired skill sets and how they applied them to life and work after college.

Transferrable Skills

> IGR has helped me communicate and be myself in an authentic way and part of my authentic self is including very strongly that social justice awareness and perspective … it has helped me bridge a vision of myself … reiterating the benefit in life skills and life experience that IGR provided is huge and I am very grateful for it. (Kiera)

During their reflections on the IGD process, facilitators spoke about the various skills they developed throughout their dialogue experiences and subsequently applied to their post-college lives. Some overlapping themes included their ability to (1) recognize nonverbal cues and interactional dynamics, (2) listen actively, (3) monitor airtime and voice, (4) practice empathy and perspective-taking, (5) develop an extensive vocabulary regarding social justice topics, and (6) expand their leadership capacities.

86 *Heather J. Lipkin and Kristie A. Ford*

Table 8.1 Summary of Results

---

1. *Transferrable Skills*
   a. Recognizing Nonverbal Cues and Interactional Dynamics
   b. Listening Actively
   c. Monitoring Airtime and Voice
   d. Practicing Empathy and Perspective-Taking
   e. Building a Vocabulary
   f. Strengthening Leadership Capacities
2. *Programmatic Benefits*
   a. Increased Self-Confidence When Speaking about Social Justice Issues
   b. Critical Thinking and Recognizing Systems of Oppression
   c. Expanding Social Networks and Fostering Cross-Racial Relationships
   d. Supporting Facilitators

Recognizing Nonverbal Cues and Interactional Dynamics

Beginning with the first theme, Maxwell, Nagda, and Thompson (2011) argued that facilitators "need to understand how communication styles, responses to conflict, and signs of respect can vary across cultures or identities" (p. 29). The ability to read body language and facial expressions also enables facilitators, within and outside the classroom, to know when and how to intervene, if necessary (Maxwell, Nagda, & Thompson, 2011, p. 28).

Highlighting this point, Talia and Savannah spoke about their ability to identify nonverbal cues and remain attentive to group dynamics in their post-college lives:

> I would say that facilitation skills in general ... learning to listen, learning to kind of guide a conversation or learning to pick up on nonverbal cues ... I think that was extremely useful in my job now. (Talia)

> With the team at work, I sit in a meeting and ... look around at people's faces and see how everyone's responded to the person who's speaking. (Savannah)

Elaborating on how she learned the importance of "reading the room" as a way to navigate difficult situations, Savannah cited various challenges that arose during the dialogue process. Facilitating, she stated, "taught me to constantly, constantly have that awareness because, as a facilitator it's always just looking at this group and analyzing them in a way and analyzing myself at the same time." As Savannah noted, it was not only crucial for her to be aware of participants' reactions when facilitating, but to also be in touch with her own emotions. Savannah described this simultaneous awareness as an "epic struggle," but one that contributed to her success as an IGD facilitator. Continuing with this idea, she cited the significance of the skill set she acquired through IGD:

> I think [these skills] are important in understanding interpersonal dynamics and interacting with people as you move through life ... and adding the

social identity element to that [is] being aware of people having different backgrounds and experiencing the world differently based off of their different social identities.

According to Savannah, by being conscious of group processes and social identities, she was able to recognize power dynamics that come into play in everyday situations.

Talia's and Savannah's reflections on interpersonal dynamics and navigating interactions across differing social identities serve as an exemplar for one of the important skills facilitators developed through IGD. These results also align with Hackman's (2005) discussion of the essential components of social justice education: "[an] element for effective teaching for social justice involves understanding group dynamics of the classroom and the socially constructed identities of the teacher and students" (p. 108). Likewise, by being attentive to nonverbal cues and group dynamics, these facilitators strengthened their facilitation skills.

Listening Actively

Moreover, most of the participants reflected on their development of active listening skills in relation to the IGD process. Frederick, for instance, noted: "[I] use active listening to hear people out and communicate across individuals or groups in a way that it affirms what is being said; it affirms that I've listened and considered what they are talking about and how I or others can incorporate an idea … in conjunction to what the person is saying." In other words, for Frederick, actively listening to others required hearing people's voices and carefully reiterating his understanding of what was said.

This approach to listening highlights one of Nagda's (2006) four key components of IGD: "appreciating difference," which "involves an openness to learn from others through intentional listening, asking questions, and appreciating life experiences and perspectives different from one's own" (in Nagda & Maxwell, 2011, p. 6). Frederick modeled this through active listening; he worked to bridge connections between statements while simultaneously showing those around him that they were being heard and appreciated. Active listening is key to the IGD process, and, in fact, "it is the emphasis on active listening that makes this process distinctive" (Schoem, Hurtado, Sevig, Chesler, & Sumida, 2001, p. 9). Frederick corroborated the distinctiveness of active listening as a skill by stating: "my experiences outside of college have just told me that people aren't so prone to use active listening." Similarly, as Schoem et al. (2001) noted, "people are always ready to talk, and they do, but there are few instances in which people listen, and listen intently" (p. 9). Having developed the skills to engage in active listening, in conjunction with an understanding of the impact such listening can have, Frederick astutely distinguished conversations in which active listening occurred from those in which it did not.

88   *Heather J. Lipkin and Kristie A. Ford*

In addition to Frederick, other interviewees, like Jeremy, recognized the importance of understanding others and taking the time to truly listen:

> The skills I learned [in IGD] helped me a lot ... it's incredible ... you really learn to listen to people ... not just hearing what they say, but what they feel and what they mean ... you can pick up on those nuances. [*Can you give me a concrete example of this?*] Recently I had one co-worker who was overwhelmed and didn't know how to handle it well ... I really just sat there and listened ... she just broke down in tears ... I was digging deeper into why she was feeling this way ... it was worth it because now I kinda understand how she feels and how to help her.

Based on the above reflections, former IGD facilitators continue to be aware of the manner in which they are listening to others; even in their post-college lives, they model the active listening skills they learned in IGD in the hopes of helping others feel heard. As Schoem et al. (2001) noted, in the dialogue setting, "through the open acknowledgement of the importance of listening and, more importantly, the use of structured exercises that force and reinforce an emphasis on listening, dialogue participants finally begin to 'hear' and understand one another's stories and perspectives" (p. 9). Further, truly engaged listening can be "eye-opening" for both the listener and the speaker, as both are "almost always struck by the difference that is made when another person actively and seriously listens to one's words" (Schoem et al., 2001, p. 9). Supporting this concept, as the participants in our sample emphasized, it is important to understand others and take the time to truly listen to everything being said – as opposed to just selectively hearing or putting words in others' mouths. As another facilitator, Kiera, noted, "learning how to respond rather than react is a skill or way of being that I do my best to use in every situation." To this end, the interviewees' application of active listening in their professional and personal lives, along with their understanding of its importance, suggests the value they place on this acquired skill – both within the dialogue setting and in their everyday conversations.

Monitoring Airtime and Voice

Also integral to the active listening process was participants' ability to monitor their levels of voice and participation within a space; within IGD, this is often referred to as the practice of "stepping up" and "stepping back." To that end, Leah spoke about her awareness of navigating conversations differently as a result of her participation in IGD. She shared: "I definitely feel like I learned how to sit back and collect my thoughts and practice active listening right, and then be able to speak up ... but then also that mediator role is I am constantly putting myself in a situation where I am trying to get both sides." As Leah suggested, through IGD, she learned how to simultaneously play the role of a mediator (stepping back) while sharing her own opinions (stepping up) in various situations. As a facilitator, finding a balance between guiding the dialogue and participating is crucial: "Facilitation requires sharing control and inviting participants to take an active part in class activities ... it requires that instructors be willing to incorporate pedagogical strategies that shift the classroom focus away from facilitator expertise to participant-centered learning" (Griffin & Ouellet, 2007, p. 89). Leah's explanation of "stepping up" and "stepping back" illustrates the complexity of the facilitator role – she was expected to engage in the dialogue in some moments, and to be mindful of the group dynamics, the time constraints, and the direction of the conversation at the same time.

Similar to Leah, Renee learned the step up / step back skill in her facilitator training: "I think the biggest thing I took away as a facilitator was listening and the importance of just letting someone speak their piece." Continuing, she shared that in her role as a facilitator she realized that "it's not about correcting people as much as it is kind of guiding and dialoguing." As Leah and Renee both explained in their interviews, a key skill they learned in IGD was negotiating between speaking and listening, a skill that applies to every day communication as well. Both in facilitator and participant roles, as the interviewees mentioned, it is crucial for individuals of differing identities to share their opinions; however, it is equally important for dialogue participants and leaders to allow others to speak, and to practice active listening throughout the entire process.

In her interview, Melissa further elaborated on the importance of "stepping up" and "stepping back" in her professional life, especially when working with large groups. As a teacher in the United States and abroad, Melissa noted, "just learning how to work with a larger group of people and to step back as a facilitator is something that when you're making partnerships with people from abroad, or even domestically, facilitating skills are really important." Once again, in her interview, Melissa recognized the value of her IGD skills, and, like other interviewees, exemplified utilizing this skill set in the "real world." Clearly, while IGD skills are fundamental to the dialogue setting – and are even required in this type of classroom environment – they are also useful and relevant outside of IGD. Elaborating this point, Kiera noted, "[I]f you are able to communicate consciously, honestly, and compassionately in a room where you are talking about your deep social identities, then you can communicate in any situation." In sum, active listening can be enhanced through the practice of stepping up and stepping back in dialogue settings as well as in everyday contexts (Diaz & Perrault, 2010; Schoem et al., 2001).

Practicing Empathy and Perspective-Taking

Another shared skill mentioned across the interviews was learning to be empathetic and understand others' points of view. As supported in their

90 *Heather J. Lipkin and Kristie A. Ford*

reflections, taking the time to apply the key dialogic skills mentioned in the previous sections often helped facilitators master perspective taking and listening with the intention of understanding. Regarding his IGD learnings, John stated:

> Being empathetic and being detached at the same time, which might be the other side of the coin. But, being able to check your own gut reactions to things ... I don't agree with a lot of things people say but being able to now ask: "why do they think that way?" ... [taking a] broad skill approach ... by thinking about people's life experiences and where they are coming from allows you to hit the real issues ... what is the root, where are they coming from?

In the above passage, John shared that through IGD, he learned not to push aside others' opinions and statements solely because they did not align with his own. Instead, he employed an empathetic approach in which he tried to better understand where other people were coming from before forming his own opinions. This method highlights a key component of listening with empathy; as McCormick (1999) acknowledged, "suspending judgment of someone's feelings ... helps us to become more empathetic. We need to set aside evaluating whether it is right or wrong or good or bad" in order to truly be empathetic (p. 58). John's intentional use of empathy, a skill he learned in IGD, helped him become a better facilitator as he was able to listen with the intent of understanding instead of judging. It also continued to benefit him in his post-college life as he practiced perspective-taking to understand others' opinions.

Like John, Reagan discovered why being empathetic and trying to understand others' points of view were crucial – even beyond the dialogue setting. As a White female social worker, Reagan interacted with clients who came from different socioeconomic and racial backgrounds. In reflecting on her professional interactions, she shared, "it [IGD] has helped me 'conceptualize my work' ... when it comes to different types of inequality ... it's helped me recognize where patients are coming from ... for example, different races, undocumented immigrants, underserved areas, privileged backgrounds." In order to be effective in her job, Reagan approached her clients with empathy and with the intention of understanding, which fostered a positive working relationship. According to McCormick (1999), "empathy usually reduces alienation and isolation, resulting in a person feeling 'valued, cared for, accepted as the person that he or she is'" (p. 57). In accordance with this quotation, Reagan sought to understand her clients' needs and the unique situations they were in, which she attributed to the skills she developed in IGD. Clearly, John and Reagan appreciated the importance of working with others and trying to understand their situations instead of relying on stereotypes or preconceptions. This skill continued to aid them in their post-college lives, as it is a tool they utilized in their everyday encounters at work and at home.

Building a Vocabulary

As Bell and Griffin (2007) explained, building a social justice vocabulary through "readings, videos, lectures, and discussions" and gaining background knowledge in the field is essential to becoming effective facilitators, as it helps them to "analyze current examples of oppression in our society as well as identify ways people have struggled to resist oppression in every historical period" (p. 71). In alignment with this premise, some participants reflected on their ability to communicate effectively about race, and attributed this skill to their IGD training. As Vivian stated, "I think IGR gave me the tools to definitely be more articulate in how I talk about race, how I can explain different concepts of race ... and how to pull in different systems of inequalities and how they connect to race." Vivian's focus on content parallels the "knowledge" component of the Passion, Awareness, Skills, Knowledge (PASK) model (Beale, Thompson, & Chesler, 2001). As Beale, Thompson, and Chesler (2001) noted, "[a] kind of knowledge important in this setting [IGD] is information about the nature of prejudice, discrimination, and institutionalized privilege and oppression" (p. 229). Through her expanded vocabulary, Vivian was able to explain the intersections between various forms of inequality. She further noted: "[I can] connect the dots, so to speak, between different things that have happened, but then also knowing some historical contexts behind it ... like power, privilege, [and] oppression." With this IGD background knowledge about systems of oppression, as Vivian shared, she was able to speak about race as a social construct within broader systems of power.

In her interview, Vivian even recalled some of the texts included in her IGD experience and attributed them to shaping her social justice knowledge: "I still remember some of the texts we've read ... I don't go back to them every day, but I still remember some of the things we've looked at." Clearly, while the IGD experience requires sincere self-reflection and attention to others' opinions, learning historical background and reading relevant literature is equally useful and informative. This type of social justice knowledge helps facilitators "identify fact from falsehood, be knowledgeable of pressing current and historical concerns, and be alert to sensitive and provocative issues" (Beale & Schoem, 2001, p. 273). In fact, striking a balance between content and process through the PASK model "requires combining and applying ... awareness, knowledge, and passion – in a timely and strategic fashion in order to enhance learning and growth opportunities for dialogue participants" (Schoem et al., 2001, p. 231). Building a social justice vocabulary, along with developing an understanding of the historical background of the field, were clearly memorable skills that interviewees reflected on three to five years after graduation.

92   Heather J. Lipkin and Kristie A. Ford

Like Vivian, other participants also referred back to their IGD readings, activities, and notes as references – even in their post-college lives. For instance, Mia discussed her use of IGD's "Forced Choices"[1] exercise in her job: "I definitely use those skills. We do activities like that, and I definitely bring up a lot of social issues in the class and use what I learned in IGR to be able to facilitate conversations with my kids." Used to help surface and explore similar and different viewpoints, this activity enabled Mia to facilitate difficult social justice-related conversations with English Language Learner (ELL) high school students in her classroom.

Moreover, as a White woman, Melissa reflected on how helpful it was to draw upon her vocabulary when discussing race and other social justice topics. She shared: "It's just ... the hardest part of having a white identity, when I first started the [IGD] program was just having the vocabulary to even talk about how I felt ... it was a huge barrier." Likewise, Eliott, a White man, noted that "being able to talk about social justice and talk about issues with race and not feel ultra-uncomfortable ... and to have the vocabulary ... it is not as over-whelming as the first time when you are realizing what privilege is and how deep it goes ... and how differently you can be treated because of the color of your skin or your gender ... I am not debilitated ... I can [now] engage in those types of conversations."

As Melissa and Eliott indicated, they initially struggled with participating in conversations about race. Since many White participants had never thought much about race prior to IGD (Ford, 2012), building a vocabulary was cru-cial to their experience, as it enabled them to vocalize their opinions in an informed way. Given the complexity of race and racism, language is critical to the dialogue setting as "miscommunication and misunderstanding can easily arise" (Bell, Love, Washington, & Weinstein, 2007, p. 385). Building on this idea, some White participants were initially afraid to speak up in IGD because they did not want to offend others. According to Hardiman, Jackson, and Griffin (2007), this fear is not uncommon: "Many participants come into social justice education courses with some fear that they will 'make a mistake' by trig-gering someone else" (p. 56). For Melissa and Eliott, having a vocabulary of words and phrases that were respectful toward other races and cultures eased this fear. In sum, building a vocabulary rooted in social justice concepts, while simultaneously studying the real-life implications of such terms, was one specific skill that these facilitators developed through IGD.

Strengthening Leadership Capacities

Further, by undergoing the facilitation training process and actually facilitat-ing race-focused dialogues, several participants of differing social identities reported building effective leadership skills. By definition, a facilitator moni-tors the dialogue process, is mindful of reactions within the room, and inter-jects with literary background knowledge when appropriate (Maxwell, Fisher, Thompson, & Behling, 2011; Nagda & Maxwell, 2011). Hardiman, Jackson,

Communicating Differently Post-College   93

and Griffin (2007) recognized the multifaceted role of dialogue facilitation in this way: "The role of the facilitators is to help create a class environment in which participants can share their experiences, express their beliefs, ask questions, and listen respectfully to the experiences and questions of others" (p. 51).

For Logan, a Black man, attending to the facilitation principles highlighted by Hardiman, Jackson, and Griffin (2007) was a challenging, yet rewarding endeavor. Reflecting on his growth as a leader because of his responsibilities as an IGD facilitator, he stated:

> [IGD] helped me be a really effective leader because I had to pretty much run the class with another student and then the students come to class and they look at us. [I] had to pretty much I guess run everything, make sure they get the assignments, make sure they feel comfortable speaking up in a class. So it definitely helped me become an effective leader, gave me great communication skills, and it gave me the confidence to be a bigger role than just sitting in class and listening to the professor speak.

In this role, Logan not only developed communication and organizational skills, but he also became more self-assured. In fact, Logan attributed his confidence running programs in his post-college job to his IGD experience:

> My past job and other jobs I've applied to, they're usually supervisory roles so I'll be in charge of students, I'll have my own staff. So ... I felt very comfortable talking to people, interacting with people ... IGD also gave me the confidence to run the programs that I created at [higher educational institution]. And it helped me to deal with that easily and not feel nervous or anything like that as well.

Due to this increased confidence developed through the facilitation experience, Logan was able to apply his IGD leadership skills to his post-college professional life. Like Logan, other interviewees' also discussed how IGD enhanced their leadership capacities within the classroom and beyond.

For instance, in her HIV prevention work, IGD helped Reagan, a White woman, better communicate with and support staff who were often frustrated with changing office protocols. Using the leadership skills she acquired and taking the initiative to speak up, she encouraged other co-workers to "recognize where these individuals [staff] are coming from" and asked: "[H]ow do we help staff who are overworked and underappreciated, and being told every day another set of rules? How [do we] empower them to do their best work? How can we simplify it [the protocols]?" Attributing this intervention to her IGD training, Reagan was able to embrace a leadership role in order to improve the work environment for office staff and the clients who utilize their services.

As these examples suggest, by drawing on their IGD knowledge and skills, interviewees identified tangible ways in which they were applying and

94 *Heather J. Lipkin and Kristie A. Ford*

strengthening their leadership abilities in their chosen career fields. In the next section, we describe four overarching themes that the facilitators identified when discussing the value of IGD.

Programmatic Benefits

Most notably, when speaking about the benefits of IGD, participants positively reflected on (1) increasing their self-confidence when speaking about social justice issues, (2) thinking critically and recognizing systems of oppression, (3) expanding their social networks and building cross-racial relationships, and (4) valuing the supportive nature of the program.

Increased Confidence When Speaking about Social Justice Issues

As briefly touched upon in the *"Strengthening Leadership Capacities"* section of this chapter, many facilitators in our sample identified their heightened sense of self-confidence when speaking about social justice issues as an important out-come of the IGD process. Accordingly, with her newly developed vocabulary and IGD frameworks, Melissa elaborated on this IGD benefit: "I've found that nowadays, since my time in IGR, I'm able to kind of confidently take a stance on how I feel about certain issues of oppression and what my role is in that and also how I'm affected by them." Melissa continued:

> Just having that background has set me up to feel so much more confident talking to newer people about those issues because they do play a role ... and then also reflecting on myself and seeing how much I was able to grow into a more confident social justice advocate, [I'm] able to talk about issues of race and other kinds of social justice. It was just really amazing to ... be a part of that and to see how much change I went through.

Other facilitators also attributed their confidence in speaking about and grappling with social justice issues to IGD. Sophie, for instance, noticed herself purposely engaging in conversations about social justice after college:

> It [IGD] just made everything so much easier because I wasn't scared of having hard conversations ... I wasn't scared of popular things that are messy and I think that that really helped me and my students connect and we could talk about these issues of race and class and identity ... I wouldn't even know how to do that if I wouldn't been through IGD and had those same conversations.

As Melissa and Sophie's examples suggest, interviewees' increased confidence led them to engage in difficult conversations and raise social justice topics in various settings – whether it was at work, in the classroom, or among family and friends. The link between social justice knowledge and increased confidence in speaking up against injustices complements Bandura's (1986) Social Cognitive Theory. Bandura argued that the "development of self-efficacy or self-confidence in interpersonal interactions promotes increased levels of (behavioral) change" (in Mayhew & Fernandez, 2007, p. 56). Applying this theory to Melissa, Sophie, and other IGD facilitators, increased knowledge led to higher levels of confidence; ideally, this newfound self-confidence should also result in a higher frequency of social-justice-oriented actions. (For more on social justice advocacy in practice, see Chapter 9.)

Critical Thinking and Recognizing Systems of Oppression

In addition to being more confident when speaking about social justice issues, several participants reflected on their ability to identify and label systems of oppression. They attributed their ability to think critically and reflect on unjust systems to their IGD experience, noting that a clear benefit of the program was teaching students and facilitators to develop a critical awareness of these systems. To this end, Melissa compared her understanding of oppressive and unequal systems before her IGD involvement to now:

> [N]ow that I've gone through the IGD sequence, I mean, it was like a year and a half basically of training ... so to have been on the end of that cycle and then try to remember the very first things that I did where someone first introduced me to these ideas is sort of difficult 'cause my brain is just trained in a certain orientation now, where it's like, "Oh, of course that's obvious! ... of course there are systems of oppression!"

The quotation above is extremely powerful as Melissa recalled the progress she made after a year and a half of IGD training. She attributed her understanding of oppressive systems to this training, in which she learned to critically view the world and question existing structures. Thinking back to her initial grasp of social justice concepts before becoming involved in IGD, Melissa now finds it "difficult" to reflect on her previous understanding of structural inequalities. Comparatively, as she stated, she is "trained in a certain orientation now," or in thinking critically, and as a result, she recognizes (and cannot unsee) systems of oppression.

Similar to Melissa, Mia modeled a larger understanding of systematic inequalities: "Honestly, I think I was realizing ... that feeling I had in front of me that society wasn't as it was before or knowing that the reason why I experience the sense of poverty or discrimination wasn't just an isolated situation." She continued, demonstrating her awareness of unjust systems that affect society at large, and not just her alone: "[this] is something that develops systematically and it is developed in our society due to other factors." This reflection during her interview exemplifies Mia's ability to critically think about the systems in which she lives. Arguably, Mia's social justice education resulted in this newfound awareness of individual, interpersonal, and structural oppression. Lopez,

96 *Heather J. Lipkin and Kristie A. Ford*

Gurin, and Nagda's (1998) research discussed the type of individualized thinking Mia spoke about before engaging in IGD: "Many studies have demonstrated the tendency to see human behavior as caused by the internal qualities of individuals" (p. 306). Due to her IGD education, however, Mia gained a broader understanding of society at large. This line of thinking, similar to Melissa's and other participants within our sample, highlights one of the benefits of participating in IGD.

Beatriz further echoed the benefit of critical thinking due to her IGD background, and even claimed that her education was "engrained" within her. She stated: "I feel that what I've learned, especially at Skidmore, and especially in IGR, that stuff is very engrained in me … there are a lot of moments where I catch myself questioning things, and I know that it's because of the education that I've received." This sentiment supports Lopez, Gurin, and Nagda's (1998) study in which they recognized the continuing affect of critical thinking and analysis beyond the IGD classroom. As they noted, their results "suggest that students [in their study] were not merely adhering to course ideology (specific to the topics covered) but were using a method of analysis they learned in the course to think critically about other types of group inequalities and new intergroup situations" (Lopez, Gurin, & Nagda, 1998, p. 322). Further emphasizing this idea, Nagda et al. (2009) noted that "the communication processes [developed in dialogue courses] were significantly related to increased critique of inequality and commitment to post-college action to redress inequality" (p. 52). As Beatriz commented above, the type of thinking she learned in IGD was "engrained" within her, and helped her to astutely notice and continuously question the structural inequalities and systems of oppression she encounters post-college.

It is important to recognize that Beatriz, as a trained facilitator, completed a series of intensive courses where she learned the skills and tools to become an effective facilitator. However, as Lopez, Gurin, and Nagda's (1998) research revealed, even those involved in social justice education for a short period of time can benefit from it, particularly in regard to certain ways of thinking: "we found evidence that a change in causal thinking, toward more structural analyses of inequality and intergroup situations, may occur in an even shorter period of time – in response to an intense semester-long course on intergroup relations as opposed to several years of a social science curriculum" (p. 323). While facilitators have more exposure to social justice pedagogies given their intensive involvement with the IGD program, it is encouraging that students who are (even minimally) involved can also demonstrate similar learning outcomes.

In sum, as Beatriz said, "what I'm trying to say is how I perceive the world is that I still question everything that I pick up along the way." This tendency to question and be reflective reinforces the ability to think critically in the hopes of understanding systems of oppression, a clear benefit of IGD that many participants noted within our study. Moreover, this learned process of critical thinking often extends into the post-college world: "Communicative interactions and alliance building, informed by critical analysis and engaged relationships,

Communicating Differently Post-College 97

opens the possibility of 'doing with' in building a just community" (Nagda et al., 2009, p. 54). Similarly, by developing a critical awareness of systems of oppression, the majority of participants in our sample remained actively engaged in social justice actions post-college. (For more, see Chapter 9.)

Expanding Social Networks and Fostering Cross-Racial Relationships

In addition to cultivating their social justice proficiency and confidence, as well as thinking critically about systems of oppression, several participants mentioned their expanded social networks as another result of IGD. Nagda and Gurin (2007) noted, "In IGD, community is built across difference and through the deep exploration of differences and conflicts" (p. 39). Along these lines, Beatriz, a Latina woman, reflected on her ability to form friendships with people of other races/ethnicities: "I'm even able to relate now to people that I thought I could never relate to ... because I used to just, I only knew to hang out with other Hispanics and other African Americans, and now that's expanded so much." As Beatriz remarked, not only has she gained friends of other races/ethnicities, but she has also found commonalities and ways to "relate" to people who appear different from her. Building these friendships was an eye-opening process for Beatriz, and was one that she attributed to her IGD involvement: "I'm able to have really great relationships with White people and people with other cultural backgrounds and that is because of my experience at Skidmore and IGR, so I'm very conscious of that." Beatriz's reflection supports Nagda, Gurin, Sorensen, and Zúñiga's (2009) finding that "dialogue increased students' positive intergroup relationships ... [and they] showed significantly greater motivation to bridge differences and greater increases in empathy" (p. 5). Further, Beatriz's cross-racial friendships highlight Nagda and Gurin's (2007) statement that "involving students in intellectual and affective interactions with fellow classmates [through dialogue] ... can contribute to democratic living not just politically but personally as well" (p. 43).

Similar to Beatriz, Mia, a multiracial woman, spoke about the qualities she looks for in her friends. She attributed these friendship values to her IGD experience and social justice knowledge, and stated:

> I think, for me, it is important to have that racial diversity, but I think what is more important is to have people who are aware ... I don't think I can be very close to someone who can't see the struggles of people of color in society ... [I need people] who are willing to look at my experience and not judge me.

Based on the above statement, through IGD, Mia realized that racial diversity is important in her social networks; however, she also wanted her friends to be socially aware and open to seeing other points of view. By building relationships

98   *Heather J. Lipkin and Kristie A. Ford*

with "aware" individuals, Mia surrounded herself with a supportive, socially cognizant circle of friends who recognized injustices and sought to combat them. Moreover, she looked for friends who were "willing to look at [her] experience" and not place judgment on the ways in which she experienced the world as a multiracial woman. As Nagda and Gurin (2007) found, "IGD research shows strong evidence for students' increased critical consciousness" (p. 36), and having an expansive IGD social network who recognized structural racism and inequality provided Mia with a valuable cross-racial support system.

Supporting Facilitators

Finally, related to broadening their interpersonal support networks, many facilitators spoke about the overarching programmatic support they received throughout the IGD process. In fact, many participants cited support as one of the most beneficial and memorable aspects of their IGD experiences. To that end, Frederick and Talia respectively stated:

> There is such a strong support within the whole IGR sequence and beyond. You are kind of within this community in that when you're on campus you feel so connected – and you feel like you can talk with someone to really engage with these issues, talk to other people about best practices and really formulate them so that it makes sense for you. (Frederick)

> The most memorable part [of IGD], I would say, was the support between the students and from the faculty and the instructors' approaches …it was just amazing to be able to come together [in Practicum] and reflect on what was happening in our classes … and just to be around people who actually got it, rather than constantly trying to speak up or trying to convince people that … there's an issue. (Talia)

Both quotations highlight the dynamic relationships often formed among students, staff, and faculty within the IGR program. As Talia noted, it was reassuring to be surrounded by fellow peers and instructors who "got it," or understood that social injustices are embedded within everyday life. Accordingly, Griffin and Ouellett (2007) explained, "Teaching social justice education courses is more rewarding if you have colleagues and friends with whom you can discuss issues, challenge your awareness, receive help, and commiserate when things don't go as planned" (p. 90). Building on this statement, as Talia stated, instead of "trying to speak up" or "trying to convince people" that issues exist within society, her Practicum course offered a safe space to unpack what happened in dialogue each week. (For more on the Practicum course, see Chapter 2.) Ultimately, by taking the time to reflect on emergent themes and debrief group dynamics that surfaced in the dialogues, student facilitators and faculty/staff instructors learned with and from one another, while also supporting one another through the process.

Gabriel also highlighted the supportive friendships he developed with his classmates through IGD. He stated: "Most of the friends that I have – that I keep [in] close contact with and I see – are friends that went through the IGR process with me … when we all come together, I feel like we could talk freely and we know what we're talking about with each other." He continued: "when you have people that are willing to have conversations with you about different subjects and they tell you what they think or how they feel about something, you can relate to them." As Gabriel shared, through his IGD courses, he established a close-knit friendship network. Similar to Talia and Frederick, it was beneficial for Gabriel to engage with people who shared an interest in social justice issues due to their IGD involvement. With a group of people who understood the dialogue process, Gabriel's friendship network offered a safe space to grapple with difficult issues. For Gabriel, this support even extended beyond the Skidmore campus, as the friendships he maintained with his IGD classmates offered a strong support group outside the classroom setting in his post-college life. As he noted, many of his peers – with whom he is still in touch three years post-college – are people he could talk with "freely" and to whom he could relate.

As this section demonstrates, being strongly supported in college was reportedly one of the most beneficial aspects of the IGD process, and one that should not be taken for granted. Savannah summed this up nicely when she said: "it's harder to find the outlet I had when I was at Skidmore … [I had my] IGR family which was always this really great support network to turn to." (See Chapter 11 for recommendations on how to foster this type of support with alumni facilitators.)

Summary of Results

As evidenced in this chapter, the majority of participants in our sample utilized their IGD skills and appreciated the benefits gained from their IGD experiences in their post-college lives. For many, this line of thinking became second nature. As Katie explained, by the end of the IGR process, "a lot of it isn't even applying skills we were taught, it was applying habits that were taught through repetition." Specifically, three to five years post-college, participants continued to hone their IGD practices, such as listening actively and with empathy, being attentive to group dynamics, balancing voice within a space, applying appropriate social justice terminology, and developing as effective leaders. Additionally, interviewees acknowledged the overarching benefits of IGD, including sureness in speaking about social justice topics, understanding systems of oppression, attention to racially diverse social networks, and programmatic support.

Together, all of these factors were instrumental in furthering facilitators' developmental process as socially aware and engaged citizens in their post-college workplaces and communities. Nagda, Gurin, Sorensen, & Zúñiga (2009), however, remind us that "developing and acting on a sense of personal and social responsibility are lifelong endeavors" (p. 6). As such, in Chapter 9,

100   Heather J. Lipkin and Kristie A. Ford

we elaborate further on the facilitators' post-college engagement in social justice work. Specifically, we focus on the ways in which participants attempted to define, apply, and remain motivated to continue their journeys of social justice education and advocacy. Participant reflections on the challenges they faced and the support they required reinforce the notion that the IGD experience is one step in a lifetime of committed social justice efforts.

Note

1   In this interactive activity, students are read a series of provocative statements and are asked to make a choice by moving to one side of the room if they agree with the statement and to the other side of the room if they disagree. By physically asking students to choose a side, this activity can surface disagreement or conflict within a dialogic space.

References

Bandura, A. (1986). *Social foundations of thought and action*: A social cognitive theory. Englewood Cliffs, NJ: Prentice-Hall.

Beale, R., & Schoem, D. (2001). The content/process balance in intergroup dialogue. In D. Schoem & S. Hurtado (Eds.), *Intergroup dialogue: Deliberative democracy in school, college, community, and workplace* (pp. 266–279). Ann Arbor, MI: University of Michigan Press.

Beale, R., Thompson, M., & Chesler, M. (2001). Training peer facilitators for intergroup dialogue leadership. In D. Schoem & S. Hurtado (Eds.), *Intergroup dialogue: Deliberative democracy in school, college, community, and workplace* (pp. 227–246). Ann Arbor, MI: University of Michigan Press.

Bell, L. A., & Griffin, P. (2007). Designing social justice education courses. In M. Adams, L. A. Bell, & P. Griffin (Eds.), *Teaching for diversity and social justice* (pp. 67–87). New York, NY: Routledge.

Bell, L. A., Love, B. J., Washington, S., & Weinstein, G. (2007). Knowing ourselves as social justice educators. In M. Adams, L. A. Bell, & P. Griffin (Eds.), *Teaching for diversity and social justice* (pp. 381–393). New York, NY: Routledge.

Diaz, A., & Perrault, R. (2010). Sustained dialogue and civic life: Post-college impacts. *Michigan Journal of Community Service Learning*, Fall, 1–12.

Ford, K. A. (2012). Shifting white ideological scripts: The educational benefits of inter- and intraracial curricular dialogues on the experiences of white college students. *Journal of Diversity in Higher Education*, 5(3), 138–158. Adapted with permission of APA.

Griffin, P. & Ouellett, M. L. (2007). Facilitating social justice education courses. In M. Adams, L. A. Bell, & P. Griffin (Eds.), *Teaching for diversity and social justice* (pp. 89– 113). New York, NY: Routledge.

Hackman, H. W. (2005). Five essential components for social justice education. *Equity & Excellence in Education*, 38, 103–109.

Hardiman, R., Jackson, B., & Griffin, P. (2007). Conceptual foundations for social justice education. In M. Adams, L. A. Bell, & P. Griffin (Eds.), *Teaching for diversity and social justice* (pp. 35–66). New York, NY: Routledge.

Lopez, G. E., Gurin, P., & Nagda, B. A. (1998). Education and understanding structural causes for group inequalities. *Political Psychology*, 19(2), 305–329.

McCormick, D. (1999). Listening with empathy: Taking the other person's perspective. In A. L. Cooke, M. Brazzel, A. S., Craig, & B. Greig (Eds.), *Reading book for human*

Communicating Differently Post-College   101

relations' training 8th edition (pp. 57–60). Alexandria, VA: NTL Institute for Applied Behavioral Science.

Mayhew, M. J., & Fernandez, S. D. (2007). Pedagogical practices that contribute to social justice outcomes. *The Review of Higher Education, 31*(1), 55–80.

Maxwell, K. E., Fisher, R. B., Thompson, M. C., & Behling, C. (2011). Training peer facilitators as social justice educators. In K. E. Maxwell, R. A. Nagda, & M. C. Thompson (Eds.), *Facilitating intergroup dialogues: Bridging differences, catalyzing change* (pp. 41–54). Sterling, VA: Stylus Publishing.

Maxwell, K. E., Nagda, B. A., & Thompson, M. C. (Eds.). (2011). *Facilitating intergroup dialogues: Bridging differences, catalyzing change*. Sterling, VA: Stylus Publishing, Inc.

Nagda, B. A. (2006). Breaking barriers, crossing boundaries, building bridges: Communication processes in intergroup dialogues. *Journal of Social Issues, 62*(3), 553–576.

Nagda, B. A., & Gurin, P. (2007). Intergroup dialogue: A critical-dialogic approach to learning about difference, inequality, and social justice. *New Directions for Teaching and Learning, Fall*(111), 35–45.

Nagda, B. A., Gurin, P., Sorensen, N., & Zúñiga, X. (2009). Evaluating intergroup dialogue: Engaging diversity for personal and social responsibility. *Diversity and Democracy, 12*(1), 4–6.

Nagda, B. A., Gurin, P., Sorensen, N., Gurin-Sands, C., & Osuna, S. M. (2009). From separate corners to dialogue and action. *Race and Social Problems, 1*(1), 45–55.

Nagda, B. A., & Maxwell, K. E. (2011). Deepening the layers of understanding and connection: A critical-dialogic approach to facilitating intergroup dialogues. In K. E. Maxwell, R. A. Nagda, & M. C. Thompson (Eds.), *Facilitating intergroup dialogues: Bridging differences, catalyzing change* (pp. 1–22). Sterling, VA: Stylus Publishing, Inc.

Schoem, D., Hurtado, S., Sevig, T., Chesler, M., & Sumida, S. H. (2001). Intergroup dialogue: Democracy at work in theory and practice. In D. Schoem & S. Hurtado (Eds.), *Intergroup dialogue: Deliberative democracy in school, college, community, and workplace* (pp. 1–21). Ann Arbor, MI: University of Michigan Press.

Yankelovich, Daniel. (1999). *The magic of dialogue: Transforming conflict into cooperation*. New York, NY: Touchstone.

9 Working Towards Social Justice Advocacy

Kristie A. Ford and Heather J. Lipkin

What is your vision for the next five, ten, and/or fifteen years? What do you hope to be doing personally and professionally?

I guess ten or fifteen years down the road I would like to still be in this career field. I would like to be Vice President of Student Affairs. I've always thought that the more power you have the better control you can have over an environment … I can still see myself engaging in diversity … I think that, you know, just having that type of power, you can pretty much use it for good and create a more inclusive campus. (Logan, Black man[1])

5 years down the road? I think my social justice would look like working with for-profit developers, real estate developers, who are interested in building in underserved communities … working along the side of them to make sure that they understand the culture of that community and also make sure that the individuals in that community are … take advantage of this deal, of that development, or any other development that comes or that's built in their neighborhood. That's gonna be my social justice. I'm going to focus on making sure that lower income, poverty level, minority individuals are not pushed to the side and instead given a chance to speak and to take advantage of all the resources that are coming to them or provided to them or accessible. (Elise, Latina woman)

Doing a career that I'm passionate about, whether it be Church Ministry, or … I'd love to be doing something along those lines, affecting change in my community. I would love to be living in the same place that I'm working so that, you know, it's not like I'm, I'm leaving to go to work and not leaving to go somewhere else but just to be a face in a community, help to raise up leaders in that space, people who want to affect change in their environment and also raise my kids to be people that are compassionate for others … yeah, and in ten years I think that's what I'd like to be doing. (Isabelle, Black woman)

I hope to sprinkle some of the principles of higher ed in different domains where it doesn't feel like you have to only go to college to get information …

Working Towards Social Justice Advocacy 103

How do we make it accessible? How do we make it just? (Jennifer, Black woman)

The above quotations highlight Logan, Elise, Isabelle, and Jennifer's long-term visions for the social justice work they hoped to engage in in the future. Like them, most of the participants in our sample intended to continue advocacy work, in some form, in their personal and/or professional post-college lives. Taken from the 28 qualitative interviews in which facilitators reflected on their IGD experiences and its impact on their post-college lives, this chapter highlights four central themes and related sub-themes that inductively emerged in the data analysis process: (1) definitions of social justice advocacy, (2) how the facilitators have applied social justice to their personal and professional lives, (3) the challenges of engaging in this work, and (4) the motivation to continue working for change. (See Table 9.1.) For organizational purposes, we have delineated the results in this way, while also recognizing that the themes were not necessarily mutually exclusive, as they were often overlapping and/or interrelated. Finally, it is important to note that the IGD courses at Skidmore College focused on race specifically, with attention to social justice issues more broadly, and therefore many of the quotations include a racialized lens on issues of justice.

Defining Social Justice Advocacy

When asked to explain what it means to be a social justice advocate, facilitators provided a range of definitions that were informed by the content knowledge they gained in IGD. The following quotations by Melissa, Gabriel, and Isabelle

Table 9.1 Summary of Results

1. *Defining Social Justice Advocacy*
   a. Enhancing Personal Awareness
   b. Maintaining Commitment
   c. Taking Action
   d. Practicing Accountability
2. *Applying Social Justice Advocacy*
   a. Professional and Personal Examples of Engagement
   b. Counter examples
3. *Assessing Impact Challenges of Social Justice Advocacy*
   a. Prioritizing Issues and Feeling Overwhelmed
   b. Taking Risks and Dealing with Resistance
   c. Engaging Social Justice from a Position of Privilege: Navigating Whiteness
   d. Assessing the Consequences of an Action: Navigating Racial "Otherness"
   e. Lacking a Support System
4. *Motivation to Continue Social Justice Advocacy*
   a. Understanding the Importance of Social Justice Work
   b. Recognizing One's Privileges and Wanting to Give Back
   c. Wanting to Understand More about Social Inequalities
   d. Considering the Impact on Current or Future Families

104   *Kristie A. Ford and Heather J. Lipkin*

capture two common themes across the interviews – recognizing the humanity of people and working towards equality for all social identity groups:

> [A] social justice advocate I think means treating everyone as fully human and then trying to take actions to carry that out ... justice is doing something that people deserve, like what's right by the law. But *social* justice is about human relationships ... [and] realizing how to treat people within a social community, human cultural context. (Melissa, White woman)

> I would say social justice is fighting for any of the social identities we carry around with us every day, even though they might not pertain to you. (Gabriel, Latino man)

> [Social justice advocacy has] the ability to restore what has been wronged; to bring back balance to what has been unbalanced due to history. (Isabelle, Black woman)

In addition, other participants spoke about more specific characteristics that they believed qualify an individual as a social justice advocate, including (1) enhancing personal awareness, (2) maintaining commitment, (3) taking action, and (4) practicing accountability.

Enhancing Personal Awareness

Regarding awareness, Talia, a multiracial woman, stated:

> I think it means that you understand – or at least are willing to understand – that there are structures ... that are much larger than us, and that you can see that someone's affected by things that are beyond their control ... and also that a person is able to look within themselves and recognize their own privileges or disadvantages.

Talia's response suggests that social justice advocates must be aware of how people with varying social identities experience the world. Further, as Talia pointed out, social justice advocacy requires awareness of others as well as oneself. Likewise, Hackman (2005) noted, "personal reflection reminds teachers to reflect critically on themselves and the personal qualities that inform their practice" (p. 106). Making a point to be self-reflective is therefore important, not only for facilitators and teachers (Vaccaro, 2013), but also for advocates in general; it requires advocates to be aware of identity-related privileges and how individuals and groups are impacted by larger systems (Edwards, 2006; Reason & Broido, 2005). This is especially crucial given that, as Landreman, Edwards, Balon, & Anderson (2008) argued, "we do not live in a just and equitable society, [and thus], we must be aware that our own social, historical, and political experiences in an unjust and

Working Towards Social Justice Advocacy 105

inequitable society shape our conscious and unconscious perspectives" (p. 3). Consequently, for Talia, being aware of social justice issues and the ways in which they played out – in her life and in the lives of others – was crucial to being an effective advocate.

Maintaining Commitment

Building on the idea of continual awareness, several facilitators cited commitment as a key component to social justice advocacy. This requirement echoed many participants' discussion of social justice work as a lifelong process. Accordingly, Savannah (White woman) believed that commitment to social justice must be embedded within one's lifestyle: "it's hard to believe sometimes that people don't move through the world that way, you know, considering all of these very complex parts of yourself and the people around you that really just affect how you do everything … [IGD] taught me to constantly, constantly have that awareness." Clearly, for Savannah and Talia, learning how to be aware and reflective were not only IGD skills that extended into the "real world," but were also vital for social justice advocacy more broadly (Hackman, 2005; Landreman et al., 2008).

Taking Action

Other common themes evident in facilitators' definitions were related to taking action, becoming a visible leader within a community, and allying towards collective change. For Jennifer, social justice advocacy simply meant "to do" or to take an active role in the change process. Likewise, Beatriz and Isabelle stated:

> A social justice advocate is someone who … is really at the forefront of issues of social justice … I think that's someone who's not just challenging their [sic] friends, but is also, participating in community-based organizations … leading kind of the way … so someone who is visible to a group of people or a community. (Beatriz, Latina woman)

> For me that would be the ideal thing – to partner with people … who historically have been voiceless … and empower them to use it to better their environment and better their situation. (Isabelle, Black woman)

As these quotations suggest, active and visible engagement in working to create social change were central to their definitions. Perhaps it was not enough, then, to simply be aware of and committed to social justice work: "the possession of information alone does not necessarily provide students with a pathway for action" (Hackman, 2005, p. 105). Instead, as Beatriz shared, active devotion to advocacy and fighting oppression were also key. It is also important to note that action is one of many components that help advance social justice work and progress. According to Schoem, Hurtado, Sevig, Chesler, & Sumida (2001), "Dialogue involves talking, but taking action often leads to

106 *Kristie A. Ford and Heather J. Lipkin*

good talking, and dialogue often leads to action" (p. 14). Based on this quote, Schoem et al. (2001) identified a dynamic, reciprocal relationship between dialogue and action – both of which are productive and help achieve the end goal. Many interviewees echoed this idea, and demonstrated it in their post-college careers, which was a core concept that they learned in IGD.

Practicing Accountability

Finally, the participants overwhelmingly spoke about the importance of accountability and responsibility when trying to create social change. Accordingly, Sophie and Frederick shared:

> I think what it means is to holding ourselves accountable to have hard conversations about identities and to know the ways in which your identity and the perception of your identity impacts your role in the world. (Sophie, White woman)

> I think a social justice advocate is someone who is willing to stand up and fight for the greater good of groups of the society in whatever context they're in … anyone, in any role that you're in, you can be an advocate for social justice … be it … you see something problematic in your workplace or your social circle and … being okay and comfortable with confronting someone and … challenging them on their perspectives and their actions. (Frederick, Latino man)

For Sophie, Frederick, and many others, a commitment to social justice advocacy required holding oneself accountable for addressing injustices in the world. Similar to Talia's account of the importance of self-reflection, Frederick, for instance, spoke about feeling responsible for challenging "problematic" moments that arise, even within his own friend group. In sum, the results suggest that social justice advocacy requires a combination of awareness, commitment, active engagement, and a sense of responsibility to create change within personal and professional interactions. While framed in slightly different terms, these definitions align nicely with previous literature in the field (e.g., Bell, 1997; Hackman, 2005; Waters, 2010).

Applying Social Justice Advocacy

> I am a proud social justice advocate … I cannot separate it from who I am … I have been living social justice to the best of my ability each day. (Kiera, multiracial woman)

According to their definitions, most of the facilitators considered themselves to be social justice advocates and/or working towards that ideal due, at least in part, to their college involvement with IGD. To that end, Elise and Melissa noted:

Working Towards Social Justice Advocacy 107

I'm not gonna say I'm a social justice advocate at every moment of my day … I try my best to be a social advocate and think I strive – I am a social advocate, I consider myself one. Although at times I may not be very proactive about it … I think I still work and try to … translate what it is. (Elise, Latina woman)

I realized that I've made certain decisions post-college with social justice in mind and with my desire to be a social justice advocate in mind … so when we set up the interview I began to reflect on my past experiences and … it was kind of cool, just a nice opportunity to reflect on … just how IGD has changed me as a person … and how I'm making choices now without even really thinking about what I'm doing … it's who I am. (Melissa, White woman)

Professional and Personal Examples of Engagement

Specifically, 24 of the 28 participants reported engaging with social justice work in their personal and professional lives, to varying degrees. Professionally, 24 participants maintained jobs connected to social justice – such as working in nonprofits, social work, and education. Specific areas of focus included work related to HIV prevention, homelessness and housing, domestic violence and abuse, women's mental health, incarceration and the criminal justice system, poverty and educational disparities, international education, deaf and hard-of-hearing communities, urban ministry, and youth empowerment. In addition, participants were involved in various diversity and social justice initiatives, such as facilitating dialogues in other higher education programs or within the workplace, joining action committees, creating professional development workshops, publishing related research, challenging homogeneous hiring practices, supporting underserved clients as they navigate governmental bureaucracy, and advocating for racial justice within the law. These results also mirror some of the workplace diversity initiatives and advocacy work reported by Sustained Dialogue[2] students after graduation (Diaz & Perrault, 2010).

In our study, John, for instance, shared how IGD has made him a "better lawyer":

Law school is an interesting place to practice these [IGD] skills … it has made me a better lawyer. Lawyers are very adversarial and trying to win at all costs. This has allowed me to understand where they [opposing council] are coming from, and respect them more … let's try to unpack what their position is. (John, White man)

In this example, John used the perspective taking skills he developed in IGD to better understand the range of experiences and opinions that might impact a particular legal case. Coming from a different professional vantage point, Julia, a social worker for domestic violence survivors, highlighted the advocacy role she played for her clients to ensure that they received appropriate support services:

108 *Kristie A. Ford and Heather J. Lipkin*

> I help them get connected with services that can lead to empowerment and countering the messages they are constantly receiving. The presence of social workers also helps to make sure that the survivor's stories can be heard and believed so that they can have a voice – I fight for them to have a voice ... With attorneys ... I have conversations like about the impact of trauma and mental health, and so if someone is not being understood ... I'm explaining why this is why they're reacting this way and that they're not crazy ... So advocating to – whether it be an attorney, to a prosecutor who means well but doesn't necessarily understand, so, uh, enlightening them I guess ... So that idea is more individual, that individual basis as well – not only with clients who I'm helping ... empower themselves, but also with people who interact with these marginalized populations who might not understand how their identities are impacting the way that they're presenting. (Julia, White woman)

As she herself noted, Julia serves an important intermediary role between the clients she works with and the various legal representatives her clients may come into contact with during court proceedings.

Finally, Devon, a Black male K-12 teacher committed to working with marginalized populations, remained self-reflexive about his interactions with students in hopes of fostering a more socially just educational space: "In every session, I have to evaluate what I am saying and what I am doing, how I am interacting with a student ... I am constantly thinking about my own practice." This practice, however, was not shared by all of his colleagues. Devon continued by discussing the need to challenge his White colleagues who had a "savior complex" (Edwards, 2006; Ford & Orlandella, 2015; Hughley, 2010; Kendall, 2006) and would say things like: "Oh well, this kid *needs* me ... they don't have anyone else." He further explained: "For that to come from a White teacher seems like savior of the world to me ... it comes off really bad. I have addressed that in the past ... it happens all the time that teachers come with like a savior complex that is really dangerous." Needless to say, the assumption that people of color need White people to "save" or "rescue" (Edwards, 2006; Hughey, 2010; Kendall, 2006) them can feel "both patronizing and paternalistic" (Ford & Orlandella, 2015, p. 295). In addition, as Srivastava (2005) argued, "the notion of goodness can lead to an unhealthy 'preoccupation with morality and self'" (p. 31), which compelled Devon to professionally intervene in these moments.

Personally, the facilitators also reported engaging in other social justice activities such as: challenging oppressive comments made by family or friends, raising justice-related issues with their church communities, starting a LGBTQA support group, and participating in activism, like Occupy Wall Street (http://occupywallst.org/). Savannah, for instance, described the importance of remaining engaged with both the local community and national events in hopes of creating structural change:

> I was very active in the Occupy Wall street movement and ... and, just like being aware of what's around my neighborhood and talking to people and all of these things that I feel like are in this general direction of being

Working Towards Social Justice Advocacy   109

an advocate you know like teaching yourself, and knowing what's going on with the people around you. (Savannah, White woman)

In contrast, from a more interpersonal level, Renee, a White woman, used her IGD skills to challenge friends who made racialized comments about the perceived safety of her neighborhood in Harlem:

> I'll tell people where I live. And they start commenting on … "Oh do you feel safe?" or "What's a White girl like you doing there?" And I usually welcome the discussion … I try to use some of my [IGD] skills … I just want to talk about it. (Renee, White woman)

Here, Renee employed dialogue skills such as active listening, perspective taking, and leading by example (DeTurk, 2006; Diaz & Perrault, 2010; Vasques-Scalera, 2011). Further, Renee exemplified Diaz and Perrault's (2010) description of the attitudinal and behavioral changes of post-college Sustained Dialogue students, including comfort in engaging across different social identities, developing a public voice, and relocating to a more diverse area. Finally, former facilitators in Vasques-Scalera's (2011) study reported taking action on both individual and institutional levels. For instance, their facilitation experiences provided them with the tools to "raise issues openly," "counter people's discriminatory comments," "articulate social injustices," and "challenge corporate authority" (Vasques-Scalera, 2011, p. 203). Likewise, many of the facilitators in our sample took on similar actions within their personal and professional spheres of influence (Goodman & Shapiro, 1997).

Counterexamples

Not all the former facilitators, however, were actively involved in social justice efforts; a counterexample most strongly surfaced across four of the interviews, or 14% of the sample – Samantha (White woman), Reese (White man), Katie (White woman), and Jeremy (Latino man). Samantha, who worked for a marketing company, was largely unreflective about her post-college disengagement; Reese felt guilty for this oversight; and Katie indicated that she was (at best) a "lazy" advocate since her current life and work was in an unrelated field. Finally, Jeremy stated: "It's a random road [referring to his job in management and sales] … I feel like I am one of the few who are not doing anything IGR related." Jeremy further explained that he considers himself a social justice ally, rather than an advocate: "I am not actively involved in those fights. An advocate is actively fighting those fights … I am more of a social justice ally … someone who is willing to engage with people in more of a passive way." (For more on facilitator disengagement, see Chapter 10.)

Assessing Impact: Never Doing Enough

All but one participant seemed to struggle with the application of engaging in social justice work – feeling like they were never doing enough and/or recognizing things that they could do differently in the future. As a result, they were

110 *Kristie A. Ford and Heather J. Lipkin*

extremely self-critical about the impact (or lack thereof) that they believed they were making which sometimes affected morale. To that end, Isabelle, a Black woman, stated: "I am not as active as I would like, honestly ... In conversation, yes, with people that I'm able to be honest and truthful with if I do, but not, not on a public scale, not right now, no."

While outwardly engaged with issues of justice, many of the White participants – like Eliott, Savannah, and Laura – also set incredibly high expectations for themselves and thus were disparaging about their participation in meaningful social justice work since college. Admitting that his whiteness gives him the option to disengage with race issues (Kendall, 2006), Eliott, who taught in a low-income, predominately Black and Latino school, noted:

> I do feel like social justice is important to me, but I guess, I think that ... being a White straight male, it is easy to not take that action step because it is not something that is confronting me or challenging me every day ... it is not something on my mind, and in my face.

Additionally, Savannah, despite having started a staff dialogue at her workplace, did not consider herself an active advocate of change: "With the work I am doing now and some of like, the personal patterns I have fallen into ... I haven't shared my voice in a lot of moments where I think I should have." Finally, Laura, who was working to coordinate race-focused professional development opportunities for faculty at her middle school, stated:

> I wish I was more involved in movements that are going on in the community. I wish I was more involved with Black Lives Matter. I wish I was more involved in community organizations and pushing policy in our country. But, I have to tell myself one step at a time, to finish grad school, and then to jump in with both feet. And hopefully I will come back to it.

In the participants' analysis of impact, a distinction was often made between micro- (individual) and macro- (policy) level changes; Beatriz, Reagan, as well as others, seemed to give much more credence to the latter:

> Being a behavioral therapist ... I am learning a lot about myself and the people I work with, but, I do feel, there's something still in me that wants to pursue macro-work ... even though I am already advocating for marginalized populations, but macro-work in the sense that like, more of a political outlook, more of getting out there and rallying up and bringing consciousness to other people. (Beatriz, Latina woman)

> I hope that I am a part of it [social justice] and think a lot about it when I am working one-on-one with patients ... but on a large scale, I wonder how impactful it is. (Reagan, White woman)

Moreover, many participants felt conflicted that their current jobs were, in some way, reinforcing the "system" and they felt powerless to make substantive change, which is a common stage in "justice-cognizant ally identity" development, according to Reason and Broido (2005, pp. 82–83). Julia, for instance, named the cognitive dissonance she felt when striving for justice while existing within an unjust world: "I came to realize I am actually a part of the very system and institution that oppresses many target [or marginalized] groups." She further explained:

> [As a social worker], I work for the government and criminal justice system ... But I am part of the system that can knock them [people] down – and if we had social justice, people wouldn't be knocked down with messages that blamed them for the violence they experienced. Social justice work is fighting those messages. The best way I can frame my job as social justice related is that I am trying to help victims navigate through a system that can sometimes mirror society and blame the victim, as well as a system that does not always take the time to understand the victim ... So the best way I can feel good about what I do is, by thinking about how my presence and the presence of all the other social workers helps with "damage control" and how to the best of our ability we counter all of the messages they have received through the system that the violence is their fault or that they should have done something more to avoid the situation. When I say "damage control," I mean that given the current social injustice that still is very prevalent, I help provide a positive message that they all too often aren't given. (Julia, White woman)

As Julia noted, she frequently felt like she was in triage mode, or operating from a "damage control" mind-set, rather than proactively working to change an unjust system. Likewise, Frederick (Latino man) realized that even higher education is a problematic "corporate organization," Gabriel (Latino man) joked that he was "selling his soul" in his current position, and Talia (multiracial woman) commented: "I want to be doing more ... my job right now is somewhat painful because I'm noticing that I'm not doing enough to advocate for those who need it the most, and instead, I'm contributing to some of the discrimination and oppression that just exists in the education system." Finally, Leah and Eliott remarked on the challenges of working within an inherently racist structure:

> I feel like I am not really touching the problem. That idea of like, putting Band-Aids on things that may or may not heal ... I'm basically working within a structure that is racist. So ... fighting that is really difficult when structures in place ... like monetary choices right, like budget cuts and all that. And seeing the distribution of wealth in our country and just feeling ... [I feel] a little bit disheartened. (Leah, multiracial woman)

> Partly ... I go back and forth. I know that schools in low-income areas need educated educators and they don't have a lot of them ... I give a lot. At the same time, the education system has its own serious flaws and as an

112 *Kristie A. Ford and Heather J. Lipkin*

institution ... It's frustrating to see how the suspension policy contributes to students dropping out of school and ending up in prison ... especially Black and Latino kids ... I work for the enemy in a way, I work for a bad system but I like kids so I haven't figured out how to reconcile that. (Eliott, White man)

Based on the above quotations, it is not surprising that many participants felt overwhelmed by the enormity of the task at hand and disillusioned by their ability to make substantive change (for more, also see: Vasques-Scalera, 2011). The subsequent section focuses more explicitly on the ongoing challenges they faced, as the participants tried to promote social justice among family, friends, colleagues, and the institutions they interacted with.

Challenges of Social Justice Advocacy

Except for Logan, a Black man, all of the facilitators reported grappling with a range of challenges related to social justice work in their post-college lives, including (1) prioritizing issues and feeling overwhelmed, (2) taking risks and dealing with resistance, (3) engaging in social justice work from a position of privilege, (4) assessing the consequences of a particular action, and (5) lacking a support system which led to isolation and burnout.

Prioritizing Issues and Feeling Overwhelmed

As previously noted, the task of creating social change can feel daunting. Accordingly Mia, a multiracial woman, stated, "it feels very overwhelming and then I wonder what else I can do." Similarly, Reagan (White woman) recognized, "the system is so broken, I often felt burned out. I don't know what I am doing is helpful or productive," and Frederick (Latino man) conceded that "it does get tiring sometimes cause I don't want to deal with it, I don't want to have these conversations if I know where in the past these conversations have gone, or the emotions that have come out because of it." Finally, John (White man) admitted that "sometimes you want to relax or have fun with your friends. You don't want to talk about this all of the time. And [don't] have the energy to engage yourself. At 10 o'clock when get home just want to watch TV." As these quotations suggest, fatigue and emotional burnout are significant impediments to sustained social justice work (Edwards, 2006; Ford & Orlandella, 2015; Tatum, 2003). As a result, John, as well as other facilitators, across race and gender categories, were struggling to find the appropriate balance between passion for creating change and self-care. John decided that self-care meant focusing on social justice primarily within the professional realm:

Actually ... I would prefer to keep it [social justice] mostly professionally ... not turning off my brain, but I would like my job to be social justice oriented and then come home at the end of the day and kind of relax with

Working Towards Social Justice Advocacy 113

> family or friends … and not place such a huge weight on being able to have serious conversations about race with my partner or friends or whatever because that is what I do all day … [I prefer to] come home and have more of a conventional social and familial life I guess, if that makes sense. (John, White man)

While compartmentalizing this work was necessary and perhaps easier for John as a White man, Frederick (Latino man) took it "day by day, piece by piece" in an effort to "tackle one small issue at a time." Focusing on practical strategies, Vivian (multiracial woman) recommended "taking time for yourself to have fun on the weekends or whenever you can." She continued by saying: "I think those are the ways that you can sometimes take a time out from social justice work." Although self-care is crucial for effective lifelong social justice advocacy (Tatum, 2003), it was rarely mentioned by the participants without some prompting. Even then, the strategies these committed advocates mentioned for dealing with the stressors inherent in social justice work were minimal and/ or deemed, in their estimation, to be insufficient. Moreover, most participants were unable to articulate a strategy for how to best balance self-care with maintaining a critical and engaged social justice lens.

Taking Risks and Dealing with Resistance

Not only did the facilitators feel overwhelmed by how to make a difference, but they also encountered resistance to their efforts, which they did not feel prepared to handle outside of the IGD setting. This finding is also highlighted in a study by Richards-Schuster et al. (2015) in which they stated: "students expressed feeling unprepared for moving into organizational environments that differed from their experiences surrounded by other social-justice-minded students in college" (p. 378). Similarly, despite their involvement in social justice work (and IGD) throughout college, recent graduates often struggled to create social change in the larger world, leading to feelings of frustration and discontent.

Perhaps most discouraging was when family or friends did not understand their passion and commitment to these issues. Many of the participants discussed the insensitive comments that loved ones made and the psychic impact of those interactions. For instance, Melissa noted:

> So it's just a constant struggle if I try to talk to my family about it, all of whom are White … they make classic racial jokes. And it really discourages me, because I'm not really sure how to move those conversations forward in a productive way where I'm getting something out of it and so are the people I'm talking to … The problem I've had since IGD is being able to talk about race and racism and other systems of oppression with other White people where I'm taken seriously for talking about it. (Melissa, White woman)

114 *Kristie A. Ford and Heather J. Lipkin*

Unfortunately, as Melissa's comment highlights, often White advocates cannot rely on peer or familial support in their pursuit for social justice (Ford & Orlandella, 2015; Reason & Broido, 2005; Vasques-Scalera, 2011).

Engaging in Social Justice Work from a Position of Privilege: Navigating Whiteness

Like Melissa, other White participants spoke about the identity-specific challenges of being in a position of privilege and engaging in intra-racial conversations; they were also conflicted about how to meaningfully participate in antiracist actions. To that end, Sophie, who thoughtfully discussed throughout her interview how to involve privileged White people in social justice work, stated:

> I think my biggest challenge in moving forward [post-college] is to find ways to communicate better within my own demographic, to communicate my sense of urgency and my awareness of privilege as it evolves ... I get to a point where I want to shovel down on [White] people, like wake up, what are you doing here. (Sophie, White woman)

Sophie and Melissa's challenge engaging in conversations about social justice in personal or professional settings echoed Richards-Shuster et al.'s (2015) finding that "as one student put it, 'no one wants to talk about social identities and social justice as much as college students do'" (p. 378). Moreover, this feeling if often heightened in White environments in which agent group members rarely, if ever, discuss Whiteness and its societal implications (Ford & Orlandella, 2015; Kendall, 2006).

In addition to trying to be taken seriously by members of their own racial group, White facilitators in our study, like Evan, Renee, Reese, Laura, and Katie were still grappling with a range of internal questions consistent with differing, sometimes unacknowledged, regressive stages of white racial identity development (Helms, 1990/1995). Accordingly, Laura and Katie disclosed:

> I think I will always grapple with racial identity ... as a White person it is very easy to fall back into old patterns ... so I am always reminding myself to come back to that training, remember what I learned, and check myself. (Laura)

> Now when I think about IGR, I think about maybe I have lost it ... I was so socially aware in college...I wonder if ... am I am different person now? Is it one of those things, if you don't use it, you lose it? Have I lost that [White] awareness and that ability to dialogue and to be aware of how I am coming off to people, you know? (Katie)

Further, beyond questioning if they have "lost" their critical awareness, some White facilitators dealt with feelings of racial guilt as they made sense of their position within a system of white domination and then figured out how to best ally with, not for, people of color (Eichstedt, 2001; Ford & Orlandella, 2015; Helms, 1990/1995; Jensen, 2005; Waters, 2010). Renee, for instance, stated: "It's almost too easy not to think about what IGR gave me or what I took away from IGR. It's like the white guilt just comes back tenfold." Ultimately, however, Jensen (2005) argued that guilt is "irrational and counterproductive" as it immobilizes White people and hinders progress (p. 47). Based on this premise, Jensen (2005) invited White people "to live on the edge of the guilt, to use it to challenge ourselves and each other to do better" (p. 51).

In contrast to dealing with white guilt, others, like Sophie, wrestled with being seen as "undercover within my own people" or an unfamiliar entity by loved ones who "don't know what a White antiracist activist looks like." Similar to the notion of a "race traitor," which is described by Bailey (1998) as "privilege-cognizant Whites who refuse to animate the scripts Whites are expected to perform, and who are unfaithful to worldviews Whites are expected to hold" (p. 2), people like Sophie are threatening to the social order (Bailey, 1998; Eichstedt, 2001). Consequently, the choice to adhere to social justice values was painful for some facilitators, especially if it resulted in isolation from White friends or family members (Reason & Broido, 2005; Vasques-Scalera, 2011).

Finally, one participant also contended with an opposing, but equally problematic script: the "White savior" narrative, a theme that also emerged in the case studies (Edwards, 2006; Ford & Orlandella, 2015; Hughey, 2010; Kendall, 2006). As a social worker, Leah explained that she felt uncomfortable with people's reactions to her work, which included statements like, "Oh wow, you are really doing God's work" or "Thank God for people like you." Perceived in divergent ways – as a guilt-stricken White liberal, a traitor to the White race, or a rescuer of underprivileged populations for their social justice work – the White participants in this study had to constantly figure out how to (re)negotiate their understanding of and relationship to white allyhood (Eichstedt, 2001; Ford & Orlandella, 2015; Jensen, 2005; Waters, 2010).

Assessing the Consequences of a Particular Action: Navigating Racial "Otherness"

Moreover, beyond these internal and external struggles, facilitators grappled with the potential consequences of their actions. For multiracial facilitators and facilitators of color in particular, fear of backlash from friends or employers was cited as a reason to censor oneself and/or proceed cautiously around social justice topics. Talia, a multiracial woman, for example, revealed that she needed to "fluff it up" at times, or use "softer words" and not "show my emotions" among co-workers. In addition, these young professionals of color felt the need to prove themselves in order to be taken seriously (Ford, 2011; Gutiérrez y Muhs, Flores Niemann, González, & Harris, 2012; Johnsrud & Sadao, 1998); they also worried more about the professional ramifications of disrupting the status quo. To that end, Frederick and Vivian shared:

> Some of the challenges professionally ... [are] being mindful of how and what you say can be perceived by other individuals – especially if they are upper management ... and trying to do good work, trying to do meaningful

work, and being okay with challenging others but not coming across as insubordinate and/or putting your professional career at risk, you know, from making a comment that may make others feel uncomfortable. (Frederick, Latino man)

One of the greatest challenges I guess is knowing when to engage ... professionally there are certain fights you can't fight depending upon your own power ... in an organization. There are only certain things you can do without risking loss of employment. (Vivian, multiracial woman)

As these quotations both highlight, working within a hierarchical system can be challenging, especially for recent graduates who are trying to balance their idealistic goals (i.e. social justice) with the practicality of maintaining employment and a steady income.

Lacking a Support System

Finally, beyond fear of reprisal, the lack of a support system and social justice community caused most participants, across identities and career fields, to feel isolated and physically and/or emotionally burned out (for more on emotional burn out, see: Edwards, 2006; Ford & Orlandella, 2015; Reason & Broido, 2005; Vasques-Scalera, 2011). As noted in Chapter 8, during college IGD provided the facilitators with a close-knit community of socially engaged students; once they graduated, however, it proved difficult to reproduce that level of cognitive and affective support. This challenge highlights the value of support systems in the lives of IGD facilitators (specifically) and recent college graduates (generally). Emphasizing this point, Murphy et al. (2010) note the importance of "relational support in enhancing or inhibiting emerging adults' transitions from college to career" (p. 179).

Lacking this type of support in her transition, Kiera, a Black woman, noted: "I don't always feel like I have advocates ... the challenge is wanting to live a social justice lifestyle but also picking your battles." Also reflecting on her IGD experience, Katie reported:

In college it is a think-tank of expressing ideas ... everyone is in that educational mind-set so they would love to engage with you about it, but in the "real-world" people are not likely to talk with you about issues ... I miss that sort of 24-7 you can talk about your feelings and curiosities and it was fostered and I just don't think that is what the real world is post-college. (Katie, White woman)

As these reflections suggest, a major benefit of the IGD experience in college was the uniqueness of the situation – sitting in a room with fellow participants,

Working Towards Social Justice Advocacy 117

all of whom were invested in discussing social justice issues. Further highlighting this point, Savannah (White woman) shared: "At the College like I was more of a bigger fish I guess in a smaller pond and now I feel like the tiniest fish in like an ocean … so that falls under the umbrella of isolation." As many participants noted, personal, interpersonal, and structural factors often impacted their ability to more fully engage in social justice advocacy in their post-college lives. For example, lacking a close-knit support system, being mindful of challenging superiors in the professional workplace, and trying to maintain harmony between social groups further complicated these facilitators' advocacy efforts. Reason and Broido (2005), however, reminded allies that missteps and barriers are part of the learning process and allies should be compassionate with themselves and others as they figure out how to apply their social justice values to the world around them (pp. 87–88).

Motivation to Continue Social Justice Advocacy

> I think there's so much going on that there's just days where I don't like want to think about it because it's so stressful but sometimes you just open the news, go on Facebook, you just read a comment about someone's ignorance, it just re-sparks my motivation automatically you know … that's going to motivate me to speak up, to have, to engage with others for the greater good. (Frederick, Latino man)

Despite the noted challenges above, participants shared motivators for continuing to engage in social justice work. Major themes included (1) understanding the importance of social justice work, (2) recognizing one's privileges and wanting to give back, (3) wanting to understand more about social inequalities, and (4) considering the impact on their current or future families.

Understanding the Importance of Social Justice Work

Beginning with the first theme, John, for instance, noted:

> It's kind of the type of thing where I don't understand people who don't want to do it. Once the mask has been removed from society … once you realize, "Oh my God, this is it," I don't see how you can then not want to do it … it is so obvious to me … this is so unjust. This is so ridiculous. How is this our society now? How it is backsliding now? There is no choice. The energy is almost immaterial. This is an obligation, like a passion. (John, White man)

With the heightened awareness of existing structures that he gained through IGD, John recognized injustices, which fueled his passion for this work.

118   *Kristie A. Ford and Heather J. Lipkin*

Recognizing One's Privileges and Wanting to Give Back

In a slightly different way, Talia, a multiracial woman, reflected on the complexity of her social identities and how they motivated her to create change:

> It's really important work and the struggles and the resistance is just another evidence of the necessary work … if I am struggling, I know that there are people out there that are struggling so much worse than I am … I'm really privileged to not only be a college graduate and know what I'm talking about with the actual like systems and structures, and … be able [to] use words that describe what people are experiencing … the fact also that … I'm part White and that people don't see me as a threat or whatever.

As this passage suggests, Talia understood her privileges as a college graduate, and recognized that many people are "struggling" more than her, especially given the power structures in which we live. As a multiracial individual with a lighter skin tone, her ability to not be viewed as a "threat" also gave her leverage to fight battles that those who feel more oppressed and disadvantaged by systematic injustices are less likely to risk fighting.

Wanting to Understand More about Social Inequalities

In addition to recognizing their privileges, several interviewees referenced their desire to learn more as a motivator to engage in social justice work. As Melissa (White woman) stated, "I want my knowledge of social justice and my involvement in it to continue to grow and expand." This comment highlights the core of IGD practices: the combination of content and process: "Freire's (1970) praxis loop is a wonderful example of how information needs to be combined with tools for critical thinking to bring the power of that information to fruition" (Hackman, 2005, p. 106). DeTurk (2006) also echoed this notion and argues that change-makers require the reasons and resources to act. Arguably, Melissa's reason to act stemmed from a desire to combat injustices as she learned more about them.

Like Melissa, Logan (Black man) also sought to understand more about social justice issues after graduating from college. He shared, "just because I'm a straight male doesn't mean that, like, I shouldn't … try to understand a lot more about what a gay or lesbian or bisexual or transgender person would go through on a daily basis." Logan's recognition of his privilege as a straight male, coupled with his acknowledgement that he did not fully understand heterosexism and transphobia, inspired him to learn more. In sum, as many of the participants affirmed, developing and employing a social justice lens often brought into focus inequalities that require persistence to alter.

Considering the Impact on Current or Future Families

Personally, there was also motivation to continue social justice work as the female facilitators, in particular, considered the impact of such work on their current and/or future families. It is significant to note that the theme of care-taking and child-rearing, which often has differential gendered implications within U.S. society (Riina & Feinberg, 2012), only emerged in some of the interviews with the women in our sample. One of the participants, for instance, who is married to a person of a different race, discussed the pain of dealing with her partner being racially profiled. Isabelle (Black woman) shared, "For me, it hurts. It just hits home because they believe he's something that he's not ... I would love to go to the police station and give them a piece of my mind [laughter], or it's not even like one place, it's an issue within the whole system." Isabelle then pondered the impact racial stereotyping might have on her future children and asked: "like how do we talk to our kids about that?" As a result she indicated that she wanted to raise her "kids to be people that are compassionate for others." Like Isabelle, other participants also hoped to instill social justice values in young children. For example, Talia, Vivian, and Samantha respectively, said:

> I hope to have a family that really, really is passionate about those issues, and I can imagine that my future kids or whatever would be able to have some sort of discussion around social justice. (Talia, multiracial woman)

> I think that my understanding of a lot of these issues will be a part of creating that new generation ... Even, with my newest family member [my niece] who is going to be one soon, I have already bought her a book about her identity ... So, in little ways, I am being subtle personally about what I think is important. (Vivian, multiracial woman)

> I think like as far as having children and like how I teach them about the world and how I teach them to engage in this. You know talk about race and talk about social justice. You know I'm definitely going to use what I learned in IGR in that sense. (Samantha, White woman)

In hopes of creating a better world, approximately 25% of the participants, all self-identified as women, were consciously thinking about how to apply IGD skills to the next generation; this finding also aligns with Diaz and Perrault's (2010) study on Sustained Dialogue. Moreover, Brett (2011), a former IGD instructor and administrator, published a book entitled *Parenting for Social Change*, which begins this conversation from her own perspective and experiences. More systematic and empirical research, however, is needed to understand the longitudinal impact of social justice education on family building, parenting styles, and child outcomes.

Summary of Results

In sum, this chapter documents how former facilitators are conceptualizing, applying, and struggling with the challenges and possibilities inherent in social justice work in their personal and professional post-college lives. For most interviewees, being involved in IGD reportedly impacted their perspectives on race

120 *Kristie A. Ford and Heather J. Lipkin*

and justice; they were now more attentive to social inequities, had a better understanding of how their target (marginalized) and agent (privileged) identities intersected, and maintained a strong desire to learn more. These factors acted as motivators, energizing the facilitators' commitment to continually challenge oppression in their post-college lives. As Leah (multiracial woman) stated, "I think I just really hate the problem. I want to be some piece in the really big puzzle ... and figuring that out I guess is still what keeps me going." While difficult, many also remained motivated to create change in hopes of realizing a more just and equitable world for future generations. To that end, Gabriel noted:

> One of the major challenges is keeping perseverance ... knowing that you have to pursue what you believe in, in terms of social justice, and knowing that one day what you're doing will make a change, even if you don't see it right now. (Gabriel, Latino man)

Ultimately, participating in a movement toward equality – slow as it might be – led most of the interviewees to stay engaged in social justice work in the hopes of making at least a small difference. Although ally and advocacy work are developmental, lifelong processes (Edwards, 2006; Reason & Broido, 2005; Waters 2010), the facilitators found different ways to apply their IGD skills on personal, interpersonal, and structural levels, including self-work and continued education, intervening when racist comments or jokes arise, and protesting instances of oppression and structural disadvantage. To continue in their journeys, however, Vivian reminded aspiring advocates to "rejuvenate yourself and come back ready to go again."

Not all former facilitators were "ready to go again," however. As pathways toward social justice action (or inaction) are varied and complex, the next chapter, "A White Male's Post-College Reflections on Race, Resistance, and Social Change," highlights Reese's case study as the most prominent counter-example within the data.

Notes

1 Throughout this chapter, differing raced and gendered patterns in experience are noted, when appropriate. To facilitate this process, this chapter includes the race and gender demographic information also listed in Table 2.1.
2 The Sustained Dialogue is a "multi-stage conflict resolution process in which small diverse groups of people meet over time and dialogue across differences" (Diaz & Perrault, 2010, pp. 33–34). While the Sustained Dialogue model differs from IGD, both focus on sustained intergroup interactions.

References

Bailey, A. (1998). Locating traitorous identities: Toward a view of privilege-cognizant white character. *Hypatia*, *13*(3): 27–42.
Bell, L. A. (1997). Theoretical foundations for social justice education. In M. Adams, L. Bell, & P. Griffin (Eds.), *Teaching for diversity and social justice: A sourcebook* (pp. 3–15). New York, NY: Routledge.

Brett, T. G. (2011). *Parenting for social change.* Tucson, AZ: Social Change Press, Learning Enterprises, LLC.

DeTurk, S. (2006). The power of dialogue: Consequences of intergroup dialogue and their implications for agency and alliance building. *Communication Quarterly, 54*(1), 33–51.

Diaz, A., & Perrault, R. (2010). Sustained dialogue and civic life: Post-college impacts. *Michigan Journal of Community Service Learning,* Fall, 1–12.

Eichstedt, J. L. (2001). Problematic white identities and a search for racial justice. *Sociological Forum, 16*(3), 445–470.

Edwards, K. (2006). Aspiring social justice ally identity development: A conceptual model. *NASPA Journal, 43*(4), 39–60.

Ford, Kristie. (2011). Race, gender and bodily (mis)recognitions: Women of color faculty experiences with white students in the college classroom. *The Journal of Higher Education, 82*(4), 444–478.

Ford, K. A., & Orlandella, J. (2015). The "not so final remark": The journey to becoming white allies. *Sociology of Race and Ethnicity, 1*(2), 287–301.

Freire, P. (1970). *Pedagogy of the oppressed.* New York, NY: Seabury.

Goodman, D., & Shapiro, S. (1997). Sexism curriculum design. In M. Adams, L.A. Bell, & G. P. Griffin (Eds.), *Teaching for diversity and social justice: A sourcebook* (pp. 89–113). New York, NY: Routledge.

Gutiérrez y Muhs, G., Flores Niemann, Y., González, C. G., & Harris, A. P. (Eds). (2012). *Presumed incompetent: The intersections of race and class for women in academia.* Boulder, CO: Utah State University Press.

Hackman, H. W. (2005). Five essential components for social justice education. *Equity & Excellence in Education, 38,* 103–109.

Helms, J. E. (1990). *Black and white racial identity: Theory, research, and practice.* Westport, CT: Greenwood.

Helms, J. E. (1995). An update of Helm's white and people of color racial identity models. In J. G. Ponterotto, J. M. Casas, L. A. Suzuka, & C. M. Alexander (Eds.), *Handbook of multicultural counseling* (pp. 181–198). Thousand Oaks, CA: Sage.

Hughey, M. (2010). The white savior film and reviewers' reception. *Symbolic Interaction, 33*(3), 475–496.

Jensen, R. (2005). *The heart of whiteness: Confronting race, racism, and white privilege.* San Francisco, CA: City Lights

Johnsrud, L., & Sadao, K. C. (1998). The common experience of 'otherness:' Ethnic and racial minority faculty. *Review of Higher Education, 21*(4), 315–342.

Kendall, F. (2006). *Understanding white privilege.* New York, NY: Routledge.

Landreman, L, Edwards, K. E., Balon, D. G., & Anderson, G. (2008). Wait! It takes time to develop rich and relevant social justice curriculum. *About Campus,* September–October.

Murphy, K. A., Blustein, D. L., & Bohlig, A. J. (2010). "The college-to-career transition: An exploration of emerging adulthood." *Journal of Counseling & Development, 88*(2), 174–181.

Reason, R. D., & Broido, E. M. (2005). Issues and strategies for social justice allies (and the student affairs professionals who hope to encourage them). In R. D. Reason, E. M. Broido, T. L. David, & N. J. Evans (Eds.), *Developing social justice allies: New directions for student services* (pp. 81–89). San Francisco, CA: A Wiley Company.

Richards-Shuster, K., Ruffolo, M. C., Nicoll, K. L., Distelrath, C., Galura, J., & Mishkin, A. (2015). Exploring challenges faced by students as they transition to social justice work in the "real world": Implications for social work. *Advances in Social Work 16*(2), 372–389.

Riina, E. M., & Feinberg, M. E. (2012). Involvement in childrearing and mothers' and fathers' adjustment. *Family Relations, 61,* 836–850.

Schoem, D., Hurtado, S., Sevig, T., Chesler, M., & Sumida, S. H. (2001). In D. Schoem & S. Hurtado (Eds.), *Intergroup dialogue deliberative democracy in school,*

122 Kristie A. Ford and Heather J. Lipkin

college, community, and workplace (pp. 1–17). Ann Arbor, MI: University of Michigan Press.

Srivastava, S. (2005). "You're calling me a racist?" The moral and emotional regulation of antiracism and feminism. *Signs, 31*(1), 29–62.

Tatum, B. (2003). *"Why are all the black kids sitting together in the cafeteria?": And other conversations about race.* New York, NY: Basic Books.

Vaccaro, A. (2013). Building a framework for social justice education: One educator's journey. In L. Landreman (Ed.), *The art of effective facilitation: Reflections from social justice educators* (pp. 23–44). Sterling, VA: Stylus Publishing.

Vasques-Scalera, C. (2011). Changing facilitators, facilitating change: The lives of intergroup dialogue facilitators post-college. In K. E. Maxwell, B. A. Nagda, & M. C. Thompson. (Eds.), *Facilitating intergroup dialogues: Bridging differences, catalyzing change* (pp. 201–212). Sterling, VA: Stylus Publishing.

Waters, R. (2010). Understanding allyhood as a developmental process. *About Campus,* Nov–Dec., 1–8.

10 A White Male's Post-College Reflections on Race, Resistance, and Social Change

Kristie A. Ford

> Perhaps the most telling indicator of facilitators' understanding and commitment to social justice is their willingness to continue to work despite the challenges (Vasques-Scalera, 2011, p. 209).

While most of the participants in our sample were trying to actively engage with issues of social justice post-college, it is also important to acknowledge the exceptions in hopes of better understanding the complexities of various personal and professional pathways. Of the four facilitators who were not involved, on any level, with social justice work post-college, one self-identified as Latino (Jeremy) and three identified as White (Reese, Samantha, and Katie). Although it is difficult to extrapolate from such a small sample, previous research suggests that agent group members who benefit most directly from patriarchal and racist structures feel less incentive to challenge the status quo (Bonilla-Silva, 2014; Feagin, 2013; Johnson, 2006); this could also help explain why more of the White participants, even those who expressed some commitment to creating change, seemed to struggle more with the meaning and implications of social justice work. (For more, see Chapter 9.)

As a self-identified White heterosexual man, Reese's interview, in particular, reflects the most distinct and contrary interview in our sample. In some ways, Reese was cognizant of this when he agreed to be interviewed for this project. To that end, he shared: "When I agreed to do this interview I thought, 'Well, I might not have a lot to say [about my involvement in social change efforts], but sociological method, you know, whatever I say will probably still be of use.'" Reese's interview was especially noteworthy because of his brutal honesty and his reflections, which greatly differed from the majority of participants in our sample. As Reese anticipated, his story provided a unique, and important, perspective; this chapter outlines his complicated, and sometimes contradictory, relationship to race, IGD, and social justice advocacy.

124   *Kristie A. Ford*

College Years: Racial Awakening and (Eventually) Embracing IGD

Reese entered the first course in the IGD sequence for facilitators, Race & Power, extremely reluctant and skeptical. He explained:

> I remember just when I was first introduced to it ... I thought it was the most bullshit pedagogy when I was first introduced to it, and I fought it so hard. I don't even know why, I don't even know why I would ever come back. When I think about how ... I don't know why I would have ever signed up for another course. I thought, I really thought it was stupid when I was first involved in it ... And getting over hang-ups with ... just like talking in a circle with the whole dialogue pedagogy was a huge hang-up.

Once he was able to "get over those hang-ups," however, Reese acknowledged that "the rest of the work kind of opened up a bit more." Although he despised the circular seating arrangements, which are key to the dialogic model, he eventually realized that "what you are talking about with these people in a classroom ... makes a big impact." From that point on, Reese reported active engagement with IGR during college, on both an intellectual and a personal level. Intellectually, Reese's coursework in Sociology and the IGR program provided a powerful synergy in helping him better understand himself and his role in society: "when I came to school I didn't really know what to think or how to think or what to do. Sociology and IGR really helped me figure it out kind of. And helped me understand my place and understand who I was and why I was." In particular, he described working on a paper about Freire (1970) as a "waterfall moment" in which he "really got it ... it was just really [an] important moment in my life when I think about developing." From this text, he also began to realize that allying for social justice entails "working with, not for, people of color" (Edwards, 2006).

In addition, Reese noted two core lessons and/or skills that he took away from facilitating the People of Color/White People dialogue, in particular: (1) the ability to grapple with seemingly conflicting or contradictory information through critical reflection, and (2) racial humility (Edwards, 2006; Helms, 1990/1995; Kendall, 2006). Beginning with the former, Reese noted that "being able to handle two almost opposing things in your head" helped him to understand "what I think, and how I think, and where these things I think come from." In accordance with the literature, Reese described critical (or active) thinking as one of the skills he developed through the IGD process (Gurin, Nagda, & Zúñiga, 2013; Nagda & Gurin, 2007; Sorensen, Nagda, Gurin, & Maxwell, 2009). Indeed, as Sorensen et al. (2009) argued, critical reflection is a crucial component of the Critical Dialogic Theoretical Model of Intergroup Dialogue, as it allows "students to examine their own perspectives, experiences, and assumptions" in relation to others (p. 20). (For more on the Critical Dialogic Model, see Chapter 1.) By developing this critical consciousness (Freire, 1970), students learn to "analyze how their own experiences are connected to socialization by parents, teachers, peers, and communities and how they understand their group identities and positions within systems of power and inequality" (p. 14). For Reese, this critical reflection process helped him to make sense of how his world view was shaped by social and structural forces of power, privilege, and inequality.

Second, with some initial hesitation, Reese admitted:

> When I first started getting involved in IGD, I needed to be this hero. I needed to start getting involved in race for teaching all White people ... For anybody who wanted to talk to me about race or if they needed to come talk to me about race, I would have a lot to tell them. But I think, and I think this is something that came out of being a co-facilitator with a [Latina] was that, like that's not helpful.

Within the Pseudo-Independent stage of white racial identity development (Helms, 1990/1995), it is not uncommon for a White person, like Reese, to want to be the "hero" by distancing himself from whiteness and teaching uninformed White people about white supremacy and oppression (Edwards, 2006; Frankenberg, 1993/2001; Hughey, 2010; Kendall, 2006; Srivastava, 2005). To this point, Srivastava (2005, p. 41) cited Kleinman (1996), who stated, "we become so invested in our beliefs as radicals or 'good people' that we cannot see the reactionary or hurtful consequences of our behaviours." While perhaps well intended, as Reese eventually realized, assuming this "hero" label absolves White people from taking responsibility for their own participation in systems of racial inequality (Ford & Orlandella, 2015; Kendall, 2006).

During a nonlinear journey of self-discovery and change, Reese figured out how to use his whiteness in a socially just way; Reese ended his Skidmore College career committed to, and actively promoting, the foundational principles of IGD. In addition, he became closely involved with other related campus initiatives, like a grassroots change organization which formed in hopes of supporting leadership development and community engagement around social justice and sustainability issues.

Defining Social Justice Advocacy

Interestingly, Reese's post-college definition of social justice advocacy did not seem to align with his activist-focused work during college. In particular, the conversation below highlights his notion of social justice advocacy, which seems more focused on "helping" on an individual level, rather than creating institutional or structural change. Moreover, in contrast to other participants, Reese's definition of social justice advocacy did not specifically allude to racial justice.

Interviewer: How would you define social justice advocacy?

Reese: That they are an advocate for social equality. So that means that they are seeing someone or seeing a group of people

126 *Kristie A. Ford*

	that are or have, um, are being oppressed in some way or being exploited, that they stand up to them in some way and work towards solving that issue, which is the oppression of that group of people. And that obviously not restricted to race by any means.
Interviewer:	So can you give me a concrete example of what that tangibly looks like?
Reese:	What that tangibly ... ugh, well, so social justice ... um, so if you are a politician, it could be developing programs for supporting ... if we are talking about socioeconomics, supporting people who can't make enough money. I mean, it's just, a concrete example can be anywhere. If talking about socioeconomics you could be ... it can be donating food to a food bank. It could be, now I'm also thinking about the refugee situation, it could be taking a refugee into your home so they can figure out what's going on. You're advocating for social justice because you, this person, there is something that is socially unjust that is going on and you are advocating for justice.
Interviewer:	So is there a difference in your mind between charity and justice? Or are they the same thing?
Reese:	They are not the same thing. Let me think ... so charity I think, charity has a much broader definition, charity is just giving. Right? I can be charitable [giving] to a really hateful organization but I'm not being ... well, from my point of view, I'm not being a social justice advocate.

When unpacking Reese's definition of social justice advocacy, Edwards's (2006) three-stage model of ally development proves useful (for more, see Chapter 1). Within this framework, Reese's description would likely fall somewhere between the first and second stages – ally for self-interest and ally for altruism. More concretely, by operationalizing social justice advocacy as donating to a food bank or temporarily welcoming a refugee into your home, Reese ignored the structural realities that underpin rampant social problems like hunger and homelessness. Instead, he focused on individual-level interventions (ally for self-interest) from a white guilt or savior positionality of "helping" people or serving the greater good (ally for altruism). While social interventions, at any level, are necessary, Reese's inability to articulate a more nuanced definition of social justice is perhaps, in part, due to his post-college disengagement with these issues.

Post-College Years: White Guilt, Stagnation, and Entrenchment

In his four years since graduation, Reese has worked for two different unrelated organizations. As his jobs were secured through [White] social networks (which remained an unexamined consequence of his white privilege), Reese did not seem to have a clear career trajectory. He recognized his lack of focus and indicated that he was not proud of his professional life so far.

Moreover, despite the fact that his partner, a White woman, was actively involved in white racial identity work, both personally and professionally, Reese had not seriously considered or engaged with the topic since college. He found this reality difficult to admit, especially to the Director of Skidmore's IGR program. His relaxed and confident demeanor changed; he became somewhat nervous and emotional when he stated: "If I was being honest I would have to say that I don't think in any meaningful way. I'm really embarrassed saying that to you face to face. [Why?] ... Well, to be honest, because you're someone that I admire and look up to and I don't want to say that to you ... and the reason I feel embarrassed is because I feel like I was a waste of time." The guilt and embarrassment he expressed focused largely on his perceived personal failure, rather than reflecting on the nature of whiteness and institutionalized racism, which makes it easier for people in positions of privilege to step away from this work (Brandyberry, 1999).

Reflecting on his trajectory – from naïveté, to critical engagement, to disengagement – he employed the stages of white racial identity development as a possible explanation (Helms, 1990/1995). More concretely, Reese shared that he was living and working in a racial homogenous (White) area where the people around him "have never really engaged in racial identity work." Given that, based on his previously acquired IGD knowledge, Reese worried that he had regressed to the "reintegration" (Helms, 1990/1995) stage of racial defensiveness and fear, which caused a lot of cognitive dissonance and "inner turmoil." The few times race-related discussions came up in his work environment, Reese reported that he was frustrated by the conversation and therefore tried to avoid the issue. Trying to make sense of this decision, he admitted: "Ugh, yeah. I mean it could be because I have to work with these people and because I can't ... in the back of my mind, be *that* person ... I can't be that kind of person in the office. That person who annoys you about race." Pushing him deeper, the interviewer probed: "What happens if you are *that* person?" He responded:

> The fear that I have is that opportunities ... I won't be able to do my work. Opportunities won't be there. There is definitely a fear of being ostracized ... I keep coming back to this idea of community. I feel like there are not many people who would be in my community if I was as involved in this work as I had been in college. I'm afraid, I don't know. It makes me feel vulnerable to think about.

According to his own analysis, self-preservation – both on a practical and an emotional level – prevented this formally active facilitator from intervening in problematic race-related discussions in the office and within his current social circles. In particular, being *that* type of person, a "race traitor" (Bailey, 1998; Eichstedt, 2001; Reason & Broido, 2005), could have significant implications on his personal and professional relationships with other White people.

128　*Kristie A. Ford*

This theme also emerged across some of the other White participant interviews. (For more, see Chapter 9.) By "de-centering," "de-stabilizing," or "subverting" the center in an attempt to challenge dominant narratives (Bailey, 1998, p. 32), race traitors often experience feelings of isolation from their loved ones. (For more, see Chapter 9.)

In addition, Reese later mentioned that he was also afraid of inadvertently hurting people of color by engaging in problematic allying behaviors (Edwards, 2006; Eichstedt, 2001; Ford & Orlandella, 2015; Waters, 2010; also see Chapter 9). This expressed fear aligned with Waters's (2010) intermediary (or second) stage in a three-stage model of social justice ally development: "I just don't want to hurt people like, I mean ... I just don't wanna like do the wrong thing [on behalf of people of color] and make someone think negatively towards me or towards my people." He continued: "yeah, I don't feel like I am good enough." Even in how he framed this concern, however, Reese still seemed more focused on self-interest and self-presentation, evident in his reference to not wanting "me" or "my people" to be perceived in a negative light. Embedded in these comments was the fear many well-intended White people have of being called (or assumed to be) a racist (Bonilla-Silva & Forman, 2000; Tatum, 2003). Edwards (2006), citing Berkowitz (2003), reminded us that allyship should not be dependent on peer approval (p. 42) (also see Ford & Orlandella, 2015). Kendall (2006) also contended that allies should not be focused on pleasing the "other"; instead, they should be focused on individual growth and development. Rather than taking responsibility for his own learning, Reese reverted back to the idea that he needed closer relationships with people of color in order to feel more competent in his racial identity and allying work.

Moving Forward: Renewed Hope for Empowerment and Change

Interestingly, after the tape recorder was turned off, Reese mentioned that IGR made a "big impact" on him and "changed his perspectives." He then offered the metaphor of "soldiers [former facilitators] subtly spreading ideas" through their participation in the program.

Continuing a series of contradictions, despite Reese's clear disengagement with social justice work after college, when asked about his professional goals five to ten years from now, Reese immediately focused on creating organizational change from the inside out, and then eventually working "outside of the system ... I don't know what a new system looks like, but a system that is definitely more inclusive." He concluded by excitedly stating: "Yeah! This is making me feel a little bit more integrated [into the IGR community]."

Concluding Remarks

What can social justice scholars and practitioners take away from this interview? What can it help us learn about IGD facilitators' pathways toward (or away from) social justice? What does it tell us about whiteness and white entrenchment? Perhaps this interview results in more questions than answers. Nonetheless, the complexities embedded in individual counterexamples may provide a window into broader sociological phenomenon worthy of further investigation. While the exception within this sample, white guilt, resistance, and complacency are not new areas of inquiry (for more, see Bailey, 1998; Eichstedt, 2001; Jensen, 2005). The fact that a few IGD facilitators, who were highly trained, skilled, and involved in this work, chose to disengage speaks to the fragility of social justice education and the need for continual support. As Vasques-Scalera (2011) urged, "programs such as IGR provide a model for education that is individually and socially transformative. Yet helping facilitators create change requires a long-term commitment to nurture and support them after they leave the university and enter a new setting" (p. 211). Reese may have chosen the same path; Vasques-Scalera's (2011) comment, however, highlighted the importance of programmatically committing to facilitators' lifelong journey of self-discovery and change.

References

Bailey, A. (1998). Locating traitorous identities: Toward a view of privilege-cognizant white character. *Hypatia, 13*(3), 27–42.

Berkowitz, A. (2003). Applications of social norms theory to other health and social justice issues. In H. W. Perkins (Ed.), *The social norms approach to preventing school and college age substance abuse: A handbook for educators, counselors, and clinicians* (pp. 259–279). San Francisco, CA: Jossey-Bass.

Bonilla-Silva, E. (2014). *Racism without racists: Color-blind racism and the persistence of racial inequality in America.* Lanham, MD: Rowman & Littlefield.

Bonilla-Silva, E., & Forman, T. (2000). "I am not racist, but … ": Mapping white college students' racial ideology in the USA. *Discourse & Society, 11*(1), 50–85.

Brandyberry, L. (1999). Pain and perseverance: Perspectives from an ally. *Journal of Counseling and Development, 77*(1), 7–9.

Burkhardt, J., & Chambers, T. (2003). Kellogg forum on higher education for the public good: Contributing to the practice of democracy. *Diversity Digest, 1*(2), 1–2.

Edwards, K. (2006). Aspiring social justice ally identity development: A conceptual model. *NASPA Journal, 43*(4), 39–60.

Eichstedt, J. L. (2001). Problematic white identities and a search for racial justice. *Sociological Forum, 16*(3), 445–470.

Feagin, J. R. (2013). *The white racial frame: Centuries of racial framing and counter-framing.* New York, NY: Taylor & Francis.

Ford, K. A., & Orlandella, J. (2015). The "not so final remark": The journey to becoming white allies. *Sociology of Race and Ethnicity, 1*(2), 287–301.

Frankenberg, R. (1993). *White women, race matters: The social construction of whiteness.* Minneapolis, MN: University of Minnesota Press.

Frankenberg, R. (2001). The mirage of an unmarked whiteness. In B. Rasmussen, E. Klinenberg, I. J. Nexica, & M. Wray (Eds.), *The making and unmaking of whiteness* (pp. 72–96). Durham, NC: Duke University Press.

Freire, P. (1970). *Pedagogy of the oppressed.* New York, NY: Seabury.

Gurin, P., Nagda, B. A., & Zúñiga, X. (Eds). (2013). *Dialogue across difference: Practice, theory, and research on intergroup dialogue.* New York, NY: Russell Sage Foundation.

130 Kristie A. Ford

Helms, J. E. (1990). *Black and white racial identity: Theory, research, and practice*. Westport, CT: Greenwood.

Helms, J. E. (1995). An update of Helm's white and people of color racial identity models. In J. G. Ponterotto, J. M. Casas, L. A. Suzuka, & C. M. Alexander (Eds.), *Handbook of multicultural counseling* (pp. 181–198). Thousand Oaks, CA: Sage.

Hughey, M. (2010). The white savior film and reviewers' reception. *Symbolic Interaction, 33*(3), 475–496.

Jensen, R. (2005). *The heart of whiteness: Confronting race, racism, and white privilege*. San Francisco, CA: City Lights.

Johnson, A. G. (2006). *Privilege, power, and difference*. New York, NY: McGraw-Hill.

Kendall, F. (2006). *Understanding white privilege*. New York, NY: Routledge.

Kleinman, S. (1996). *Opposing ambitions: Gender and identity in an alternative organization*. Chicago, IL: University of Chicago Press.

Nagda, B. A. & Gurin, P. (2007). Intergroup dialogue: A critical-dialogic approach to learning about difference, inequality, and social justice. *New Directions for Teaching and Learning, 111*, 35–45.

Reason, R. D., & Broido, E. M. (2005). Issues and strategies for social justice allies (and the student affairs professionals who hope to encourage them). In R. D. Reason, E. M. Broido, T. L. David, & N. J. Evans (Eds.), *Developing social justice allies: New directions for student services* (pp. 81–89). San Francisco, CA: John Wiley & Sons, Inc.

Sorensen, N., Nagda, B. A., Gurin, P., & Maxwell, K. E. (2009). Taking a "hands on" approach to diversity in higher education: A critical-dialogic model for effective intergroup interaction. *Analyses of Social Issues and Public Policy, 9*(1), 3–35.

Srivastava, S. (2005). "You're calling me a racist?" The moral and emotional regulation of antiracism and feminism. *Signs, 31*(1), 29–62.

Tatum, B. (2003). *"Why are all the black kids sitting together in the cafeteria?": And other conversations about race*. New York, NY: Basic Books.

Vasques-Scalera, C. (2011). Changing facilitators, facilitating change: The lives of intergroup dialogue facilitators post-college. In K. E. Maxwell, B. A. Nagda, & M. C. Thompson.(Eds.), *Facilitating intergroup dialogues: Bridging differences, catalyzing change* (pp. 201–212). Sterling, VA: Stylus.

Waters, R. (2010). Understanding allyhood as a developmental process. *About Campus*, Nov–Dec., 1–8.

Part III
Beyond IGD Facilitation

11 "I Wouldn't Be the Person I Am Without IGR"

Implications and Conclusions

Kristie A. Ford and Heather J. Lipkin

Sometimes digging in that deep was really difficult ... I didn't always want to go there; I didn't always want to have the eyes to see some things ... but it is really worthwhile, it's just hard sometimes ... It is worthwhile to lose that sense of ignorance, or unknowing, or not seeing ... you have a fuller view of the world you live in ... it has helped me become closer to myself and know myself more. I have a better understanding of the layers underneath. (Sophie)

The co-facilitation experience is very powerful, even more powerful than being a participant in the dialogue ... it is the behind the scenes conversations where you can learn from each other. (John)

I would recommend it [the IGR program] to anyone ... learning to facilitate there is a lot of confidence in approaching social justice issues that is very helpful and can be applied to many things ... the lessons are very much across the board. It is always going to be a beneficial experience for me and one that I would recommend. (Reagan)

The IGR program gives you an amazing experience where it opens your eyes to the world ... and I really appreciated that. And I think that skill set is really great ... using that in practical terms for your future career is something people may not think of. (Jeremy)

I wouldn't be the person I am without IGR. Coming to terms with white privilege was one of the most challenging pieces of the work I did through IGR ... it's always something to be working on ... remembering that feeling is something that I hold with me. (Laura)

Summary of Results

Thinking about her experience, Melissa stated, "IGD is just within the context of a college setting, but it's so much more than just a class." The majority of participants' continued involvement with social justice issues, as evidenced by their interview and auto-ethnography reflections, supports Melissa's statement.

134 *Kristie A. Ford and Heather J. Lipkin*

Through a social justice advocacy lens, this research project sought to answer the following research questions by analyzing 28 in-depth interviews and five auto-ethnographies from former IGD facilitators three to five years post-college: (1) What are the short- and long-term implications of IGD on facilitators' personal and professional trajectory?, (2) How do IGD facilitators navigate race and social justice issues post-college?, and (3) Do IGD pedagogies help foster sustained racial identity and ally development? In the remainder of this section, we will address each question in turn:

1 *What are the short- and long-term implications of IGD on facilitators' personal and professional trajectory?*

With a newfound passion fostered by IGD, some participants went on to graduate school to study sociology, law, education, social work, and other social justice-related fields. Others took their social justice knowledge with them and continued down different paths, pursuing marketing, business, or publishing. In particular, the auto-ethnographies by Victoria, Sarah, Teshika, Luna, and Stephen serve as exemplars for the promises and limitations of applying IGD to the workforce. Clearly, all five facilitators experienced notable moments of racial awakening, and reawakening, and were making a difference in their chosen fields. IGD, however, did not fully prepare them to translate their social justice ideals into other professional contexts after college. As such, they continued to grapple with questions like, How do we use our IGD skills to empower communities to collectively work towards equity and justice, without inadvertently reinforcing oppressive narratives, attitudes, or behaviors? And, where do we go from here? What would a truly just and equitable world really look like in practice?

Most facilitators also noted the ways IGD touched their personal lives. Specifically, after facilitating a dialogue, they were more apt to intervene when they witnessed acts of oppression, initiate justice-related conversations in differing social settings, and volunteer with activist organizations or causes. In addition, some of the facilitators were beginning to think about building families and how to apply social justice values to the next generation.

Regardless of their chosen personal and professional paths, the facilitators – in both the auto-ethnography and interview data – identified tangible skills they took away from their participation in IGD, which they subsequently applied to post-college life. Demonstrable skills included the ability to recognize nonverbal cues and interactional dynamics, listen actively, balance voice within a space, empathize, and lead more effectively. Moreover, the facilitators credited IGD with providing a supportive community, which helped to foster their self-confidence when speaking about oppression and social justice issues.

While our results offer compelling evidence of the long-term impact of IGD, in reporting these outcomes, it is important to recognize that the

Implications and Conclusions 135

facilitators were active participants in the IGD process, not passive receivers of knowledge (Freire, 1970). As Melissa stated, "[IGR] was one of the most amazing experiences of my entire college career ... it taught me that, you know, an experience is kind of what you put into it and ... it's what you make of it." Echoing Melissa's statement, the individuals in our study learned valuable skills and reaped benefits from IGD *because* of their dedication to the experience, their trust in the process, and their continuous hard work during and after college. As Logan noted, "this is like a lifelong process ... there will always be room for improvement and room for me to learn a lot more."

2 *How do IGD facilitators navigate race and social justice issues post-college?*
As stated in Chapter 1, we defined social justice advocacy as "the intentional, lifelong developmental process that people embark on, both individually and collectively, in hopes of creating a more just and equitable world around a range of social issues such as racism and white supremacy, classism, and heteropatriarchy." Likewise, and in accordance with the relevant literature, most of the facilitators in this study focused on valuing the humanity of all social identity groups and working towards collective justice in their post-college lives by (1) enhancing personal awareness, (2) maintaining commitment, (3) taking action, and (4) practicing accountability (Bell, 1997; Hackman, 2005; Landreman, Edwards, Balon, & Anderson, 2008; Mayhew & Fernandez, 2007; Waters, 2010). Achieving this goal, however, was often hindered by a range of external challenges, including working within a problematic system, feeling overwhelmed by the enormity of the task at hand, dealing with resistance, and lacking a support network. Further, the facilitators continued to grapple with identity-related concerns such as how to navigate (1) whiteness and privilege in a socially just way; and (2) racial "otherness," along with its implications in the context of social change work. While striving to disrupt dominant narratives and hegemonic practices, most also worried that their efforts were insufficient to effect change in any meaningful way.

3 *Do IGD pedagogies help foster sustained racial identity and ally development?*
Despite the noted challenges, 24 of the 28 former facilitators, or 86% of the sample, remained motivated to continue social justice work and development because they understood what was at stake if they remained silent. Moreover, the interviewees wanted to make a difference in the world, and cherished this lifelong journey of learning, reflection, and engagement. Ultimately, by participating in IGD's critical-dialogic process (Sorensen, Nagda, Gurin, & Maxwell, 2009), most participants found a sense of purpose and direction as they increased their knowledge of race relations, alliance-building, and social justice advocacy. Further, many acknowledged that the IGD experience itself was beneficial and life-altering, reinforcing the necessary "passion" in the PASK model (Schoem, Hurtado, Sevig, Chesler, & Sumida, 2001, p. 230). Indeed, social justice

136   *Kristie A. Ford and Heather J. Lipkin*

advocacy "requires substantial commitment and passion ... [and the] belief in the importance of social justice education and the possibility of social change provides facilitators with visions to work toward" (Schoem et al., 2001, p. 90).

Counterexamples, like Reese's story highlighted in Chapter 10, are also important to acknowledge and unpack, especially in relation to white racial identity and ally development (Edwards, 2006; Helms 1990/1995; Reason & Broido, 2005; Waters, 2010). Although an anomaly within the sample, Reese reminded us of the nonlinear and maturational trajectory experienced by at least some, if not all, of the facilitators in differing ways (Edwards, 2006; Waters, 2010). Waters's (2010) model, for instance, highlighted the cognitive, intrapersonal, and interpersonal processes that inform alliance-building and social change across three developmental stages – initial, intermediate, and mature. For Reese, even though IGD helped him to develop a mature understanding of social justice during college, without this constant engagement post-college, he reverted to earlier stages of the model. In hopes of countering such retreats in the future, as Waters (2010) argued, "Understanding the development of ally identity as a continual process is crucial to providing students with learning opportunities that are developmentally appropriate" (p. 8).

While participating in the IGR program is only one step in a lifelong process of self-discovery and change, in the end, the majority of the participants in our sample continued to be thoughtful about their engagement with social justice work and its related challenges. They remained motivated to persist and continue their efforts in the hopes becoming allies for social justice (Edwards, 2006) – for those who are oppressed and for themselves.

Implications

Our research has several implications related to IGD specifically and social justice education more generally. In the following sections, we discuss our suggested curricular revisions and additions, and highlight the importance of ongoing social justice communities.

Curricular Revisions

Given most of the participants in our sample are continuing to grapple with how to best engage in social justice issues beyond the college setting, the IGD curricular offerings at Skidmore College and other higher educational institutions could be revised and/or expanded to best meet student needs. As Kiera, for instance, noted:

> Adulting is hard ... being out of college and growing on your own without the structure of a school environment is something you do not necessarily feel prepared for ... it has definitely been challenging, but [I am] just growing and learning in my own way.

When asked about whether a course focused on merging their theoretical knowledge and practical skills post-college would be useful, she affirmed,

> Oh my gosh, yes. Yeah, that is a really amazing idea ... before I graduated if I had been reminded or told that social justice and activism have many different forms ... that would have helped ease some of the hardness I have put on myself.

She continued, comparing her expectations for social justice involvement post-college to her reality:

> The vision in college was the idea that you have to be actively in an organization or speaking out in a public [way] ... and closely tied to my career where I can live and breathe social justice ... that is a perspective that many college students get ... I have realized that it doesn't have to be that way ... I feel like my vision for what social justice work [is] has changed ... maybe it is out of necessity ... I decided to name it and live it on my own terms, so it has been an evolution of seeing the many ways social justice can fit into a life in everyday experience.

As Kiera suggested, reframing and expanding definitions of social justice work could be instrumental to helping alumni facilitators figure out how to apply their IGD skills to their post-college lives. A course, such as the University of Michigan's IGD Capstone, "Social Justice in the Real World" (https://igr.umich .edu/courses/sequence), offers a great model. Similarly, other IGD or social justice programs might consider adding courses focused on post-college life that enhance dialogic skill sets beyond the classroom and help students connect theory and practice through action-focused projects (Broido, 2000; Freire, 1970; Mayhew & Fernandez, 2007). Specifically, such courses should (1) explore different forms of activism and their implications; (2) assess the impact of personal, interpersonal, and structural change efforts; and (3) develop community support systems. Given the participants' mention of "not doing enough," it could be helpful to provide additional references citing the range of possibilities for how to approach activism (also see: Vasques-Scalera, 2011). For example, the Action Continuum (Wijeyesinghe, Griffin, & Love, 1997), as well as similar resources, might serve as a tool to help facilitators assess their level of post-college engagement. As Domingue and Neely (2013) noted, "social action should be seen as an ongoing journey, not as one or more isolated events" (p. 233).

Moreover, given the noted struggles of White facilitators in particular, to navigate race within White settings, the People of Color/White People dialogue curriculum could be expanded to engage more deeply with intra-racial group dynamics. Sophie, a White woman, for instance, suggested:

> Something that I wished I had that wasn't explicitly kind of IGD that would have helped is about how to introduce the intergroup dialogue and

138   *Kristie A. Ford and Heather J. Lipkin*

white identity. [It] is a lot about exposing privilege, but it wasn't a lot about, at least that I recall, about engaging within our own White communities about issues of privilege. So I felt really prepared leaving IGD to go into a community that didn't look mine and feel comfortable and be able to own my privilege. But how to work in a White community ... I feel like I almost have less preparation for that.

Likewise, Melissa noted that she felt "confident at least academically and professionally in talking about these issues ... but so unconfident talking to the [White] people who I'm supposed to be the closest with." In order to help facilitators translate their learning beyond the dialogue setting, Vasques-Scalera's (2011) study also suggested that facilitators could benefit from more contact with people who are resistant to and/or not committed to issues of justice.

Interacting with people from more diverse ideological backgrounds, through work with local businesses or community organizations, for instance, might also prove useful for facilitators of color and multiracial facilitators who had to later learn how to take prudent risks in order to stay true to their social justice beliefs while navigating racial microaggressions within the workplace (Sue, Capodilupo, Torino, Bucceri, Holder, Nadal, & Esquilin, 2007).

Alumni-Facilitator Support Network

Finally, it would be advantageous to develop a robust alumni-facilitator network so that IGD facilitators can maintain a supportive community while pursing social justice work and practicing self-care in their post-college lives (Broido & Reason, 2005; Vasques-Scalera, 2011). This could also be helpful for those who are struggling to incorporate social justice advocacy into their post-college lives. A support system could remind facilitators why they joined the IGR program in the first place, and reignite their passion for this work. Perhaps, with the addition of a support network, participants would be less likely to disengage post-college. Highlighting this point, Frederick advised:

You would hope that everyone could keep strong with this kind of interest or passion at least in some kind of way, but not like become stagnant or regress in some regard so if there's some way that we can facilitate that, that would be great. I would love to like be able to talk to some other young professionals who went through IGR, see what their experiences are going through their workforce and share common practices, so we can continue to kind of grow together in some ways.

In addition to an alumni network to provide encouragement and career advice, the participants felt that support could come in other forms, including mentors, online communities, conferences, and social meet-ups. John accordingly noted that he needed a "network of people who have been there before."

Future Research

While our findings add to the limited existing literature on IGD and its post-college implications for former facilitators (e.g., Vasques-Scalera, 2011), there is much more to learn within this field by quantitatively and qualitatively analyzing a larger sample of participants from varying social identities and across differing geographic locations. In addition to expanding and diversifying the sample, interviewees could be systematically followed beyond three to five years post-college to assess the potential impact of IGD 10 or 15 years after graduation. This longitudinal approach might also provide more data in relation to how individuals are (or are not) applying their skills and social justice ideals to their interactions with partners, children, and other family members (for more, see: Diaz & Perrault, 2010).

Conclusions

According to Broido and Reason (2005), "little has been written about the impact of college experiences on social justice ally development" (p. 23). It is therefore crucial to invest in such efforts, since higher educational institutions have the responsibility to prepare future leaders for their active engagement in society. Although more research needs to be done regarding IGD and advocacy beyond the college setting, this book project begins to fill that gap. As these data suggest, IGD has the potential to foster change agents as former facilitators use their skills to confront inequality in an effort to achieve justice within and beyond higher educational settings (Maxwell, Nagda, & Thompson, 2011).

In alignment with our initial premise, we contend that the peer-facilitation role, in particular, may yield more significant and lasting outcomes (Maxwell et al., 2011; Vasques-Scalera, 2011). Accordingly, Vivian stated, "The time that I spent in the classroom as a facilitator I think I grew the most." Moreover, this research supports other empirical studies that "highlight the importance of social justice courses in the development of social justice attitudes" (Broido & Reason, 2005, p. 26). At a time when students are increasingly demanding that U.S. colleges and universities offer more diversity-focused courses and workshops (Libresco, 2015), IGD facilitators' post-college reflections can provide insight into some of the challenges and opportunities associated with social justice education.

As noted in Chapter 1, the issues that emerge within IGD on college campuses are also ripe for serious work in K-12 education, community settings, and within businesses (Dessel, Rogge, & Garlington, 2006; Groth, 2001; Walsh, 2006) (for more, see Chapter 12). For example, K-12 teachers need to learn how to have conversations about sensitive justice-related topics in their classrooms, social work graduate students need to develop multicultural competencies in order to serve a diverse clientele in their chosen fields, and CEOs need to understand how to manage a company within a global market. The breadth of the phenomenon in question is thus transferrable to a variety of settings;

140 *Kristie A. Ford and Heather J. Lipkin*

it should not be limited to dialogic courses. Irrespective of the context, at its best, social justice education – and, in particular, IGD – can be a transformative experience; as Laura simply noted: "I wouldn't be the person I am without IGR."

References

Bell, L. A. (1997). Theoretical foundations for social justice education. In M. Adams, L. Bell, & P. Griffin (Eds.), *Teaching for diversity and social justice: A sourcebook* (pp. 3–15). New York, NY: Routledge.

Broido, E. M. (2000). The development of social justice allies during college: A phenomenological investigation. *Journal of College Student Development, 41*, 3–18.

Broido, E. M. & Reason, R. D. (2005). The development of social justice attitudes and actions: An overview of current understandings. In. R. D. Reason, E. M. Broido, T. L. David, & N. J. Evans (Eds.), *Developing social justice allies: New directions for student services* (pp. 17–28). San Francisco, CA: A Wiley Company.

Dessel, A., Rogge, M. E., & Garlington, S. B. (2006). Using intergroup dialogue to promote social justice and change. *Social Work, 51*(4), 303–315.

Diaz, A., & Perrault, R. (2010). Sustained dialogue and civic life: Post-college impacts. *Michigan Journal of Community Service Learning*, Fall, 1–12.

Domingue, A. D., & Neely, D. S. (2013). Why is it so hard to take action?: A reflective dialogue about preparing students for social action engagement. In L. Landreman (Ed.), *The art of effective facilitation: Reflections from social justice educators* (pp. 231–252). Sterling, VA: Stylus Publishing.

Edwards, K. (2006). Aspiring social justice ally identity development: A conceptual model. *NASPA Journal, 43*(4), 39–60.

Freire, P. (1970). *Pedagogy of the oppressed*. New York, NY: Seabury.

Groth, G. A. (2001). Dialogue in corporations. In D. Schoem & S. Hurtado (Eds.), *Intergroup dialogue: Deliberative democracy in school, in college, community, and the workplace* (pp. 195–209). Ann Arbor, MI: University of Michigan.

Hackman, H. W. (2005). Five essential components for social justice education. *Equity & Excellence in Education, 38*, 103–109.

Helms, J. E. (1990). *Black and white racial identity: Theory, research, and practice*. Westport, CT: Greenwood.

Helms, J. E. (1995). An update of Helm's white and people of color racial identity models. In J. G. Ponterotto, J. M. Casas, L. A. Suzuka, & C. M. Alexander (Eds.), *Handbook of multicultural counseling* (pp. 181–198). Thousand Oaks, CA: Sage.

Landreman, L, Edwards, K. E., Balon, D. G., & Anderson, G. (2008). Wait! It takes time to develop rich and relevant social justice curriculum. *About Campus, 13*(4), 2–10. Hoboken, NJ: John Wiley & Sons, Inc.

Libresco, L. (2015, Dec. 3). Here are the demands from students protesting racism at 51 colleges. *FiveThirtyEight*. Retrieved May 30, 2016 from http://fivethirtyeight.com/features/here-are-the-demands-from-students-protesting-racism-at-51-colleges/.

Maxwell, K. E., Nagda, B. A., & Thompson, M. C. (Eds.) (2011). *Facilitating intergroup dialogues: Bridging differences, catalyzing change*. Sterling, VA: Stylus Publishing, Inc.

Mayhew, M. J., Fernandez, S. D. (2007). Pedagogical practices that contribute to social justice outcomes. *Review of Higher Education, 31*(1), 55–80.

Reason, R. D., & Broido, E. M. (2005). Issues and strategies for social justice allies (and the student affairs professionals who hope to encourage them). In R. D. Reason, E. M. Broido, T. L. David, & N. J. Evans (Eds.), *Developing social justice allies: New directions for student services* (pp. 81–89). San Francisco, CA: A Wiley Company.

Schoem, D., Hurtado, S., Sevig, T., Chesler, M., & Sumida, S. H. (2001). Intergroup dialogue: Democracy at work in theory and practice. In D. Schoem & S. Hurtado (Eds.),

Intergroup dialogue: Deliberative democracy in school, college, community, and workplace (pp. 1–21). Ann Arbor, MI: University of Michigan Press.

Sorensen, N., Nagda, B. A., Gurin, P., & Maxwell, K. E. (2009). Taking a "hands on" approach to diversity in higher education: A critical-dialogic model for effective intergroup interaction. *Analyses of Social Issues and Public Policy*, 9(1), 3–35.

Sue, D. W., Capodilupo, C. M., Torino, G. C., Bucceri, J. M., Holder, A. M., Nadal, K. L., & Esquilin, M. (2007). Racial microaggressions in everyday life: implications for clinical practice. *The American Psychologist*, 64(4), 271–286.

University of Michigan, IGR Course Sequence. Retrieved June 1, 2016 from https://igr.umich.edu/courses/sequence.

Vasques-Scalera, C. (2011). Changing facilitators, facilitating change: The lives of intergroup dialogue facilitators post-college. In K. E. Maxwell, B. A. Nagda, & M. C. Thompson. (Eds.), *Facilitating intergroup dialogues: Bridging differences, catalyzing change* (pp. 201–212). Sterling, VA: Stylus Publishing, Inc.

Walsh, K. C. (2006). Communities, race, and talk: An analysis of the occurrence of civic intergroup dialogue programs. *The Journal of Politics*, 68(1), 22–33.

Waters, R. (2010). Understanding allyhood as a developmental process. *About Campus*, Nov–Dec., 1–8.

Wijeyesinghe, C. L., Griffin, P., & Love, B. (1997). Racism curriculum design. In M. Adams, L. Bell, & P. Griffin (Eds.), *Teaching for diversity and social justice: A sourcebook* (pp. 82–107). New York, NY: Routledge.

Wise, Andrea. (2012). New minor in intergroup relations now available. Retrieved May 30, 2016 from http://www.skidmore.edu/news/2012/3551.php.

12 The Dialogue Continues

The Future of IGR

Stephen A. Bissonnette and Victoria K. Malaney

> Never doubt that a small group of thoughtful, committed citizens can change the world; indeed, it's the only thing that ever has – Margaret Meade (in Lutkehaus, 2008, p. 261).

Recognizing and Re-Socializing the Self

Through the Intergroup Relation (IGR) program's strategic process, engagement with the content presented in Intergroup Dialogue (IGD), and writing our auto-ethnographies for this book, we have attained a better understanding of ourselves, our social identities, and our lived experiences. We also have a better appreciation for how all of these factors influence our interactions with others, particularly in our work as educators, social workers, and as committed lifelong social justice advocates. Without the transformative and meaningful experience that IGR provided us, we would not have been as adequately prepared to engage in sustained social justice work and effect change in our personal and professional lives. (For more, see Chapter 9.)

More concretely, the ability to create co-learning environments, build trust in our dialogue courses, and create a shared meaning of dialogue was paramount to our learning process about issues of identity, social relations, and intergroup/intragroup conflict (Ford, 2012; Ford & Malaney, 2012). Furthermore, the skills, experience, and knowledge acquired through our participation with IGR at Skidmore College has undoubtedly inspired us to work in the education, social work, and nonprofit fields, while simultaneously preparing us for social justice work. Through the IGD pedagogy, we developed a critical lens to help us to understand why social oppressions exist and to persist in hopes of disrupting them (Nagda, Gurin, & Lopez, 2003). Additionally, we came to understand the importance of acknowledging intersecting social identities. Intersectionality is defined as a "powerful tool for understanding, constructing, and deconstructing: the experience of identity, the complex and mutually constituting nature of social identities, the relationships between identity and larger social systems, and the interwoven nature of manifestations of social oppression" (Mitchell, Simmons, & Greyerbiehl, 2014, p. 17). IGD offered progressive and inclusive methods for self-discovery and helped us cultivate a

The Dialogue Continues: The Future of IGR   143

keen understanding for working within an increasingly diverse global society and economy. As Freire (2008) stated, "to no longer be domesticated from oppression you have to reflect and act upon the world in order to transform it" (p. 51). There is an immense power found through such self-reflective processes, which fosters a clarity of understanding regarding the systemic and institutionalized obstacles of those living in the margins (Brookfield, 2004). Once perceived, it is difficult to unsee. Through our work with IGD we have nurtured the capacity to understand how social systems can both cause social and physical harm as well as, conversely, offer resources and opportunities to bolster marginalized communities.

Vehicle for Social Change

IGD presents the reality of societal oppression in a way that makes connections to one's own lived experience. In this way, IGD participants can understand the opportunities they have or have not been granted as well as the obstacles they have or have not overcome. Participants' understanding is framed within a sociohistorical context that locates their own narrative and self-concept as part of, or even as a consequence of, a narrative of socially constructed and enforced oppressive systems based on social identity. IGD can be used as a vehicle for social change insofar as it challenges the perpetuating vestiges of such oppressive systems and offers alternate solutions to their existence (Nagda, Gurin, & Lopez, 2003). The IGD process also fosters a deep understanding of the multitude of different perspectives in a dialogic space.

There is a concrete status quo that most people are taught to engage in and perpetuate through various modes of socialization, such as families, religious organizations, and the media (Harro, 2000). Within this status quo is imbedded subtle, pervasive, and ubiquitous systems of privilege and oppression that are all but invisible to those in positions of social power (Smith, 2016). Additionally, those in positions of power desire their comfortable position and will often delude themselves in order to maintain this sense of comfort. Recognizing oppression is to understand the paradox that the individual is part of society, and in order to be a better member of society one must engage in the painful work of unlearning systemic oppression (Kardia & Sevig, 2001). Consequently, it is the implicit support of this comfortable social status quo that is in fact enabling our current chaotic and inequitable social institutions.

The IGD process teaches us to instead be comfortable leaning into our discomfort in order to enact positive harmonious social change. Participating in experiences like IGD facilitates our collective movement into a dialogic space by moving through the discomfort of engaging in dialogue with typically challenging topics, such as the systemic implications of institutionalized racism and white privilege. Practicing to comfortably engage with such issues further develops our capacity to deconstruct the archetypal biases of our perspectives that are produced from our social world. Consequently, such a capacity allows us as individuals, and as a society, to move toward a more equitable social world.

144 *Bissonnette and Malaney*

Refining the skills and knowledge attained via IGD are necessary for participating in the co-creation of more resilient and equitable communities and partnerships that will advance society. The process and content of IGD courses most assuredly have a place in the future of our educational curricula – for students, teachers, and administrators alike – if we are to truly enact fundamental and transformational educational reform. Furthermore, we must find ways in which such a curriculum can be interwoven into the corporate sphere, through professional development opportunities for employees, in hopes of fostering similar values outside of elite spaces in higher education. The subsequent sections will focus on higher educational spaces and the corporate sphere, respectively.

Operating within Higher Education

As our auto-ethnographies suggest, engaging with the IGD curriculum in college energized us to continue doing the hard work of recognizing and dismantling systems of oppression and white supremacy. Across higher education institutions, student-led activism continues to push the ongoing struggles in the fight for social justice. National social justice movements, such as Black Lives Matter (2016), call out higher education institutions on a systemic level to recognize how the oppression of Black lives have resulted in lower enrollment and retention rates of students of color, while reminding us that racial equality has not yet been achieved (Kingkade, Workneh, & Grenoble, 2015). Black students continue to experience unequal access to and treatment in higher education. For instance, according to Castellanos, Cole, & Jones (2002), "the proportion of minority students participating in college has been rising but still lags behind attendance rates of the national norm" (p. 20). Furthermore, the percent of ethnic minority undergraduate students at four-year institutions continues to be low when compared to their White peers, with "African Americans constituting 12.3%, Chicano/Latinos constituting 8.7%, and Native Americans accounting for less than 1% of all higher education students" (Castellanos, Cole, & Jones, 2002, p. 20). We believe that using IGD to critically dialogue about social, economic, and political oppression is one way that transformative pedagogies can inspire young people to promote change within higher education. As more young people learn and understand the deeply rooted systemic issues that encumber marginalized communities, we can further mobilize our social justice efforts. It is now becoming increasingly more important to create safe spaces for dialogue about these issues in institutions of higher education, especially given the election of Donald Trump as president of the United States and his appointments of alternative right and white supremacist political figures (Altman, 2016).

At the same time, we need to create opportunities and encourage privileged communities to have the space to critically reflect on their identities in order to recognize how to partner with marginalized communities. IGR has helped us to begin to understand the complex and nuanced intersectional lives we lead.

While IGR is just one way to help college students grapple with intersectionality and issues of social justice, we believe that the IGD pedagogy and educational transformation we experienced as undergraduates came at an important developmental moment where we were open to questioning each other and inquiring deeply about the environment, institutionalized structures, and the invisible social systems in which we live.

Placing IGR in a higher education setting presents a unique yet challenging opportunity for educators and students. As colleges/universities in the United States continue to be influenced by neoliberal policies and practices that privatize, corporatize, and commercialize higher education for profit (Slaughter & Rhoades, 2004), we believe that IGR can be utilized to directly challenge them. However, there is an inherent contradiction in neoliberal policy as it relates to diversity initiatives, because there is a tension between neoliberal theory that "disenfranchises people of color under a color-blind ideology and an administrative practice that requires diversity in order to attract and function as an acceptable institution" (Squire, 2015, p. 110). As more educational institutions contend with racial bias, administrators and faculty should be prepared to hear students voice their concerns (i.e., protesting). In being cognizant that neoliberal policies create color-blind ideology (Osei-Kofi, Torres, & Lui, 2013), skills such as active listening and perspective taking are key (McCormick, 1999) in order for college campuses and their student populations to continue striving for racial equality while aiming to enhance racial climate and improve campus climate policies (Hurtado, Milem, Clayton-Pedersen, & Allen, 1998).

In sum, IGD pedagogies can be used as a tool in higher education where students practice inquiry and critical thinking strategies within the classroom and among their peers. Palumbo-Liu (2016) argues that education and the humanities within university settings are especially positioned to create opportunities because of their ability to create avenues for healing and self-reflection. Additionally, students can use dialogic exchange, active listening, and perspective-taking while organizing around issues of social justice and creating change through student activism. Perspective-taking and active listening are crucial skills to develop in the hopes of building consensus and bringing students together to organize around unjust issues or ongoing neoliberal practices occurring on college campuses.

Operating within the Corporate Sphere

We recognize the privilege of having access to IGD pedagogies through our educational process at an elite predominantly White liberal arts college, which led to our personal transformations and our social-justice-related careers. While education is one way to do this self-reflective work, we strongly believe that IGR should also operate outside the realm of higher-educational spaces. But herein lies the challenge: In what ways can IGR expand? And, what would that look like in practice? In the era in which Yoshino (2007) argued that we still "cover" our social identities (e.g., race, sexual orientation, and religious beliefs) in the

146 *Bissonnette and Malaney*

workplace, IGR could be used to help coworkers better understand different perspectives and learn how to deal with conflict.

More concretely, the curriculum used in higher educational settings could be adapted to best meet the needs of the corporate sector, which is still predominantly and historically White albeit slowly diversifying (Rampell, 2014). Groth (2001) argues that corporations primarily focus on yielding a profit in order to keep the business operating, instead of investing in the critical thinking and communication skills of their employees. To better align with these goals, dialogue could be used as a professional development tool – helping employees improve their organizational leadership skills (Isaacs, 1993). In addition, IGD could help resolve conflicts or provide the space for deeper conversations about difference in the workplace. Successful models of corporate dialogue have occurred over the years (Ellinor & Gerard, 1998; Groth, 2001), and these corporate models have helped employees develop much needed dialogic skills, including active listening, respecting differences, and promoting critical self-reflection (Ellinor & Gerard, 1998). Nevertheless, if the higher education IGD curriculum was to be implemented in other corporate settings, we also believe that an earnest commitment, sufficient time, and monetary resources from corporations is necessary to successfully implement dialogic skills in the workplace. Most corporate settings still have much more work to do to better understand social justice issues and remove organizational barriers such as ranked hierarchies and gender-based wage gaps (Stanley & Jarrell, 1998). The persistent tension of profit over personal values in corporate settings is a direct call for sustained professional development opportunities for employees. Allowing professional development for corporate employees can help build awareness of community impact while also keeping employees invested in their work (Read, 2015). As such, we encourage companies to practice corporate social responsibility and remain conscious of how their initiatives influence the greater community (Fallon Taylor, 2015).

Operating within the World

Ultimately, dialogue is an educative process where participants try to better understand one another's perspective no matter how complicated, and perhaps hurtful, the issue at hand. We are reminded by hooks (2003):

> Education is about healing and wholeness. It is about empowerment, liberation, transcendence, about renewing the vitality of life. It is about finding and claiming ourselves and our place in the world. Since our place in the world is constantly changing, we must be constantly learning to be fully present in the now. If we are not fully engaged in the present we get stuck in the past and our capacity to learn is diminished (p. 42).

We learned how to create and engage in dialogue through our higher education experience, and we believe that hooks's message can be applied to any career field.

The Dialogue Continues: The Future of IGR   147

We are all seeking to find and claim our place in the world. Education, whether it was received formally or informally, helps us to keep going. We must seek to utilize education's healing properties, especially in the wake of such tragedies that occur from a place of ignorance and misunderstanding, such as the massacre of 49 queer-identified/allied individuals at Pulse nightclub's "Latin Saturdays" party in Orlando in 2016 (Pérez-Peña & Alvarez, 2016, p. 1) or the increase in hate crimes across the United States in response to the election of Donald Trump as president (Dickerson, 2016). Engaging in strategic dialogue is one possible mechanism to experience liberation from society's hatred and oppression in order to allow us to become transcendent and renew our vitality of life (hooks, 2003).

Our society's institutionalized oppressive systems and constructed social identities have very real implications for the lived experiences of people perceived as being from marginalized groups, such as people of color and queer-identified people. The 2016 massacre at Pulse, for instance, was fueled by an institutionalized, rampant, ubiquitous, and pervasive system of hatred, misunderstanding, ignorance, and bigotry that is deeply imbedded within the very roots of the history of our country and our planet. Likewise, the hateful responses of Trump supporters toward marginalized groups is fueled by the divisive, derogatory, and abusive language of the Trump presidential campaign (Dickerson, 2016). It is not something we learn or are taught explicitly from any singular source, but rather absorb from a multitude of sources in our social environment (Harro, 2000). It is because of their eerily subtle, ubiquitous, and pervasive nature that we must actively and consistently recognize, oppose, and deconstruct these systems. Those whose lives were taken that night in Orlando or who are terrorized by hate crimes are simply seeking out a safe and welcoming place to freely express and radiate the beauty of their truest self. Our world should celebrate such moments instead of demonizing and destroying them.

It is from such real horrors and tragedies that we see the critical importance of programs such as IGR. Now more than ever, we need programs such as IGD in our institutions of education to directly and explicitly combat and address these issues and provide safe spaces for all students as well as opportunities to challenge our biases and prejudice in a radical way. The work we are doing in education matters, and we have to keep having dialogue about these issues with students in order to create a more equitable future. Through the strategic processes and content of IGD, we are able to develop a new perspective of our social identities and lived experiences that is contextualized within a narrative of systemic oppression. We also build a capacity for understanding the perspectives, identities, and lived experiences of those who surround us. Through this process, we develop the skills to recognize, oppose, and deconstruct oppressive ideologies and systems while working towards building bridges of understanding between the severed communities of our society in order to foster a more peaceful and equitable world. Oppression is painful and destructive to our communities; it is therefore important that social justice advocates, like ourselves, take responsibility for challenging stereotypes, discrimination, and structural inequities (Kardia & Sevig, 2001).

Onward

As we look towards the future, both as individuals and collectively as a human society, we must remember to learn from our past history to inform the present day. While there have been some strides made in moving toward equality for marginalized social identities – for instance, the ruling for federally recognized same-sex marriage in June 2015 – we still have much more work to do in regard to the oppressive violence towards the LGBTQ communities (Chappell, 2015; Pérez-Peña & Alvarez, 2016). The complex sociohistorical context responsible for both the violence toward LGBTQ communities and communities of color, as well as the social justice work of Black Lives Matter, reminds us that such incidents and movements are not isolated, but rather inextricable. IGR taught us the importance of understanding the social systems of oppression. We are now equipped to research our historical context and critically view the place in which we currently stand in history. By taking the time to know and learn the U.S. history of colonization (Zinn, 2003), we can use our collective power and privilege as educators and community organizers to stay inspired and continue engaging in the long, arduous fight for social justice. We know that we cannot keep silent about daily injustices (e.g., police brutality, racial discrimination, educational inequality). In our own ways, we will continue to be the spheres of influence to directly impact our world in order to make it more socially just and peaceful (Goodman & Shapiro, 1997).

We believe that the future of IGR lies in a sustained call for social justice coalition work that centers on intersectionality. In general, spaces that hold dialogue should frame social identities as intersectional to further shape and inform how we use our voices to recognize and challenge the privileges in our professional and personal communities. As stated in our auto-ethnographies, now that we recognize systems of oppression in our everyday lives, they are virtually impossible to ignore. But we also need to be both more explicit in voicing and acting on our commitment. We must be more capacious in our understanding of the role of the humanities and education in the world. We need to develop an insatiable desire for being more than just advocates for education – we need to become serious activists for it, especially in places beyond the campus, such as volunteering for nonprofits in support of social justice causes. However, at the same time, we must adapt our point of reference according to this new historical situation during the presidency of Donald Trump (Palumbo-Liu, 2016).

We feel compelled to continue the dialogue amongst our peers, families, and coworkers. As Freire (2008) said, seek to be the "individual [that] is not afraid to confront, to listen, to see the world unveiled. This person is not afraid to meet people or to enter into dialogue with them" (p. 39). We are not afraid to enter into dialogue with our personal and professional networks. If we are not to act from a place of fear and ignorance, we must then act from a place of compassionate understanding. In order to achieve this position, we must engage with a radical recognition of our own social identities and re-socialization to recognize

The Dialogue Continues: The Future of IGR   149

our own biases and perspectives. Our deconstructive work is radical insofar as we are simply "grasping things at the root" and reaching to the most basic source of our privilege and oppression (Davis, 1987). In this way, we can each contribute to co-creating a more harmonious, and thus equitable, society.

References

Altman, A. (2016). How Donald Trump is bringing the alt-right to the White House. Retrieved from http://time.com/4569895/donald-trump-stephen-bannon-alt-right/

Black Lives Matter (2016). *Black lives matter* website. Retrieved from http://blacklivesmatter.com.

Brookfield, S. D. (2004). *The power of critical theory: Liberating adult learning and teaching.* San Francisco, CA: Jossey-Bass.

Castellanos, J., Cole, D. & Jones, L. (2002). Examining the ethnic/minority student experience at predominantly white institutions: A case study. *Journal of Hispanic Higher Education, 1*(1), 19–39.

Chappell, B. (2015). Supreme court declares same-sex marriage legal in all 50 states. Retrieved on July 6, 2016 from http://www.npr.org/sections/thetwo-way/2015/06/26/417717613/supreme-court-rules-all-states-must-allow-same-sex-marriages.

Davis, A. (1987). Address *Let us all rise together, women, culture and politics* at Spelman College.

Dickerson, C. (2016). Reports of bias-based attacks tick upward after election. Retrieved on December 3, 2016 from http://www.nytimes.com/2016/11/12/us/reports-of-bias-based-attacks-tick-upward-after-election.html?_r=0

Ellinor, L. & Gerard, G. (1998). *Dialogue: Rediscover the transforming power of conversation.* New York, NY: John Wiley and Sons.

Fallon Taylor, N. (2015). 22 great examples of socially responsible businesses. Retrieved on June 2, 2016 from http://www.businessnewsdaily.com/5499-examples-socially-responsible-businesses.html.

Ford, K. A. (2012). Shifting white ideological scripts: The educational benefits of inter- and intraracial curricular dialogues on the experiences of white college students. *Journal of Diversity in Higher Education, 5*(3), 138–158. Adapted with permission of APA.

Ford, K. A., & Malaney, V. K. (2012). "I now harbor more pride in my race": The educational benefits of inter- and intra-racial dialogues on the experiences of students of color and multiracial students. *Equity and Excellence in Education, 45*(1), 14–35.

Freire, P. (2008). *Pedagogy of the oppressed.* New York, NY: Continuum International.

Goodman, D. & Shapiro, S. (1997). Sexism curriculum design. In M. Adams, L. A. Bell, & G. P. Griffin (Eds.), *Teaching for diversity and social justice: A sourcebook* (pp. 89–113). New York, NY: Routledge.

Groth, G. A. (2001). Dialogue in corporations. In D. Schoem & S. Hurtado (Eds.), *Intergroup dialogue: Deliberative democracy in school, in college, community, and the workplace* (pp. 195–209). Ann Arbor, MI: University of Michigan.

Harro, B. (2000). The cycle of socialization. In M. Adams, W. Blumenfeld, R. Castaneda, H. Hackman, M. Peters, X. Zuniga (Eds.), *Readings for diversity and social justice* (pp. 16–21). New York, NY: Routledge.

hooks, b. (2003). *Teaching community: A pedagogy of hope.* New York, NY: Routledge.

Hurtado, S., Milem, J. F., Clayton-Pedersen, A. R., & Allen, W. R. (1998). Enhancing campus climates for racial/ethnic diversity: Educational policy and practice. *Review of Higher Education, 21*(3), 279–302.

Isaacs, W. N. (1993). Taking flight: Dialogue, collective thinking, and organizational learning. *Organizational Dynamics, 22*(2), 24–39.

Kardia, D. & Sevig, T. (2001). Embracing the paradox: Dialogue that incorporates both individual and group identities. In D. Schoem & S. Hurtado (Eds.), *Intergroup dialogue: Deliberative democracy in school, in college, community, and the workplace* (pp. 247–265). Ann Arbor, MI: University of Michigan.

Kingkade, T., Workneh, L., & Grenoble, R. (2015). Campus racism protests didn't come out of nowhere, and they aren't going away quickly. *Huffington Post*. Retrieved on June 20, 2016 from http://www.huffingtonpost.com/entry/campus-racism-protests-didnt-come-out-of-nowhere_us_56464a87e4b08cda3488bfb4.

Lutkehaus, N. C. (2008). *Margaret Mead: The making of an American icon*. Princeton, NJ: Princeton University Press.

McCormick, D. (1999). Listening with empathy: Taking the other person's perspective. In A. L. Cooke, M. Brazzel, A. S., Craig, & B. Greig (Eds.), *Reading book for human relations' training* (pp. 57–60). Alexandria, VA: NTL Institute for Applied Behavioral Science.

Mitchell, D., Simmons, C., Greyerbiehl, L. (Eds.) (2014). *Intersectionality and higher education: Theory, research, and praxis*. New York, NY: Peter Lang.

Nagda, B., Gurin, P., & Lopez, G. (2003). Transformative pedagogy for democracy and social justice. *Race, Ethnicity, and Education, 6*(2), 165–191.

Osei-Kofi, N., Torres, L. E., & Lui, J. (2013). Practices of whiteness: Racialization in college admissions viewbooks. *Race Ethnicity and Education, 16*(3), 385–405.

Palumbo-Liu, D. (2016). Education and activist humanities, now more than ever. Retrieved on June 20, 2016 from http://www.huffingtonpost.com/david-palumboliu/education-and-activist-humanities-now-more-than-ever_b_12904122.html

Pérez-Peña, R., & Alvarez L. (2016). Orlando gunman attacks gay nightclub, leaving 50 dead. Retrieved on June 13, 2016 from http://www.nytimes.com/2016/06/13/us/orlando-nightclub-shooting.html.

Rampell, C. (2014). Google, Apple other tech companies struggle with minority hiring. Retrieved on June 20, 2016 from http://www.oregonlive.com/opinion/index.ssf/2014/08/google_apple_other_tech_compan.html

Read, M. (2015). Why professional development matters to your employees. Retrieved on July 18, 2016 from https://learn.uvm.edu/blog-business/professional-development-matters.

Slaughter, S., & Rhoades, G. (2004). *Academic capitalism and the new economy: Markets, state and higher education*. Baltimore, MD: The John Hopkins University Press.

Smith, F. (2016). Privilege is invisible to those who have it: Engaging men in workplace equality. *The Guardian*. Retrieved July 7, 2016 from https://www.theguardian.com/sustainable-business/2016/jun/08/workplace-gender-equality-invisible-privilege.

Squire, D. (2015). Engaging race and power in higher education organizations through a critical race institutional logics perspective framework. *Journal of Critical Scholarship on Higher Education and Student Affairs, 2*(1), 105–121.

Stanley, T. D., & Jarrell, S. B. (1998). Gender wage discrimination bias? A meta-regression analysis. *The Journal of Human Resources, 33*(4), 947–973.

Yoshino, K. (2007). *Covering: The hidden assaults on our civil rights*. New York, NY: Random House.

Zinn, H. (2003). *A people's history of the United States*. New York, NY: Harper Perennial.

Contributors

Luna Malachowski Bajak, LMSW, is a Peruvian-American licensed social worker based in New York City. Luna has been working in the mental health and public health sector for the past six years, specifically with homeless and formerly homeless individuals struggling with addiction and diagnosed with mental health and chronic illnesses. Luna is now an Assistant Program Director at a supportive housing site in Manhattan.

Stephen A. Bissonnette, M.Ed., is a Boston-based college access program manager and writer who was born and raised on the south coast of Massachusetts. Stephen attended Skidmore College in New York, where he studied Sociology and Gender Studies with a focus on social justice and environmental sustainability. Stephen went on to be a corps member with Teach For America in Memphis, Tennessee, where he received his Master of Education and initiated an urban environmentalist extracurricular program for his students. Most recently, Stephen has begun to oversee college access programs across New England as well as consult with an environmental start-up in Boston, which seeks to foster resilient communities and bioregions through urban design and development.

Sarah Faude, M.S.Ed., is a Ph.D. Candidate in the Department of Sociology and Anthropology at Northeastern University in Boston, MA. Her dissertation will explore the experiences of district staff in implementing a citywide school choice policy in an effort to better understand the relationship between school segregation, student assignment policies, and district practices. She has also contributed to several projects related to equity and access gaps in education in Massachusetts, spanning from preschool to public higher education, all of which emphasize bridging research with practitioners. Before arriving at Northeastern, Sarah received her B.A. in 2009 from Skidmore College, her M.S.Ed in Urban Education from the University of Pennsylvania in 2011, and spent several years teaching middle and high school English in Philadelphia.

Kristie A. Ford, Ph.D., is an Associate Professor of Sociology and the Director of Intergroup Relations (IGR) Program and Minor at Skidmore College. She received her B.A. in sociology from Amherst College and her M.A. and

152 *Contributors*

Ph.D. in sociology from the University of Michigan, Ann Arbor. Her research and teaching interests include race and ethnicity, gender and sexuality, and social justice education. She consults widely with colleges/universities who are hoping to build IGR programs on their campuses. For her work, she has received several honors, including the President's Award at Skidmore College, the NAACP Community Service Award, and the Regional Leadership Council on Inclusion Award.

Teshika R. Hatch, B.A., is an educator and youth worker in Oakland, CA. After receiving her B.A. in Sociology-Psychology at Skidmore College, Teshika worked in the Skidmore Admissions Office as a multicultural recruiter and admissions counselor. Because of her focus on social justice and racial equality work in college, Teshika was determined to interact more directly with youth. She currently works at Juma Ventures, a college access and youth development organization that supports first-generation college-bound students get to college and develop positive work and financial habits. Starting off as a Youth Development Coordinator and now as the Bay Area Program Manager, Teshika has had the opportunity to not only work directly with youth but also oversee the programmatic services delivered by the youth advocates.

Heather J. Lipkin, B.A., graduated from Skidmore College in May 2015 with a major in Sociology and a minor in Intergroup Relations. In her time at Skidmore, she was a peer mentor to first-year students, a research assistant, and facilitated a semester-long dialogue focused on race, racism, and other social justice topics. She plans on applying to graduate school in the near future, and would like to pursue a career in social justice work. She currently works for a marketing agency, where she helps nonprofits fundraise through direct mail and digital campaigns.

Victoria K. Malaney, M.Ed., is a Ph.D. student in the department of Educational Policy, Research and Administration, focusing on Higher Education in the College of Education at the University of Massachusetts–Amherst. Victoria's research interests focus on multiracial college students, intergroup dialogue, race, and student activism. Prior to graduate school, Victoria was an AmeriCorps VISTA and VISTA Leader for two years. She also worked at Skidmore College in the Office of Student Diversity Programs. Victoria is the Chair of the American College Personnel Association's Multiracial Network (MRN) and is a proud alumna of Skidmore College.

Index

accountability and social justice advocacy 106

action and social justice advocacy 105–6; assessing consequences of actions 114–15; disengaged former facilitators 109

active listening skills 87–8

admissions office and multicultural recruitment 59–61

airtime and voice monitoring 89–91

Algonquian people 73

alumni-facilitator support network 138

alumni IGD facilitator panel 29

AmeriCorps VISTA 39–41

applying social justice advocacy 106–12

Asian-White woman's auto-ethnography 54–64

autobiography, racial 46

auto-ethnographies of former IGD facilitators 23–4; alumni IGD facilitator panel 29; Latina-White female teacher/social work practitioner 65–71; multiracial female multicultural recruiter/student advocate 54–64; multiracial woman's social justice advocacy path 36–44; Northeastern Intergroup Relations (IGR) Conference 29; themes 30–3; White female teacher 46–52; White queer male teacher 73–83

awareness enhancement and social justice advocacy 104–5

Bell, L. A. 4

Black Lives Matter 3

Brown, Michael 3

burnout 112–13, 116–17

Catholic school 74–5

charter schools 48–9, 79, 81

College for Every Student (CFES) program 61

commitment and social justice advocacy 105

communication skills, recognizing non verbal cues 86–7

competencies for social justice educators 4 *see also* skills and capabilities acquired by IGD facilitators

confidence building 97–8

continuing engagement with social justice advocacy 106–12

corporate opportunities for Intergroup Relations 146

Critical-Dialogic Theoretical Model 6, 31, 124

Critical Race Theory (CRT) 47, 73, 74–5

critical thinking/recognizing systems of oppression 95–7, 124–6

cross-cultural relationship building 97–8

curriculum-related implications of IGD facilitator study 136–8

Cycle of Liberation 55

data analysis procedures 23

Delgado, R. 73, 75

disciplinary systems in schools 79–80

disengaged former facilitators 109, 123–9

diversity recruitment 59–61

diversity training 3

emotional burnout 112–13, 116–17

empathy 66–7, 89–91

empowerment themes in facilitator auto-ethnographies 32–3 *see also* auto-ethnographies of former IGD facilitators

ethnic "purity" 75–6

154 Index

facilitation skills 86–94 *see also* skills and capabilities acquired by IGD facilitators

facilitators *see* Intergroup Dialogue (IGD) peer-facilitators

faculty/staff roles and responsibilities 20

faculty training in diversity 3

families, impact of social justice advocacy work 119–20

Ferguson, Missouri 3

financial aid 60, 81

Flake, S. 50

Freire, P. 50, 67, 76–7, 80–1, 143

future of Intergroup Relations and Intergroup Dialogue *see* Intergroup Relations (IGR), future of

Gandhi, Mahatma 36

graduate school experiences 50, 69–70

group dynamics-related skills 86–7

Hackman, H. W. 4

Harro, B. 55

hate crimes 147

higher education, IGD and operating within 144–5

higher education, minority access 59–61, 144

homophobia 74

hooks, b. 146

Hurricane Katrina 76

"I, Too, Am Harvard" 3

interactional dynamics-related skills 86–7

Intergroup Dialogue (IGD) 6; acquisition of content knowledge and voice 31–2; applying process knowledge and skills 32; critical-dialogic approach 6, 31, 56; definition 6; PASK model 8, 135; research on 6–8; as vehicle for social change 143–4

Intergroup Dialogue (IGD) peer-facilitators: defining social justice advocacy 103–6, 125–6; faculty/staff roles and responsibilities 20; interviews with 22; long-term visions 102–3; research on 8–9; skills acquired 86–94; study limitations 24; study methodology 21–4; training and support model 8, 20; White disengaged male's reflections 123–9, 136; *see also* auto-ethnographies

of former IGD facilitators; skills and capabilities acquired by IGD facilitators

Intergroup Dialogue (IGD) peer-facilitators, study results *see* Intergroup Dialogue (IGD), study results

Intergroup Dialogue (IGD), skills acquired from *see* skills and capabilities acquired by IGD facilitators

Intergroup Dialogue (IGD), study implications 136; alumni-facilitator support network 138; conclusions 139–40, 142–3; curricular revisions 136–8; future research 139; *see also* Intergroup Relations (IGR), future of

Intergroup Dialogue (IGD), study methodology 21–4; future research 139; *see also* auto-ethnographies of former IGD facilitators

Intergroup Dialogue (IGD), study results 133–4; applying social justice advocacy 106–12; defining social justice advocacy 103–6; implications 136–9; navigating race and social justice issues 135; programmatic benefits 94–9; short- and long-term personal and professional impacts 134–5; social advocacy challenges 112–17; summary of 99–100, 119–20; sustained racial identity and ally development 135–6; transferrable skills 86–94; *see also* skills and capabilities acquired by IGD facilitators

Intergroup Relations (IGR), future of 142–3, 148–9; critical need in trying times 147; IGD as vehicle for social change 143–4; operation beyond educational sphere 145–6; operation within higher education 144–5; research directions 139; *see also* Intergroup Dialogue (IGD), study implications

Intergroup Relations (IGR) program: faculty/staff roles and responsibilities 20; minor program 17–19; peer-facilitation model and training 20; pilot program 17, 55–6, 74–5; Practicum course 19, 20, 56–7, 98; Race and Power course 18, 55, 124; Racial Identities: Theory and Praxis course 19, 38, 55–6; University of Michigan's program 5–6, 137; *see also* Intergroup Dialogue;

Index 155

Intergroup Dialogue (IGD) peer-facilitators
Intergroup Relations (IGR) program, former facilitators' reflections *see* auto-ethnographies of former IGD facilitators
Intergroup Relations (IGR) program, skills acquired by facilitators *see* skills and capabilities acquired by IGD facilitators
intersectionality of identities 73
interviews with IGD facilitators 22
isolation and burnout 116–17

jail inmate mentoring 39–41

Latina-White female teacher/social work practitioner's auto-ethnography 65–71
leadership skills 92–4
leaning into discomfort 10, 143
Lewis, A. E. 49
Life Coach mentoring 39–41
listening skills 87–8
longitudinal approach to IGD research 139
long-term impacts of inter-/intragroup pedagogies 6, 134–5
long-term visions of former facilitators 102–3

mental health advocate 68–71
mentoring jail inmates 39–41
microaggressions 36–7, 55, 58
minority access to higher education 59–61, 144
minor program in Intergroup Relations (IGR) 17–19
Mississippi Delta 77–8
Montessori school 81
Moore, W. L. 48
motivations of social justice allies 5
motivation to continue social advocacy 117–20, 135–6
multicultural recruitment 59–61
multiracial women's auto-ethnographies 36–44, 54–64

National Conference on Race and Ethnicity in American Higher Education (NCORE) 37
nonverbal cue recognition 86–7
Northeastern Intergroup Relations (IGR) Conference 29

Occupy Wall Street 108
Office of Student Diversity Programs (OSDP) 41, 55
oppression: developing skills for recognizing 95–7; IGD as vehicle for social change 143; IGD pedagogical approach 6; interacting systems 74; mental illness stigma 70, 74; Race and Power course 18, 55, 124; "reverse oppression" 66; "self-depreciation" 80; shelter residents' experiences 68; shifting the paradigm 82–3; stages of social justice advocacy 5; teachers and 76–7; themes and observations in facilitator auto-ethnographies 31, 33, 37–8, 41–3, 49, 57–9, 62, 63, 65–6, 68–70, 80, 82–3; violence and 62; *see also* privilege; social justice advocacy

Passion, Awareness, Skills, and Knowledge (PASK) 8, 135
peer-facilitators *see* Intergroup Dialogue (IGD) peer-facilitators
personal awareness enhancement 104–5
perspective-taking skills 89–91
police interactions and White privilege 71, 78
police interactions with mentally ill persons 70–1
Practicum course 19, 20, 56–7, 98
prioritizing issues 112
privilege 41; challenges of working from position of 114–15; empathy and 66–7; IGD as vehicle for social change 143; recognizing and social justice advocacy engagement 118; themes and observations in facilitator auto-ethnographies 32–3, 38, 41, 46–52, 65, 66–7, 73, 78, 82–3; White persons' police interactions 71, 78; *see also* oppression
Pulse massacre, Orlando 147

queer White male's auto-ethnography 73–83

Race and Power course 18, 55, 124
racial-autobiography assignment 46
racial awakening, themes and observations in facilitator auto-ethnographies 31, 37, 49
Racial Identities: Theory and Praxis course 19, 38, 55–6

156 Index

racial identity development, White 75–6, 127 *see also* privilege

racism: Critical Race Theory (CRT) 47, 73–5; IGR minor program addressing 18; microaggressions 36–7, 55, 58; School to Prison Pipeline 79–80; themes and observations in facilitator auto-ethnographies 37, 47–9, 57–8, 73–6, 78; "What are you?" question 31, 36, 37, 41, 54; *see also* oppression; privilege; social justice advocacy

recruiting diverse students 59–61

resistance, risk-taking and dealing with 113–14

"reverse oppression" 66

risk-taking 113–14

safe spaces 32, 57, 58, 66, 68, 98–9, 144, 147

School to Prison Pipeline 79–80

"self-depreciation" 80

self-reflexivity 23

shelter residents 68–9

Skidmore College 16–17; admissions office and multicultural recruitment 59–61; dealing with racism at 57–8; first cocurricular student group 41; Intergroup Relations (IGR) minor program 17–19; Intergroup Relations (IGR) Pilot Program 17; Northeastern Intergroup Relations (IGR) Conference 29; peer-facilitation model and training 20; working for Office of Student Diversity Programs 41, 55; *see also* Intergroup Relations (IGR) program

skills and capabilities acquired by IGD facilitators 85, 94, 134; active listening 87–8; airtime and voice monitoring 89–91; confidence building 94–5; critical thinking/recognizing systems of oppression 95–7, 124–6; empathy and perspective-taking 89–91; leadership 92–4; recognizing non verbal cues and interactional dynamics 86–7; social justice vocabulary 91–2; social network expansion 97–8; summary of study results 99–100; support 98–9

social justice advocacy: ally motivations 5; applying and continuing engagement 106–12; burnout 112–13, 116–17; confidence in discussing issues 94–5; continuing challenges of 51–2; defining 5, 103–6, 124, 135; disengaged former facilitators 109, 123–9, 136; IGD as vehicle for social change 143–4; long-term visions of former facilitators 102–3; maintaining commitment 105; motivation to continue 117–20, 135–6; personal awareness enhancement 104–5; practicing accountability 106; shifting the paradigm 82–3; summary of facilitator study results 135–6; taking action 105–6; themes in facilitator auto-ethnographies 31–3; White Savior complex 33, 77, 82, 115

social justice advocacy, challenges of 112; assessing consequences of actions 115–16; lack of support and isolation 116–17; prioritizing and feeling overwhelmed 112–13; risk-taking and resistance 113–14; working from position of privilege 114–15

social justice advocacy, former facilitator's reflections *see* auto-ethnographies of former IGD facilitators

social justice advocacy skills development *see* skills and capabilities acquired by IGD facilitators

social justice awareness 104–5

social justice education: benefits of 96; defining 4; educator competencies 4–5; IGD and higher education 144–5; Program on Intergroup Relations 5–6; *see also* Intergroup Relations (IGR) program

Social Justice in the Real World course 137

social justice vocabulary 91–2

social network expansion 97–8

social welfare policy and programs 71

social work practitioner 68–71

Sorensen, N. 6, 31

special education volunteer 67

Stefancic, J. 73, 75

"stepping up" and "stepping back" 88–9

student development advocate 62–3

support: IGD benefits for students/facilitators 98–9; lack of, isolation, and burnout 116–17; suggested alumni-facilitator network 138

Index   157

teachers and oppression 76–7
Teach for America 48, 77–82
teaching experiences 48–51, 67, 77–82
training model for IGD peer-facilitators
 8, 20
Trump, Donald 144, 147

University of Massachusetts (UMass)
 Amherst 41–2
University of Michigan (UM) Intergroup
 Relations (IGR) Program 5–6, 137
University of Missouri 3

VISTA volunteer 39–41
voice and airtime monitoring 89–91
Volunteer in Service to America
 (VISTA) 39–41

Wampanoag Nation 73
"What are you?" question 31, 36, 37,
 41, 54

White and Asian mixed-race woman's
 auto-ethnography 54–64
White disengaged male's reflections
 123–9, 136
White female's reflections on identity
 and privilege 46–52
White privilege *see* privilege
White queer male teacher's auto-
 ethnography 73–83
White racial guilt 114–15
White racial identity 75–6, 127 *see also*
 privilege
White Savior complex 33, 77,
 82, 115
women's shelters 68–9

Young, I. M. 62–3
youth development advocate
 62–3

Zuñiga, Ximena 41–2